God Hides in
Plain Sight

God Hides in Plain Sight

How to See the Sacred in a Chaotic World

Dean Nelson

BrazosPress

a division of Baker Publishing Group
Grand Rapids, Michigan

Published by Brazos Press
a division of Baker Publishing Group
P.O. Box 6287, Grand Rapids, MI 49516-6287
www.brazospress.com

Printed in the United States of America

Library of Congress Cataloging-in-Publication Data
Nelson, Dean, 1954–
    God hides in plain sight : how to see the sacred in a chaotic world / Dean Nelson.
        p.   cm.
    Includes bibliographical references (p.   ).
    ISBN 978-1-58743-233-0 (pbk.)
    1. Grace (Theology) 2. Nelson, Dean, 1954– 3. Sacraments—Miscellanea.
I. Title.
BT761.3.N46 2009
234′.1—dc22   2009016986

To Marcia,
who let Rilke be our guide from the beginning,
so we could live the questions together,
and love each other forever

Contents

Acknowledgments

This book started as an idea that repeatedly sent me back to my former professor and current friend, mentor, and colleague, Maxine Walker. She kept reading sample chapters and kept encouraging me and kept giving me valuable suggestions. She also supported this project financially through the Wesleyan Center for 21st Century Studies at Point Loma Nazarene University.

Dale Fetherling, an extraordinary editor and an even better friend, transformed this manuscript from an idea into a book. He put up with a lot of my whining and was grace-filled throughout.

Three groups of supportive loved ones helped develop this book. The first is what I call "My Two Mikes"—Michael Leffel and Michael McKinney. Every time I had good news or bad news about this project, they listened, encouraged, challenged, and believed in me. They kept me on task, read drafts, and wouldn't let me give up when I was very discouraged.

The second group is "The Jebus Seminar." Jebus is a reference to a Simpsons episode, where Homer is forced to become a missionary because he didn't pay his public television pledge. That's all you need to know. The Seminar members are Randy Beckum, Rick Power, and Gary Morsch. They agreed to read the manuscript at one of our annual meetings in Hawaii, and also gave me valuable advice and support, even though they never thought it would get published.

The third and most important group is my family. My daughter Vanessa and my son Blake are the two most creative people I know, and they believed from the beginning that this was an idea worth pursuing. I had hope because of them. My wife, Marcia, though, is the one who had the most faith in this book and has always had the most faith in me. The book faced a lot of rejection from publishers— for years. It was too spiritual for some, too worldly for others, and too irreverent for many. My wife's response was always, "Well, then they're not the right one." She never seems as surprised as the rest of us when something goes right. On our first date as college freshmen she said to me, "People say you're funny. So make me laugh." I loved her fiercely then and even more so now. She even still thinks that my screenplay about senior citizens playing fast-pitch softball will someday be made into a movie.

Rodney Clapp at Brazos Press is the one who rescued this manuscript (and me) from the Dumpster. He helped shape it, gave me expert advice, and made me a better writer.

To these and others, I am grateful.

Introduction

Learning to See

To become aware of the possibility of the search is to be onto something. Not to be onto something is to be in despair.

Walker Percy[1]

Stepping out of my hotel room in Bombay, India, I paused as I pulled the door shut behind me. The piano player in the lobby twelve floors below me was playing "Für Elise" by Beethoven. It was not particularly noteworthy other than the fact that I had heard my son play it at a piano recital the night before I left for India. I stopped, and instead of heading toward the elevator, I leaned against the wall and listened to the entire song. I replayed the tape in my head of my son playing it. He was only thirteen at the time, and was in his last year of piano lessons. I knew he would never play concert halls or even hotel lobbies. But the song brought back warm memories of sitting in a university concert parlor, French tapestries on the walls, listening to my son play the recital piece that I had heard him practice hundreds of times.

It also made me feel far away from home.

I was in Bombay to teach a creative writing course to a group of adult students. I jumped at the chance to be part of their development. And even though I had spent time in major cities around the world, Bombay made me feel very alone and uneasy. Shortly before the course began, a major earthquake hit just a few hundred miles from where I would be teaching. Speculation about aftershocks predicted that they would impact the region I was in.

Taxi rides from my hotel to the school were great adventures. I counted the number of times my driver used his horn. He averaged approximately 40 times per minute—more than once every two seconds. Taxis bumping each other as they jockeyed for position on the too-small roads reminded me of playing faculty basketball at my university—no blood, no foul. We upgraded that policy to no autopsy, no foul when it became obvious that one of the guys got chronic nosebleeds at the slightest provocation from an elbow, a skull, or an errant pass. At one point the side molding on my taxi got ripped off in a too-close encounter with another taxi. The drivers didn't even stop. At traffic lights, beggars approached the window where I sat. I waved off one young girl holding a baby who had evidence of an infection running from his eyes and nose, and when I did, as if on cue, the baby sneezed on me.

My initial cab ride from the airport was much smoother, since the hotel had sent the driver. He could speak a little English, and he asked if I wanted some music for the forty-minute ride. I said yes, and he put in a cassette tape of Yanni playing mind-numbing piano monotony. I tried as hard as I could to ask the driver for some authentic Indian music, but he didn't understand my English that well, and he had it in his head that, since I was American, I would want to listen to one of our awful exports. Finally, when the tape clicked off and the radio came on with Indian music, I insisted he leave it there. He looked very confused.

Even though I had been all over the world either teaching or writing stories for newspapers, magazines, and books, for some reason I was feeling very far away from home on this particular trip. Maybe it was because of what I was reading. I knew that, soon after I returned to my work in San Diego, I would be interviewing the legendary writer Ray Bradbury on television, in front of a live audience. I was trying to prepare by immersing myself in his writings. For the India trip I brought *The Martian Chronicles*. But I was the one who felt like someone from another planet.

The feeling intensified. The morning after I heard my son's recital song, I departed my hotel room and the piano player was playing again—this time he was playing "The Spinning Song," which my daughter had just played at that same recital. She was ten. Everyone plays "The Spinning Song" at some point in their piano lessons. Even I did, forty years before. To this day, it is the only song my dad can play on the piano. Still, I paused again, thinking about the coincidence of my hearing those two songs in the hotel on different days, and that they were the last songs I had heard my kids play. They were popular songs, and the odds were high that I would hear familiar songs of some sort in a hotel that catered to out-of-towners, the way I heard a lounge singer belting out "Bye, Bye Miss American Pie" as I was checking in to the Great Wall Sheraton in Beijing the year before. (The day *that* music died was when it started getting played in lounges around the world by singers who were eventually mocked by Bill Murray.) But I could live with these coincidences in Bombay. And in sort of a self-amusing thought that would have fit well in the movie, *Bruce Almighty*, I remembered thinking, "It would *really* be a coincidence if something reminded me of my wife. Then I would *really* be impressed."

This was because of my wife's limited piano repertoire. She can only play one song, an old church chorus that she learned growing up in a pastor's home in small towns in Wisconsin and South Dakota. No one in the hotel lobby would be playing it—of this I was certain. Don McLean might be in every lounge lizard's Fake Book worldwide, but not "He Is Able."

In the writing class that morning, I asked the students to read their assignments out loud to the group so that we could critique and offer suggestions. The assignment was for each writer to take an incident from childhood and recount it with concrete and significant details, showing how it had helped shape future events in his or her life. The stories were entertaining, sometimes painful, and mostly inspiring. The last one to read was a missionary from the U.S. who had been in South India for twenty-seven years. As he read his story, I felt my jaw fall open. When he finished, I was speechless.

He told of how a pastor in Eau Claire, Wisconsin, had helped him as an eleven-year-old boy understand that God was calling him into full-time Christian service. What shocked me was that the pastor was my father-in-law, who was in his last months of life while I was in India.

In a hotel lobby, and then in the Mumbai Central YMCA, something connected me with each member of my family.

Signals

My purpose in telling these events is not to tell you that I believe in magic. I do think that coincidences occur. But I also believe that grace goes before us as a way for God to say, "Welcome! I got here before you. I've been expecting you." That's exactly how I felt when I heard this missionary read his assignment in Bombay. I was alone, feeling like a Martian, a little bit afraid, and I sensed God saying to me, "See? You're with me, and you're going to be fine."

God's welcome gave me courage. It even amused me. In a way, God was testing me, asking, "Are you paying attention? Do you see me all around you? Can you see me at work?"

This incident got me thinking about the signals God sends us—through events or each other—that we simply miss because we aren't tuned in to looking for him or his activity in everyday life. When I heard that missionary read his story, and it began dawning on me who he was writing about, a mundane assignment took on a completely different nature. It became sacred. Something holy.

I don't use the words sacred and holy lightly. They refer to things that are uniquely of God. That's how I felt about this incident in Bombay. It was holy because God had used something routine to show me that he was on my journey with me—not just on it, but ahead of me. In fact, He had created the journey in the first place. It was an experience of the "beyond in our midst," as Bonhoeffer described encounters with God.[2] For me, this was an encounter with the sacred. It was of God, and it pointed to God. My experience in Bombay made me consider Augustine's sense of God's signals, a way of thinking he developed while he was still a partier and womanizer. Outside his window one day he heard children chanting as part of their play, "Take and read, take and read." He sensed he was being told to read the Bible, which he did, and which led him to a life-changing encounter with God. Later, in his *Confessions*, he stated, "God is always present to us and to all things; it is that we, like blind persons, do not have the eyes to see."[3]

How often does God use the occurrences throughout our day to point us to himself? My sense is that he does it continuously. The biggest variable is whether we are alert enough to get it. As Eugene Peterson said, "We are always coming in on something that is already going on."[4]

Jesus tells us that we can see God at work in the little things, like a mustard plant—the equivalent of a weed. People generally expect to see evidence of God in the big stuff—the Gee Whiz events—when in reality, according to Jesus, it's at knee or ankle level, spreading like a weed. Or like yeast in bread. It's in the everydayness, using everyday elements. Whether we see it is up to us. Instead of looking up, we should be looking around. Or down.

It is a dangerous thing to look for the activity of God in the unclean and unwashed aspects of life. The danger is that we'll have to let go of our expectations that God can be experienced only in cathedrals and big, contrived events, with only certain people in charge of dispensing that activity. What about in a hotel lobby? Or a classroom in Bombay? Or incidents that occur in everyday life? "If we really had our eyes open, we would see that all moments are key moments," Buechner said.[5]

Much of our lives, it seems to me, are spent like that of the main character in Camus' novel, *The Stranger*; we are indifferent, unmoved, unfeeling, walking dead people. Not until the stranger faced his own death did he even notice the stars in the sky. He reminds me of a lot of the people I meet. "Listen to your life," Buechner said. "See it for the fathomless mystery that it is . . . There is no event so commonplace but that God is present within it, always hiddenly, always leaving you room to recognize him or not to recognize him."[6]

I experienced this hidden presence when I was covering a story for the *New York Times*. A boy had brought a gun to his high school outside of San Diego, and murdered two students and wounded thirteen more. The newspaper asked me to rush to the school and interview as many people as I could, to try to provide some understanding during the aftermath of the horrible act. I confess that I didn't want to go. I hate covering sensational stories. A few years before, I was one of the first reporters at the house where thirty-nine members of the Heaven's Gate cult took their own lives so that they could join the secret spaceship following the Hale-Bopp comet. Stories with this kind of loss are so tragic, so sensational, so senseless, that I approach them with a certain amount of dread.

At the high school, police had blocked off several blocks to keep traffic out, so I parked a half mile away and started walking to the school. In my head I was going over what I thought readers would want to know about this tragedy. I passed some people walking away from the school, and then I heard my name being called. Two of the people I had just passed were youth pastors from the area. I knew them both. One of them taught part-time where I teach. They were leaving after having spent time with students from their youth groups who had called them when the shooting began. I talked with them briefly, and felt strangely encouraged in my own task as a result.

Across the street from the school was a strip mall with a large parking lot. That's where emergency vehicles were, along with the Red Cross, and hundreds of students milling around, waiting to be picked up by parents whose primal instincts had been triggered. I approached two girls, identified myself, and asked if I could ask them a few questions. One knew the shooter well. They had seen the bodies in the hallway. It was a terrifying sight for them, yet, through their tears, they wanted to talk about it. As I wrote down their comments in my notebook, a small crowd of reporters gathered. Television cameras zoomed in. Other reporters began asking questions. It didn't get out of control, but it did start getting very intense. While this was going on, I felt a hand on my shoulder. Usually when that happens to me in a crowd of journalists, it is a photographer asking me to move to one side or another for a better picture. Without turning around, I moved a little to my left to accommodate what I presumed to be a colleague. The hand remained. So I moved a little to the right. No change. It didn't put pressure on me. It wasn't trying to get me to move. It just stayed there, and I let it while I did my work.

When I was done talking to the girls, I thanked them, and the television people moved on. I turned around to see who was behind me. It was my neighbor, whose kids are in school with my kids in another part of the city. He is the regional director of the Young Life ministry group. He had come to the school to help the Young Life chapter respond to the attack. But he saw me, and decided to come along on my task and pray for me as I talked to witnesses of the shooting. I saw his actions as God saying, "I got here before you in Leon. I am in the middle of this whole, terrible situation, including your being one of the reporters covering it." The activity of God was present, thorough, expressed with a hand on a shoulder. "Long before I arrive on the scene, the Spirit is at work," Eugene Peterson said. "I must fit into what is going on."[7]

Jesus drives home this point with a story he tells. It is about a judge who had little regard for God or people. In his city was a widow who kept coming to the judge and saying, "Grant me justice against my opponent." He refused at first, but was worn down by the woman, so he granted her justice just so she'd stop bothering him. End of story. This had always been a confusing parable to me. The sermons I'd hear about it usually justified begging and harassing God with our requests. It was a parable of getting God to bend to our needs, I thought.

But it's really about how we are constantly confronted by grace— grace that pursues, invades, initiates. We are the judge in this story, and grace continuously approaches us, like the insistent woman, demanding that we do it justice by seeing it. Grace pursues and precedes. It bends us toward God. It is like a weed that comes from a tiny seed and grows wherever it wants. It is like bacteria that takes something traditionally predictable, and changes its nature. It says to us, "Do me justice. See me everywhere."

When we're paying attention, we see that grace is breaking into our everyday moments, making them different—sacred—drawing us into the presence of God.

It's not about us getting a hold of the sacred. It's about the sacred getting a hold of us.

Hidden in Plain Sight

When I started thinking this way (it was a slow dawning, not a moment in time), I began consciously asking God, "Okay, what are you telling me—what's the lesson here?" throughout each day. It was as if everything had a point and it was up to me to get my Burning Bush decoder ring and figure out the specific hidden message God had for me. I don't do that anymore. I just look for signs of his presence, because I know they are there. He doesn't hide. I am just blind. I don't look for "the point" of it all—just the Presence. The hand on my shoulder. I had understood the concept of grace being "pardon" and "unwarranted favor," but there is another dimension to it. Grace is the experience of God's love. All I have to do is see it and accept it. Anne Lamott said, "Maybe this is what grace is, the unseen sounds that make you look up."[8] The poet Rilke said, "If your daily round seems unrewarding, don't put the blame on it; blame yourself for not being able to evoke the riches that are to be found in it."[9]

Many years ago I played on my college's baseball team. We weren't particularly good, and to put my own talent in context, I was not a starter. To be on a lousy team, and to still begin each game on the bench, did not do much for my self-esteem. To quell the boredom of watching our miserable team get shellacked each game, I took interest in our opponents' third base coaches. It was a practice I picked up while sitting on the bench in high school and Little League earlier in my unremarkable athletic life. When the other team was at bat, the third base coach would go through a series of gyrations to secretly communicate to the batter or base runner. Or, in our college games, the base runners. I knew from my own years of playing baseball that a hand to the belt, then to the bill of the cap, might mean "bunt." A hand to the other hand or face (skin on skin), might be a signal for the runner on first to steal a base. But since everyone knows some of these universal signs, each team has its own "activating" signal, which says, "This time I mean it—all those other times were to throw off the opposition."

Since I had time on my hands, I would try to figure these signals out. Once I broke the code, I would tell our players, and we could adjust for the coming bunt, steal or other play. It's highly unethical to do this, according to some players and coaches. But mine were grateful. Challenging circumstances create new ethical standards. Think Enron. We needed every advantage we could get.

One team was not difficult to figure out at all. The third base coach gave signs *only* when he wanted the players to do something. For instance, if his team had a runner on first base, the coach would yell across the diamond, "Hey Tony!" and then grab his elbow. Tony (and the rest of us) now knew that the coach wanted him to steal second. Somehow the concept of disguising the signals was lost on this coach. I think it was the one team we could beat.

I think we treat the continuous ways God breaks into our lives the same way we look at baseball team signals. They are hidden, secret, and only for the insiders, like the clergy, or those with a lot of time on their hands, like the infirmed or elderly. Prayer "warriors" they are called. And sometimes the signals are given strictly to throw some people off course because they don't know which signal is the "activator." It is as if God is there, but he is hiding until we can figure out the signals he's sending. Philip Yancey tells of natives on the southern tip of Argentina ignoring the explorer Magellan's great ships as they passed by because they were different from anything they had seen before and assumed they were an apparition. "They lacked the experience, even the imagination, to decode evidence passing right before their eyes."[10] Similarly, John describes Jesus as being in the world without the world recognizing him (John 1:10).

But instead of trying to decode God's signals, a better approach would be to simply see him where he always is: all around us. We could be fixing our eyes on the unseen, as opposed to the seen, as the apostle Paul instructs us to do. Eugene Peterson describes the process this way: "We happen upon, we notice, we reach out and touch things and ideas, people and events, and among these the Holy Scriptures themselves, that were there all along but that our ego-swollen souls or our sin-blurred eyes quite simply overlooked—sometimes for years and years and years. And then we do notice: we sight life, we realize God and hear his word, we grab the sleeve of a friend and demand, 'Look! Listen!'"[11]

I began wondering if there were ways I could pay attention to this presence more intentionally in my life. I am well aware of the spiritual disciplines, and have underlined almost every word in Richard Foster's book *Celebration of Discipline*. But practicing the disciplines is a little different from what I was wanting. I didn't want to tune things out. I wanted to tune things in and see them differently. What I hungered for was better vision so I could see God and his activity throughout my day. I believed that his grace and love and presence were all around me, but I wasn't seeing them. I wasn't living with that knowledge at my center. I wanted the blinders off. I wanted to catch the subtleties of God's activity.

More Than Two Sacraments

It was while reading Thomas Merton's "Disputed Questions" that a thought occurred to me. Some Christian faith traditions emphasize specific practices, or means to invoke and experience the grace and mystery of God, called "sacraments." Two of these are baptism and Communion. Many Christians recognize that there is something sacred and holy about those acts. They are symbols—action symbols— that have the power to speak to us about experiencing God. We experience God in an unusual and profound way when we participate in baptism and in Holy Communion. They reflect a deeper spiritual reality. In more ancient Christian faiths there are additional sacraments where grace and God's mystery are also experienced in marriage, confession, confirmation, holy orders, and anointing. I know that focusing on these traditional means of grace is not popular in current thought because of a fear of worshipping (or at least giving too much attention) to the means themselves, instead of seeing them for what they are: ways for God to reach us. The sacraments aren't a way to manage, contain, or create walls around God. History has simply shown us that they are often how God's presence is mediated. They always point beyond themselves. They help us address the illusion that God is absent. The sacraments make all of creation more real for us, Merton wrote, "because we now see all ordinary created things in a new light."[12] They are concrete actions that bend us toward, or that reveal, God. Sometimes they take on qualities of rituals, which are not necessarily bad things as long as the rituals cause us to remember or to see. Sacraments make Mystery accessible, and help us fulfill our purpose on earth.

In his book *Doors to the Sacred*, Joseph Martos said that the sacraments are "intensification rituals. They express what people are already living and deepen their commitment to it." They are human creations, he said, but they deliberately function as doors to sacred realities. "They symbolize what people believe and move them into new phases of living what they believe."[13]

In fact, throughout civilization, people have been looking for ways to experience the sacred and holy. Christians go to church no matter how boring it is, Hindus plunge into the Ganges River no matter how foul it is, Muslims make pilgrimages to Mecca, no matter how far and how crowded it is. "So it is that monks kneel and chant, that Jews eat a Passover meal, that Polynesians dance, and Quakers sit still," writes Martos.

> So it is that Catholics kneel before a crucifix, that tribal shamans wear special clothing, that Protestants honor the Bible, that Buddhists abstain from meat. But none of these places are visited, none of these actions are performed, none of these objects are revered because of what they are in themselves. In themselves they are just locations, activities, things. But they point to or symbolize something beyond themselves—something mysterious, something that cannot be seen, something special. And in this case, they are all sacraments, symbols of something else which is mysterious and hidden, sacred and holy.[14]

The sacraments, essentially, move us from here to there.

Life in High Definition

As I looked at the Christian sacraments, it seemed that they encompassed the entire rhythm of our lives in this world. Through baptism, confirmation, communion, marriage, confession, holy orders, and anointing, our lives on earth are described and experienced. Together, the sacraments provide life's liturgy. They bear the recurring themes of each of our lives. Looking at life through these sacraments intensifies each experience and gives it meaning. I began to wonder — if the purpose of these sacraments is to more profoundly experience God during the rhythm of living, how could they possibly be limited to moments in church, or administered only by a select few, since the Kingdom of God was really more like a weed or a virus? Haven't we all participated in meals where, because of the conversation, or the sheer experience of togetherness, we sensed something that transcended ourselves and connected us to the grace of God? Where it seemed as if God were saying, "Now do you see where I can be found? Look around you! I've been here the whole time!" Those moments reveal a world that we did not previously perceive. "It is like the color added to a black-and-white television screen," wrote Thomas Keating. "The picture remains the same, but it is greatly enhanced by the new dimension of the picture that was not previously perceived."[15] The sacraments awaken us to the realities of God's activity.

As I try to understand God as Creator, for instance, I begin to realize that he is continually creating and declaring it "good." The Genesis account doesn't say that he stopped and walked away from creation, leaving it to evildoers. Unfortunately, many people have come to the conclusion that the world is evil, when what we could be doing is affirming the very things in it that God affirms. The Second Vatican Council said, "There is scarcely any proper use of material things which cannot be directed toward people's sanctification and the praise of God."[16]

Jesus used everyday material, dirt and spit, to help a blind man see.

That's not to say we don't need those prepared moments in our places of worship that are planned for and officiated by clergy. God isn't limited to those events, though. When sacred moments are limited to selected sites and people, they can devolve toward legalism, or be distorted by power and control. Liberating them to the everyday allows us to see the grace of God revealed throughout our day. "It is well to have specifically holy places and things, and days, for, without these focal points or reminders, the belief that all is holy and 'big with God' will soon dwindle into a mere sentiment," said C. S. Lewis. "We may ignore, but we can nowhere evade, the presence of God. The world is crowded with him. He walks everywhere *incognito*. And the *incognito* is not always hard to penetrate. The real labor is to remember, to attend. In fact, to come awake. Still more, to remain awake."[17] Sacraments that reveal the presence of God in our everyday lives bring light and transform our ordinary existence. They reveal grace that is at work all around us.

Grace is mystery, as God is a mystery, which makes them both difficult to describe. We can learn about grace in classes and in books like these, but that's not where the real learning takes place.

The learning takes place by paying attention. Being awake. Staying awake. Seeing grace at work in moments throughout our day, and seeing them become holy moments. These holy, or grace-filled, moments are not just for those on their best behavior. If they were, then it wouldn't be grace. In the Old Testament account, Jacob lied to his father and cheated his brother. Yet, after a dream of angels on a stairway to heaven (insert your own Led Zeppelin reference here), he declares that "God is here and I didn't know it." That nondescript place in the open country became a holy place.

The means of this presence and grace of God can be experienced in worship, prayer, and reading, as well as in conversations with other people, inspired moments, and unexpected encounters. But they are rooted in the everyday stuff of this world. Theodore Runyon said, "A sacrament uses this-worldly and material means to communicate transcendent reality . . . A sacrament intends to renew the image of God."[18] John Wesley said, "The pure of heart see *all things full of God.*"[19]

I Confess, I'm Annoyed Right Now

Awareness of the grace present in each moment is not necessarily our instinct. I'm having difficulty with it as I write this, with a roofer above me dropping bags of shingles so hard that they break pieces of the popcorn ceiling loose onto my lap and keyboard. I feel like the surgeons in the television show *M.A.S.H.* where they try to bisect a colon while shells explode around the tent hospital. Lights dim, walls shake. I'm probably inhaling invisible asbestos particles that are implanting in my lungs and I'll need to finish this from inside an iron apparatus, or I'll have to blink an eye for each letter like the guy in *The Diving Bell and the Butterfly*. No! Don't sew THAT eye shut! It's the OTHER one! The painter is also here, dropping cigarette butts throughout the yard, talking to his girlfriend on his cell phone right outside my window, making plans for the weekend. Yeah—bowling sounds great for the two of them. I wish them all the strikes in the world. Our dog is simultaneously infuriated and terrified by these sounds and strangers, and runs from window to window, unsure of

which threat to attack first. And this is the quiet part of the day before
the kids come home from school. I'm not feeling very grace-filled,
attentive, or awake to the presence of God. "Often the present moment is not a sacrament, but a burden to be endured," said Richard
Foster.[20] But Thomas Kelly said that, despite the challenges, "Within
the Now is the dwelling place of God Himself."[21]

Now.

In the noise, commotion, distraction, disruption, and interruption
of my life. Grace gives the Now more room.

Anyone can see the activity of God in the big things—the Gee
Whiz moments. In fact, where would most of modern religion be if it
didn't have big crowds, big music, big productions, big budgets, and
big names? The big Christmas productions with live animals (The
Living Christmas Tree! Angels on wires descending from ceilings!
Real camels!) and the Easter extravaganzas (Simulated earthquakes!
Real hammers and spikes! Jesus flying into the rafters like Peter Pan!)
are churches' equivalent of the holiday sales at department stores.
What they don't do the rest of the year gets evened out during the big
productions. As one of my colleagues said, as we exited the Crystal
Cathedral's Christmas production, "That was better than the real
thing!"

Jean-Pierre de Caussade, in his book from the 1700s, *The Sacrament of the Present Moment*, says that God's activity permeates all
things, even the most trivial and annoying. Look for God backstage,
he says, not center stage. "No moment is trivial," he said, "since each
one contains a divine Kingdom."[22]

"The present moment is like an ambassador announcing the policy
of God."[23]

Paying attention, staying awake, practicing mindfulness, listening
to the present moment, are all part of the bridge between developing
our interior lives and seeing the events of our days as sacred moments.
Can we live in such a way that we are more attentive to the presence
and grace that surrounds us? Can we witness the holy within the
finite? How do we experience the sacred in the here and now? How
do we celebrate the sacrament of the present moment?

When I first moved to San Diego, two other men and I began
meeting for breakfast once a week. Some months we went through

a book together, where we read a chapter before our next meeting, and allowed that to frame our discussion. Other times our meals were merely sharing where we were in our lives at that moment. Sometimes breakfast was hilarious, and we headed for our cars bent over in laughter. Sometimes it was so painful that the drive to work was clouded with tears. It was a time of somewhat relaxed confession, accountability, support, intellectual stimulation, and fellowship. Eventually, one of our three went through a painful and messy divorce. He had two young daughters. We experienced that division and his depression together. We added a couple of members to the group. Our divorced friend moved away. Then the other original member of our group, Dana, developed a brain tumor.

As he was trying to recover from surgery, we moved the group meeting to his living room, where a hospital bed replaced the furniture. When it became clear that he was not going to recover, and he began losing his vision and ability to speak, I visited him and brought books to read to him. On his better days we could discuss a little of what I had just read. In his declining days, all he could muster was a disfigured, "Wow."

I knew his life on earth was nearly over. I told him I would be gone for a few days for a speaking engagement in Detroit, but that I would come over as soon as I got back in town. With great effort he whispered, "I'll see you when you get back." As I drove away, I wondered if I would ever see him again, and tears began flowing from my eyes. I stopped my car at a traffic light, and tried to tell myself to pay attention. I heard bells from the Presbyterian Church at this same intersection. They played a song I hadn't heard in probably thirty years, so it took me a few moments to remember the words. Finally, they came: "Blest be the tie that binds our hearts in Christian love; the fellowship of kindred hearts is like to that above." It was a moment where I sensed God telling me, "I understand. I got to this intersection before you. I'm weeping too." It didn't take the pain away. It gave the pain a new dimension of meaning—God's mysterious presence preceded me, and he was with me. And with my friend.

While I was in Detroit I called home to hear the results of my son's bid for student body president of his middle school. He answered the phone and told me that he had lost the election. He didn't seem all that devastated. I wished I could have spared him from the pain. (It was not a close vote, he told me. I backed off from demanding a recount.) All I could do was bear it with him. But he didn't want to talk about it—he was insistent that I call my wife at her office. Still wishing I could have taken away his pain, I called Marcia. She told me that Dana had died. I remember little else about the conversation. I was staying with my oldest brother. He tried to help me in my pain, but we both knew that he couldn't. He could only be present and share it.

I can still hear the bells ringing, *blest be the tie that binds our hearts in Christian love* . . .

I am operating under the assumption that what we have reserved for "special" experiences of the Mystery and grace of God don't need to be confined to just those moments announced in a church bulletin or mediated by official clergy. Sacred moments occur under those circumstances, of course. That's part of our Christian tradition. But if we are a priesthood to one another (the New Testament says we are), then sacred moments can also be found outside church walls.

They are occurring all around us. Before us. Beneath us. "Life is this simple," Merton said. "We are living in a world that is absolutely transparent, and God is shining through it all the time."[24] If we live sacramentally, where we are intentionally paying attention to the activity and grace of God in everyday life, we will see it. Jesus said, "The eye is the lamp of the body. So if your eye is healthy, your whole body will be full of light" (Matt. 6:22).

True spirituality is about seeing, about letting the invisible inform the visible, about letting the internal world inform the external world, about seeing the beyond in our midst.

One of the ways we can improve our vision is by living in a way that seeks to reveal the sacred—the grace—in the everydayness of life. Recognizing the constant appearance of the sacraments provides focus. Not everyone sees this, of course, or even believes that the signs—the grace—are out there waiting to be noticed. To assume that what we can really know has to be measured or touched or felt or quantified is one of the sad curses of our age. And it has a whiff of arrogance to it.

The hunger for an experience with the sacred is universal, I believe. "The fact is that human beings cannot live happily without a framework of meaning that transcends the individualism, materialism, and selfishness of the marketplace and without the sense that a loving connection exists among us as well as to that larger experience the religious among us call God," wrote Rabbi Michael Lerner.[25]

It seemed that something from beyond my "known" world even broke through one night in 2001, while watching the Arizona Diamondbacks play the New York Yankees in the World Series. It's a big deal to watch the World Series in my house, even for the non-baseball fans, which is everyone except me. In 1987 I took my five-month son on an airplane from San Diego to Minneapolis for the opening night game between the Minnesota Twins—my boyhood idols—and the St. Louis Cardinals. We flew early Saturday morning, had three connections, and got into town a few hours before the game. After seeing a glorious victory, we flew the same route home early the next morning. I take the baseball seriously.

We all watched, stunned, in Game 5, as the relief pitcher, Byung-Hyun Kim, gave up yet another late-inning home run, allowing the Yankees to go ahead in the series. The very same thing had happened in Game 4. The Diamondbacks had the Yankees on the ropes, but the Yankee mystique looked like it would prevail. They came back, at the expense of this Korean relief pitcher. Television cameras showed Kim crouching on the pitcher's mound as Scott Brosius rounded the bases with his home run. Kim looked stunned, his eyes moist. He looked as if he didn't know what had hit him. Then something did hit him—or at least bump him. His first baseman came running over and embraced him, smiling, telling Kim that it was okay, and that things were going to work out. Kim looked as if he desperately wanted to believe his teammate. The Diamondbacks went on to win the series in seven games.

The first baseman's name was Mark. His last name was Grace.

Coincidence? Wishful thinking? Overactive imagination on my part?

I listen to a lot of music, and love to hear it live. I love the simplicity and clarity of the blues, and how it seems to inject directly into your nervous system. I love the beat of rock. One of the best things I can do for my soul, though, is to go hear some live jazz. The reason is that so much of it is improvised. The rhythm section might hold a beat for several minutes, but a soloist will step out and blast something that, to the untrained ear, might sound like so much chaos and noise. The crowd tries to follow, but after a while it seems like the only thing that matters to the musicians is what they are doing on the stage at that very moment. What is breathtaking about it, though, is when suddenly, with no visible signal, all of the musicians come together and you realize that it wasn't chaos at all, but exploration and experimentation and improvisation that all merged in a colossal surprise. I read a definition of jazz years ago that said it was "ordered disorder, with sudden bursts of revelation."

To me, that sounds like life, punctuated by the sacred and holy.

1

Handing Out Coupons

The Sacrament of Vocation

The experience of eternity right here and now, in all things, whether thought of as good or as evil, is the function of life.

Joseph Campbell[1]

When one has a literature degree and no plans for graduate school or for a career in teaching, and no real sense of what the word "vocation" means, there are few options. This was the situation I faced after I graduated from college. So I did what everyone with no marketable skills seems to do in my situation. I went to work for a church.

The church had a heart for urban life. Sort of. It owned a coffee house in the city where musicians, dramatists, and other artsy people would perform on a regular basis. People came in from the streets to hear the music and, hopefully, a good news message. This was the 1970s, and this coffee house was one of the destinations on most troubadours' itineraries. It was the kind of place you'd expect to see Bob Dylan drop into. Some of the musicians and actors who came through are still touring and are now very famous. Most, mercifully, have found other means of employment.

In addition to my assignment as manager of this coffee house, I was in charge of the youth group of the church that owned it. The thinking was that, as people came off the street into the coffee house, they would want to become part of the church. It was a good theory, but it never happened. The off-the-street gang was one kind of people (no church background, harmful personal habits, hygiene issues, missing teeth, rough around the edges, in need of basics like clothing, food, and shelter, maybe a little Satan worship in their past, some schizophrenia, other flashes of mental illness) and the church group was a different kind (born into churchgoing families, more secretive about their harmful personal habits, very smooth skin, clear eyes, straightened teeth, monogrammed sweaters, maybe a little plastic surgery, but similarly desperate for attention and love). The two groups were different economically, socially, sometimes racially, and spiritually.

The church ended up with a type of identity crisis—who are we really reaching out to? The upper class folks who drive in from the suburbs and pay the bills, or these street people, who seem to be on fire for their faith?

The easy solution to the church's identity crisis was to sell the coffee house to a convenience store (keeping the neighborhood well stocked in alcohol, tobacco, and condoms; maybe they'll get that license to sell guns before too long) and move the church to the suburbs. My own crisis only deepened.

Thank You, Uncle Ed

During this time of confusion, my newlywed wife and I visited her great uncle and aunt in Indiana. The uncle, Ed Blair, was a Bible scholar. He had taught at major theological seminaries, had an Ivy League education, had led archeological expeditions in the Middle East, and was the author of the Methodist church's gigantic work, *The Abingdon Bible Handbook*. Smart guy. A bit intimidating. A theological force of biblical proportions.

He was so smart and intimidating that, during our visit with him and his wife Vivian, he sent our wives off on an errand so that it was just him and me sitting in his study.

"How long do you plan on doing this coffee house/church job?" he asked.

I didn't have a clue. I'm not a planner. I barely knew what I was going to do on the weekend.

"Beats me," I said, looking at the bookshelves, lined with books he had written. "Why?"

"Have you ever thought about the fact that this kind of job is not something one does long term?"

Actually, I had not thought of that. I was failing his little quiz.

"Is Marcia happy in Detroit?"

Ah. Now I was getting it. We weren't just having a chat. He was concerned about his vulnerable little niece in big bad Detroit.

"Not really," I said. "Since our grocery clerks are behind bullet-proof glass and the third grade teacher was gunned down in front of the students at the school down the street and my office is robbed routinely, I wouldn't say she's headed for serenity." I assumed he knew that Detroit was the murder capital of the world that year.

Uncle Ed and I had a long moment of looking into one another's eyes at this point.

"What do you know how to do?" he finally asked.

No one had ever asked me that question before. I thought for a while before I spoke. I squinted, and shifted in my chair.

"I can write," I said.

"How do you know?"

"Because I've been published in magazines and in my college newspaper."

"That proves nothing."

Ouch! Here's a guy who had written books and hundreds of scholarly articles, along with hundreds more for the popular press. I guess he should know. Actually I had a better reason for my answer than just that I had been published. During college I had hired myself out to students to write papers for them (even autobiographies, without bothering to ask them any questions about themselves—now that's talent!). I wrote my own major academic papers in a fraction of the

time it took others. I wrote poems, plays, and stories. A congressman
visiting our campus (a Republican, of course, given the conservative
bent of that school—its post office box number was 1776) asked if I
wanted to come to Washington and join his staff of speechwriters.
More fiction fun!

Uncle Ed suggested I consider journalism.

I could envision the jaws dropping on my Nixon-worshipping college alma mater if they knew I was considering journalism. I could
see them investigating me for un-American activities.

What Uncle Ed did was, as author Parker Palmer describes, surround me with a force field that made me want to grow from the inside
out—"a force field that is safe enough to take the risks and endure the
failures that growth requires . . ." where I could experience my true
vocational call. Uncle Ed created a space that both encouraged and
inspired me to take the inner vocational journey. "In such a space,
we are freed to hear our own truth, touch what brings us joy, become
self-critical about our faults, and take risky steps toward change."[2]

My first day of class in journalism school was one of the most
exciting days I remember. At first I was terrified, as if I was entering kindergarten all over again, knowing that everyone else in the
class was more prepared than I because they had gone to preschool
and learned the secret language of kindergarten teachers while poor,
deprived me, I stayed home with my mom for the first five years. I
remembered that old *National Lampoon* comedy routine based on
the drippy Desiderata poem everyone used to have on posters in their
dorm rooms. This one was renamed Deteriorata, and said: "You are
a fluke of the universe. You have no right to be here."

Likewise, I knew I was out of my league in grad school. I knew they
would soon discover that the admissions office had made a mistake—I
had spent the last three years working for a church, after all—and
would declare me an imposter. But when the professor began talking
about how he had covered the civil rights movement for a New York
newspaper, and how we were going to become storytellers to help
the world talk to itself and understand itself, it was as if a shaft of
sunlight broke through the ancient ceiling of this oldest journalism
school in the country, and illuminated my desk and me. It was like a
Franco Zefferelli film, where one defined beam of light and fresh air

cut through the gray stuffiness of that rarified atmosphere. I was in
the right place. It was a fulfillment of Palmer's definition of vocation:
"This is something I can't not do, for reasons I'm unable to explain to
anyone else and don't fully understand myself, but that are nonetheless
compelling."[3] This clarity was a means by which I experienced God,
where what I was good at met up with what the world needed—that's
the sacrament of vocation.

After our talk in his study, I spent the rest of the day breathing,
"Thank you, Uncle Ed, thank you!"

The Secret of Life

To know that we fit into the world is a wonderful gift. To use the
gifts each of us is given creates a sense of great purpose. The ancient
sacrament of receiving a vocational call centers on seeing a greater
purpose for using our gifts, skills, and interests instead of just practicing a trade. The vocational call is discovering that we can best use
our skills, gifts, and interests for the good of others. It is one of the
ways we experience Mystery, and one of the ways we help the world
experience Mystery. The vocational call on all of us is to continue and
extend the work of grace and love in the world. Those are our "holy
orders." As we accept the work we are to do, or search for the kind
of work we wish to do, the sacramental approach to it is to allow the
search to come under the umbrella of this sacred call. The work we do
and wish to do is one of the means of discovering who we are and what
our role is in the world. Our unique talents, desires, and backgrounds
are the means by which we fulfill that calling. And by seeing it as a
calling, we experience the sacred throughout our day. We experience
the presence of God through the exercise of our abilities.

This sacramental view of calling took an increasingly exclusive
turn, as did most of the sacraments, as religious practice evolved.
Instead of the vocational call being on all of us, it became more of
the territory of those called into certain kinds of service. As the term
"holy orders" evolved, it became interpreted to mean "withdrawn"
and "dedicated," usually into the cloister of a convent or monastery.
It grew into a type of elitism.

But it wasn't always that way, and it doesn't have to be that way now, if we truly believe that the Mystery of God is breaking through into every moment, and is visible to those who are paying attention. Virtually anyone can become a priest—one who is called to do holy work—in the sense of pointing people to God, and we can be priests to all we come in contact with. It is a vocation we discover when we are paying attention. The true call on all of us is not to withdraw, but to engage. Work and worship can be woven into the same cloth. The whole world becomes our monastery. Everyone can have a priestly role in our communities, for the chief purpose of being a priest is to reveal the connections we all have to God.

"The secret of life is to have a task, something you devote your entire life to, something you bring everything to, every minute of the day for your whole life," said the sculptor Henry Moore. "And the more important thing is—it must be something you cannot possibly do!"[4]

Our vocation doesn't always occur in the form of our occupations, however. For many people, vocation and occupation are two different things. "There are jobs, there are chores, and there is work," Donald Hall said.[5] Our vocation can permeate them all. Sometimes we can see a relationship between our jobs (occupation) and our work (vocation), but not always. If we can, it is something to be thankful for. If we can't, it is not cause for despair. There is opportunity for vocation in every occupation, because the vocation of everyone is to point to the presence of God, with or without a script of a specific job.

Marcia, my wife, is an accountant. That's her occupation. She has an MBA from a major university, and has used her accounting and finance skills to help construction companies build buildings and make money. Her employers are not in business to build shelters for the homeless, or churches for the devout, although, since her present bosses are spiritually minded, that is part of what they do. Mostly, though, they do construction. It is a responsible, fair company. And until recently, she felt that her vocation was to help that company stay in a strong, financial position, as well as be a positive influence to those she encountered throughout the day.

Then she was introduced to an organization called Stephen Ministries. With some training, Stephen Ministers provide compassionate care to someone in personal crisis. The relationship between the minister and the one in need can last weeks, months, or longer. The ministers don't provide money or advice. They are trained to avoid the temptation to solve problems and meet specific needs. They simply provide compassionate presence to people who can't continue on their own. They give people the opportunity for their troubled hearts to rest. The only thing that Stephen Ministers can promise is that they will listen to those who need them, and that they will pray for them. Marcia's initial experience with Stephen Ministries was the same as mine when I went to journalism school. "I know what I am put on earth to do," she told me.

She spends most of her time being a wife, mother, daughter, sister, aunt, accountant, and financial advisor. One hour per week she provides presence to her "care receiver." But it is during that hour that she feels most "called," or "ordained." That's when she experiences the visible form of the invisible Spirit. That's what a sacrament is.

Listening to Our Lives

"Vocation does not come from willfulness. It comes from listening," Palmer writes.[6] The occupations most of us prepare for are often not the result of listening to our lives, or to the spirit within us, or to the uncles that ambush us. They often come from listening to advice from parents and school counselors, from taking standardized tests that measure our "true" interests (I took one and it said I was especially suited for farming or for selling insurance), and maybe from reading publications in career center offices that have articles with titles like, "The Ten Hottest Jobs for You!!!"

An occupation is something we pursue. It is a goal we set out to achieve ("I am *applying* for a job . . ."). But a vocation is revealed from within. As Palmer says, "Before I can tell my life what I want to do with it, I must listen to my life telling me who I am."[7] Vocation comes from the inside out.

Looking at vocation this way, we can see that it is a means of discovering who we *really* are, and what we are *really* to be about. It is a means of discovering our true selves and our true purposes in the world.

Even though I had this breakthrough in journalism school, this vocational calling was not always smooth in its manifestation. I worked for a while in newspapers, and found it fascinating and fulfilling (despite its low pay), for the most part. Journalists get backstage passes to the world. Simply because I was a journalist, people let me hang out with them; they told me private, personal things. Journalists get to observe, interpret, and explain the world by telling stories. Jazz great Dizzy Gillespie let me hang out with him for a couple of days as he did workshops and concerts. Basketball great Julius Erving let me play some one-on-one basketball with him (it was close, but he eventually beat me. I really didn't foul him as often as he whined that I had). Firefighters let me be with them as they tried to protect their own homes from a forest fire. Comedians let me observe how they prepare for an audience (see me later about the bending spoon trick). Musicians let me be on stage with them, acting as if I were one of the performers (they minimized the risk by taking the mouthpiece out of the trombone, though). Illegal workers let me spend time with them as they tried to sneak into this country without getting caught by the Border Patrol. The Border Patrol let me go with them as they tried to stop the illegal workers from sneaking into the country. Parents of kids dying of cancer let me spend Christmas Eve with them. A person who was in transition from one gender to another talked with me about what it felt like to live as one gender yet feel trapped in the body of another. Residents whose homes were terrorized by a serial killer let me talk with them—one even made me lunch! A man tortured by police in China for twenty-seven years because of his association with the Dalai Lama let me sit in his apartment and drink yak butter tea with him in Tibet. A man whose children all had birth defects because of the radiation he was exposed to during the Cold War let me hang out with his family. A woman whose children were chronically ill because of the Dominican Republic's contaminated water fed us lunch. People in pain, people in ecstasy, people in the public eye, people who mostly get ignored, all have given me access to their lives. I have gotten to travel throughout the world, simply because I knew how to find and tell stories.

For a three-year hiatus, though, I saw how else my writing ability could be used, when it was only an occupation, and not a vocation.

When I first went to journalism school, the only way I could qualify for in-state tuition status was if Marcia worked full-time within the university system. So we cut a deal with one another. She would take any grunt job in order to get me the reduced tuition, as long as I would do the same for her when I was finished. She wanted to get an MBA at the University of Minnesota. I would get a job in the Twin Cities area, I promised, when she was ready to go back to school. So while I was studying journalism, she worked as a secretary, and then a bookkeeper. The work was well beneath her ability as a businesswoman, but it was a means to an end, and a deal is a deal.

When I was finished and she was ready to go to school, the job I got in Minnesota wasn't in that state's university system. It was much higher paying, so we could afford Marcia's tuition. The job wasn't actually in journalism, either. It used my journalism training, but it emphatically was not journalism. It was in a field called "corporate communications" at the headquarters of one of the largest companies in the world at the time. I started out as a staff writer for the monthly employee magazine, and eventually became editor of the magazine. I wrote articles about individuals, new businesses, philanthropic efforts; I wrote speeches; I brainstormed marketing plans and new product applications. I traveled throughout the country, schmoozed with the elite class, was on a fast management track; I made a lot of money.

And I was miserable.

I was a propagandist.

We didn't tell all of the truth all of the time, which had been my training from my parents and my professors. We told employees just enough to keep morale up so they would remain productive and loyal. The rest of the story about the company, such as whether we were gross polluters or were misleading the public about defense contracts, or whether we were being fair to the employees, we let those pesky, leftist, commie journalists dig up if they could. And if they could, it was just as easy to shoot the messenger rather than deny or confirm the accuracy of their message. I felt like a character in an Orwell or Kafka novel, part of a machine that ground down individuals until they were mindlessly serving a system that they didn't question. I was a Stepford Writer.

But as Marcia's and my agreement stated, it was a means to an end, and a deal is a deal. She didn't like being a secretary or bookkeeper in Missouri, either. I tried to keep my misery from distracting Marcia's studies, tried to read something other than depressing Russian literature in my spare time, yet she will readily point out that I didn't do that great a job of hiding my downward spiral.

I know that I could have used my time in that corporate arena more productively. I could have looked beyond whether I was being fulfilled, and tried to live up to my higher vocational calling. I could have bloomed where I was planted. I could have made lemonade out of the lemons. I could have been a happy face for Jesus. I could have had a better attitude as I blew sunshine up everyone's corporate dress. But I didn't. Pain is inevitable, the rock climber Tim Hensel used to say, but misery is optional. I chose misery.

It wasn't the Minnesota weather, either. I had grown up in that stuff. Even as an adult I loved to play outside during the winter. I simply feared that I would be in this hamster-wheel of a job forever, and somewhere in the deep recesses of my heart, I knew that I was nowhere near my vocation. I knew that I could not live out my true self in that corporate world. Some can. Praise God for them. The Big Wheel keeps on turning because of them. I couldn't. In my quest for vocational integrity, which I did not even know I was on, I knew I could not last in that job much longer.

I saw myself in the introduction of Studs Terkel's book, *Working*. "Work, by its very nature, is about violence—to the spirit as well as to the body. It is about ulcers as well as accidents, about shouting matches as well as fistfights, about nervous breakdowns as well as kicking the dog around. It is, above all (or beneath all) about daily humiliations. To survive the day is triumph enough for the walking wounded among the great many of us."[8]

Joseph Campbell tells of being in a restaurant, and at the next table were a father, mother, and a skinny young boy. The father said to the boy, "Drink your tomato juice."

"I don't want to," said the boy.

"Drink your tomato juice," the father said, in a much louder voice.

The mother intervened.

"Don't make him do what he doesn't want to do," she pleaded.

"He can't go through life doing what he wants to do," the father said. "If he does only what he wants to do, he'll be dead. Look at me. I've never done a thing I wanted to in all my life."

Campbell said he uses this example to urge his students to, "Go where your body and soul want to go." He said that within each of us is a "bliss," and that when we are paying attention, we can see that hidden hands help guide us into that bliss. "Follow your bliss and don't be afraid, and doors will open where you didn't know they were going to be."[9] When that happens, it doesn't feel like work.

Fortunately, Marcia and I had been meeting with three other couples regularly to go to movies together, read books and discuss the chapters, share meals, and go on cross-country ski weekends. They had become our community. During these lengthy discussions, the talk invariably turned to what we were doing with our lives, and in a friendly and supportive banter, each of us eventually was called upon to defend how we were living. Somehow, each gathering was done in a spirit of support and togetherness, not competitiveness or moral superiority. The gatherings weren't planned with any objective. But they emerged as a way we could help each other share our true vocations, or maybe even discover them. We were present for one another without violating one another, or doing violence to each other. There was no illusion of trying to save one another; more accurately, we illumined one another. We were priests for one another as we continued on our journey. This community helped us understand and articulate and pursue our true vocations.

Eventually jobs opened up in San Diego that suited our bliss better. Okay, suited *my* bliss better.

What God Wants

After I had been a college professor for a while I was invited to be the speaker at a retreat for freshmen just as their new educational venture was getting under way. I ended up doing this for several years. They piled into buses and traveled to a campground outside of San Diego. It was a time of bonding and recreation for them. There were worship services at night, and we all slept in a meadow under a blanket of what looked like snow millions of miles away. Nowhere else could one see so many stars. I brought my kids to the event, and it was one of the highlights of the year for us.

During one of the worship times in this informal, rustic setting, I talked to the freshman class about what God wants for them. Many of them had been raised in conservative religious cultures. I told them that they had probably been told that God wanted them to have a specific career, college, occupation, spouse, etc. They nodded enthusiastically. Then I told them that, not only did I think that this message of "God's blueprint" was overrated, it was also probably not true. We spend way too much energy on trying to uncover the tracks of a hidden God who may or may not have left us clues as to what he wants us to do with our lives, I told them. We treat God's "plan" like Bigfoot, I said.

I could tell by their facial expressions that they were nearly horrified by what I told them.

Then I told them that there was something we knew for sure about what God wanted for us, and that our focus should be there, instead of trying to play *Where in the World is Carmen San Diego?* with our divine calling. What we know, according to the Bible, other ancient writings, saints, and scholars, is that God wants us to love extravagantly. That's God's will for everyone. Everything else is secondary. That doesn't mean other pursuits are not important. But careers, spouses, etc.—the particulars of our lives—make more sense when they are seen within the context of loving. And if the students didn't believe me, I knew they'd believe Bono, the rock star, who was once asked if he asked God to bless the humanitarian efforts he was involved in. Bono said, and I am paraphrasing, that we get it backward if we do something and ask God to bless it. Find out what God is already doing in the world and participate in that, he said. That's already been blessed.

My message just didn't seem to be enough certainty for some of those freshmen. And yet, one or two would always pull me aside later and thank me for taking the pressure off.

What I hoped they heard was an encouragement to focus less on their occupation and focus more on their vocation. Listening to our true calling may mean that the pursuit of a particular occupation in law, education, medicine, the arts, engineering, agriculture, manufacturing, or parenting is just the thing for us—as long as we know we are there to love.

In the wonderful novel *Lying Awake* by Mark Salzman, the main character, Sister John of the Cross, becomes confused in her spiritual calling at the convent where she lives. The visions she used to have no longer occur, now that her epilepsy has been successfully treated by a doctor. (An interesting sub-theme in Salzman's writings is that he links spirituality to mental illness.) At the end of the novel, her Mother Superior approaches and asks if she will give a novice sister spiritual direction on God's will.

"I don't feel I know anything about God's will, Mother," said Sister John.

"Yet you're still here, trying to do his will anyway," Mother Emmanuel said. "That's the kind of understanding I meant. The doing kind, not the knowing kind."

Both women then watch as birds busily work and call around the fountain in the garden. The birds "seemed to have the best understanding of all," Salzman writes. "They answered yes to everything."[10]

Our vocation is what we are called to spend the rest of our lives doing.

"We can speak of a man's choosing his vocation, but perhaps it is at least as accurate to speak of a vocation's choosing the man, of a call's being given and a man's hearing it, or not hearing it," Buechner said.[11]

Real Work

In a university setting, it is tempting to measure our effectiveness by charting the careers of our alumni. When I talk about the journalism program where I teach, a great selling point is the success of our graduates—where they are getting published, where they are producing television programs, etc. One was part of a team of journalists that won a Pulitzer Prize—not bad for a college student! That's what gets the attention of students and their parents. A harder dimension to measure and discuss is whether our institution is helping students find their true calling—responding to the bliss. If the gospel we are teaching is one of status, safety, and self-reliance, then I'm sure we're doing as good a job as anyone else. Whether we are helping students hear the call to go where they are most needed, and where they most need to go, I wonder.

Maybe we should start granting degrees in listening. Every school loves to proclaim that it is preparing the world's leaders. What we really should be preparing are its followers.

While it is obvious that not everyone's occupation can be the *same* as their vocation, it should be just as evident that everyone's vocation can be lived out *within* one's occupation. I missed that piece of insight while I was rallying the corporate militia to sell their souls to the company store. The call on our lives is to give form to the invisible spirit in all that we do. The Spirit can be evident in our work, play, family, and society, whatever our circumstances. "When our work becomes real, our jobs will follow suit," says author and former Catholic priest, Matthew Fox.[12]

Tony Campolo tells the story of a friend of his who was in a Nordstrom store in a wealthy Los Angeles suburb around Christmas time. She was on the top floor, where the most elegant dresses cost thousands of dollars, when the elevator doors opened and a bag lady from off of the streets emerged. Tony's friend expected the employees to notify security and have the woman returned to the streets, from which she obviously had come. Instead, a stately saleswoman greeted the bag lady and said, "Can I help you madam?" The bag lady said she wanted to buy a dress. A party dress. "You've come to the right place, the saleswoman said, brightly. "We have the finest dresses in the world." The two women looked at several racks and decided on two to try on.

Campolo's friend was flabbergasted. She knew that the bag lady couldn't afford clothes from this store. But the saleswoman and the bag lady went into the fitting room. After a while, the bag lady said, "I've changed my mind. I'm not going to buy a dress today."

"That's quite all right, Madam," the saleswoman replied. "But I'd like you to take my card. Should you come back to Nordstrom, I would consider it both a privilege and a pleasure to wait on you again."[13]

Selling expensive clothes as a vocational call? When it's done this way, it is.

Christopher Wren, the architect who designed St. Paul's Cathedral in London, told of touring the cathedral site during its construction. He asked each of the workers what he was doing. One said he was cutting stones. Another said he was a carpenter. Another said he was hanging stained glass. When Wren came upon a laborer stirring cement, he asked the same question. The laborer, not knowing who Wren was, said, "Why sir, I'm building a great cathedral to the glory of God."[14] That's a person who was able to see his everyday work as his vocation.

Journalists often have to cover distasteful subjects. Sometimes the people involved in the stories are distasteful—even reprehensible. More times than I can remember, I have had sources look me in the eye with apparent sincerity and lie to my face. It happens more to me as a journalist than it does to me as a college professor, listening to creative excuses for missed exams and assignments. In my journalism practice, if it weren't for the discipline of verification, some of my stories would have been mostly false because of all the liars I talked to. And while my occupation is to tell the most balanced and complete story that I can, my vocation, my calling, is to love the people I am interviewing. I don't always like them, but the vocation in the present moment is to try to love them regardless of how they are acting.

My vocation is the same when I deal with students. Some are easier to connect with than others. My vocation is to love them all, including those who don't seem very lovable. Worship and work are inseparable, Eugene Peterson said. "What we're after is a seamless world of work and worship, worship and work . . . Work is the primary context for our spirituality." We are introduced to God in scripture, as he is going to work. When Jesus stood up in the synagogue to preach, he was announcing that he was going to work. The spirit has *anointed* me, he said. And being anointed by God, Peterson said, means given a job by God. There's a job to be done, we're told to do it, and we're equipped to do it. "Anointing is the sacramental connection linking God's work with our work," he said. Our present day task is to "recover work as vocation—as holy work. Every Christian takes holy orders." But not every job, or work, is going to be perfectly suited for this sacrament. And that's the point. "The key to living vocationally—that is, being 'God-called,' Spirit-anointed—isn't getting the right job or career but doing kingwork in whatever circumstances we find ourselves."[15]

Discovering that we all have holy orders means that our everyday tasks have meanings and connections beyond the tasks. That they are ways we participate with what God is already doing. Without the anointing, we lead "lives of quite desperation," as Thoreau described it, or, as the Grand Inquisitor proclaims in Brothers Karamazov, "Without a firm notion of what he is living for, man will not accept life and will rather destroy himself than remain in earth . . ."[16]

Stealing Soup

Peter van Breemen, a German theologian, tells of a woman who went into a restaurant with high tables where patrons could stand for a quick lunch. She bought a bowl of soup and a sausage sandwich and carried them to an empty table. She put her purse underneath, and went back to the counter to get a spoon for her soup. When she returned, a dark-skinned stranger was standing at the table, happily eating her soup. At first she was shocked. Then furious. Within seconds, she decided that, if this man wished to be so bold, then so would she. She stood at the opposite side of the table and began eating from the same bowl. But instead of being embarrassed or intimidated, the man continued to eat. He did not speak German, so he couldn't understand what the woman was saying to him, but he kept a smile on his face as they ate together.

Seeming to provoke her further, the man offered her half of the sausage sandwich. When they were finished, he, still smiling, offered his hand across the table in a handshake. Still flabbergasted, the woman shook his hand. Then the man left the restaurant. When she looked under the table for her purse, it was gone. She knew it! He was a thief! All of her money, credit cards, personal information—taken by this brazen man!

As she scanned the room to call out for help, she noticed a nearby table, with a bowl of now-cold soup, a sausage sandwich, and her purse underneath. It had never occurred to her that she had gone to the wrong table!

What is our true vocation? To be the man who, although he could not understand what was being said about him, makes room at his table. "Vocation is a dynamic reality, constantly interacting with every aspect of the here and now," van Breemen said.[17]

On days when my schedule permitted, I volunteered at my daughter's middle school. The teachers didn't need classroom assistants, the way the elementary school teachers did, when my wife and I volunteered there. At middle school, the most desperate need was for help during the lunch hour. Crowd control. When I checked in at the front office, I was given a button that said, in large letters, "Dads At Lunch." On my first day of volunteering, the receptionist gave me some coupons, good for a free cheeseburger at the local McDonald's.

"These are if you catch one of the kids being good," she said, as she doled out a few into my hand. Interesting premise, I thought. "Catching" kids being good? I noticed the drawer where the coupons were kept must have had a thousand in there. At the rate she was handing them to me, my grandchildren would be students here before the coupons were used up.

"What do you mean by 'being good'?" I asked.

"If they speak to you, or if they throw away some trash," she said. "Just don't give coupons to kids with plastic bags who are picking up trash. They are being punished for something." Apparently they had already been caught for doing something other than good.

"Do I have to have a reason to give one of these coupons out?"

She thought for a moment, and shrugged.

"I guess not."

"Then can I have some more?"

She gave me a pocketful.

I didn't really have any expectations as I approached the lunch area. My daughter had told me that it was mostly loud and messy, and offered no counsel other than to not embarrass her. I got there about ten minutes before the bell rang, so I stood off to the side of an outdoor concrete slab with metal picnic tables and a patio roof, waiting for the kids to arrive. About fifty crows and gulls had also gotten there early, but they took their places patiently on the roof so that they could have the best access to the leftovers. They acted as a type of ornithological security camera. They jockeyed for position with one another as I assumed the kids would do once the cafeteria windows were open for business.

What I didn't anticipate was how my own memories of school lunches came flooding back, nearly causing an out of body experience.

There have been times in my life when I have intentionally gone back to specific places in my past, just to stand in their midst and see if any ghosts were still there. I sat in my elementary school parking lot remembering a teacher drawing blood out of my chin with her thumbnail for my misbehaving, and walked through the rink where I got my jaw broken and teeth knocked out playing hockey, and tarried at the spot on the way home from junior high school where I lost a fight, and went to the Senior Room of my high school where I was terrorized as a freshman and then terrorized freshmen three years later, and went to graves of friends who have left us too early, and stood in the Library of Congress where I did my dissertation research, just to see if there were any ghosts lingering there. I found mostly good memories, but no ghosts.

So it really caught me off guard at this middle school when, waiting for the sixth, seventh, and eighth graders to pour into the lunch area, the jungle drums began to pound. I remembered how painful the school lunch hour could be at this age. It is the hour when it is unquestionably clear who the popular kids are and who they aren't. In the classroom, it isn't quite as clear because the teachers can compensate through judicious treatment. Even in P.E., the kids are divided into groups, not according to ability or popularity, but according to the teacher's sense of equality.

In the lunch area, though, the Invisible Hand that shakes the Sifter, sorting out who is In and who is Out, is unmistakable. I was not necessarily one of the school rejects when I was this age. I just remember seeing them everywhere, and thanking God, or Whoever, that I wasn't one of them. That the Big Snapper hadn't dragged me under yet. If you got too close to the social lepers, people might think you actually *knew* them, which meant you were potentially as weird as them, or that whatever their personality disease was could possibly leap off of them and onto you like an infected flea. You kept your distance.

Those fleas could jump. Regardless of what your pastor told you about befriending the friendless, you knew you were just going to have to accept the consequences of ignoring his instruction during lunch. You simply did not cross that imaginary line.

All my own adolescent social fears and misgivings came hurtling back during the moments I waited for the lunch bell to ring. Entire cemeteries of ghosts emptied into the patio. I could see in this place the people I had tried to avoid years ago. And I thought of how probably nothing had changed, that the evolution of the species would not have included changing the brutal selection process that isolates the fat, or non-English speaking, or severely acned, or hostile, poorly hygiened, or socially backward from everyone else. Genetic engineering hadn't figured this one out yet. I would have to see it all over again. The drums became deafening.

I was right.

The Cool Kids sat together. So did the Rich Kids. So did the Athletes. So did the Cheerleaders. So did the Girl Scouts and Boy Scouts. So did the Bible Club with their *Left Behind* books. Sometimes the groups divided along racial lines. And sure enough, there were the kids eating alone, or with maybe one other person, unable to deny the reality of what the invisible lunchroom Sifter was telling them. They did not fit in. They would be either ignored or picked on. I still don't know which is worse.

I sat briefly with many of them and tried to engage them in conversation, trying hard not to act with condescension or pity. I asked them about classes and teachers and books. Some were very talkative, even effusive, revealing some of the reasons why people steered clear of them. One barely seemed to endure my questioning and said, finally, "I prefer to be by myself, if you don't mind."

"Really?" I said. "Why?"

"Because people annoy me. They're so stupid."

At the end of each brief conversation I would produce one of these coupons.

"What is this for?" they would ask. I told them it was for a free cheeseburger.

"No, what did we do to deserve it?"

"Nothing. I just wanted you to have it. No reason. Just because I want to."

The reaction to this kind of senseless dispensation of goodness was wonderful to watch. Some were thankful. Some walked away quizzical. Some showed their friends, and those friends would come to me and ask for a coupon. At this point I felt comfortable attaching requirements.

"You see that kid sitting over there by himself? Walk over there, sit down by him and tell him something good about himself," I would say before giving the coupon.

Now *that* was fun to watch.

Some kids caught on to the coupon gig pretty quickly, and, when they saw me, would start acting like Eddie Haskell from *Leave It To Beaver*—helping others with their backpacks, throwing trash away, always looking my direction out of the corners of their eyes. One girl made sure that she was always in my line of vision, and that I saw her do something nice. She got a coupon, but I was less excited about handing out coupons to suck-ups. It's boring.

If I saw trouble brewing in a group (shouting, cursing, shoving, name-calling, and backpack swinging were pretty good indicators), I would walk into the middle of the circle with the coupons. "Look at this," I'd say. "Free cheeseburgers. Anybody want one?" They all did. Crisis averted.

Some of the tables had checkerboards painted onto their surfaces, so some days I brought checkers from home. All it took was sitting down and setting the checkers on the board, and kids would appear, wanting to play. The sound around the game was deafening. The kids played against me by committee: "No, don't move there, stupid! He'll jump you!" Every move a kid made was followed by the obligatory declaration: "You suck!" Still, it was fun. And everyone got a coupon just for being in the crowd.

The noise and chaos of the lunch period built to ear-bleeding decibels, and then the bell rang, signaling a return to classes. The kids cleared out as quickly as cockroaches when you turn on the kitchen light. Then the crows and gulls parachuted in like the 101st Airborne Division, and created a chaos of their own. None of them were interested in playing checkers.

Each of our vocations involves activities similar to my coupon routine. It isn't as if we go find the misfits and give them a trinket and a pat on the head. But we can look for those in our families, our places of work, and our communities who routinely are ignored, passed over, or taken advantage of. Loneliness can be the most devastating disease in the world. But we can, in one way or another, say to the people around us, "I see you. I notice you. You're not invisible. You matter."

We really don't need much to be equipped to fulfill our vocation. Jesus sent his followers out with nothing except instructions. As Barbara Brown Taylor says, vocation

> is simply what you do, when you know who you are and who you are working for, when you are sent out to proclaim the kingdom and to act it out with no money, no shoes, not even a walking stick. Because when it comes down to being a provider of God's love, there is really only one provider, who sends us out with nothing at all and with everything we need: healing, forgiveness, restoration, resurrection. Those are the only things we really have to share with the world, which is just as well, since they are the only things the world really needs.[18]

I suspect that God works in a similar manner to this coupon business. Something is constantly breaking through our dulled senses, telling us that we matter—that grace surrounds us.

Several years ago the novelist Chaim Potok gave a lecture at Johns Hopkins University, and told the crowd that he knew he wanted to be a writer from an early age, but when he was about to go to college, his mother took him aside and said, "I have a better idea. Why don't you be a brain surgeon. You'll keep a lot of people from dying, you'll make a lot of money."

"No, mama," he said, "I want to be a writer."

When he came home for a vacation, his mother went through the same routine, and so did he. "You'll keep a lot of people from dying; you'll make a lot of money," she said. He replied, "I want to be a writer."

Every vacation, every holiday, every visit home, the same dialogue occurred, until finally it exploded. "Chaim, you're wasting your time.

Be a brain surgeon. You'll keep a lot of people from dying; you'll make a lot of money."

"Mama," he said, "I don't want to keep people from dying. I want to show them how to live!"[19]

A Hungry Man

One night Marcia, Blake, and Vanessa and I were driving home from an event, and everyone was struck with hunger almost at once. We were almost home, and I argued the point that it would make more sense (and be less expensive) to eat something when we got home. But three other people pointed out that we were about to pass a fast-food drive-through, and that we should stop there. Overruled, I pulled in. It was about 9 p.m., and as I drove toward the drive-through lane the headlights briefly illuminated a homeless man stretching out a blanket under a tree on the other side of the parking lot. We ordered our food, and I asked for an extra few hamburgers and coffee in a separate bag.

"Suddenly hungry?" my wife asked, thinking I had experienced a change of heart from my desire to wait until we got home.

"No. I just need to do something."

I pulled out of the drive-through lane and back to the parking lot. I got out of the car and brought the bag to the man in darkness I had seen under the tree.

"You looked hungry," I said.

That night, as I was putting Vanessa to bed, I asked her what the favorite part of her day was. It is a custom Marcia and I have done with our kids since they could converse with us. We want them going to sleep thinking about something good that had happened.

"Watching you give that man some supper," she said. "Homeless people usually scare me. I never thought they might be hungry."

It was my best part of the day, too, because, perhaps it was the only point during my waking hours that I had responded to the vocational call within me.

Sometimes our vocational call is simply to be a parent, a brother, a sister or friend, even at the expense of doing "God's work." Eugene

Peterson tells of an evening at home when he was a pastor, where he was riding the crest of a wave of successes. The financial goals had been met, a sanctuary built, and he was the object of great affirmation from his congregation and his superiors. His five-year-old daughter asked him to read her a story.

"I told her I couldn't because I had a meeting at the church," he said.

"This is the thirty-eighth night in a row that you have not been home," she said.

Peterson said that this brief exchange awoke him out of a cultural slumber of listening to the wrong vocational voices. "I realized I was not doing what I had been called to do."[20]

My friend Don Walter told me about how, at Christmas time several years ago, he and his wife loaded their two little girls into their car to drive from the small Ohio town where he was a pastor, to spend the holiday with his parents in Iowa. It was a freezing day, and after a few hours he pulled the car into a highway rest stop so they could stretch their legs.

As Don approached the rest room, he saw a sign taped to the door. It was written in pen, on the back of a remnant of a cardboard box. It said, "We're stranded, and want to get home for Christmas. Could you help us?" The sign described the car these people were in.

"I thought about it for a minute," Don said. "It sounded like a scam. But what if it wasn't? It was so cold that day."

Don turned around and looked for the car. He saw it immediately. It had seen better days. When he got to the car he noticed that there was a man and a woman in the front seat, and a sleeping baby in the back. The man behind the wheel rolled his window down, and Don handed him a $10 bill. What the man said shocked my friend. The man said, "Thanks, Don."

"Did I know him from somewhere?" Don said. "Was he a member of my church? A high school acquaintance? Did he hear my wife call my name from the car? I don't know. All I know is that you can choose to accept Mystery, or assume there must be a logical explanation."

Don responded to his holy orders—the call—and the sacred broke through. Like Bethlehem at that time of year. The way it does for all of us throughout the year, if we are paying attention. Martin Luther said that "the works of monks and priests, however holy and arduous they be, do not differ one whit in the sight of God from the works of the rustic laborer in the field or the woman going about her household tasks."[21] For Luther and for us, the peasant and the merchant, "the business person, the teacher, the factory worker, and the television anchor—can do God's work (or fail to do it) just as much as the minister and the missionary."[22]

Frederick Buechner said that in our culture, people have so many voices calling to them that it is hard to discern which are worthy of our attention. One of the unfortunate ideas we retain from our Puritan forefathers, he said, is that work is supposed to be a kind of penance to work off the guilt we accumulate when we're not working. The world is full of people whose work brings no pleasure or purpose to themselves or anyone else. They listened to the wrong voice, he said.

"We should go with our lives where we most need to go and where we are most needed," he said. "What can we do that makes us gladdest, what can we do that leaves us with the stronger sense of sailing true north and of peace, which is much of what gladness is? . . . If it is a thing that makes us truly glad, then it is a good thing and it is our thing and it is the calling voice that we were made to answer with our lives."

How do we find this voice and this place? Buechner says, "If we keep our lives open, the right place will find us."[23]

2

Setting the Table

The Sacrament of Communion

We are not here to show something to God. We are here because God—
the One who wants to be completely known—has something to show
to us.

Robert Benson[1]

There is something about a meal together. The very act of breaking bread, whether it takes place at home or a restaurant or a
picnic, is a time of sharing, of experiencing something in common.
Often we use meals to perform their strictest duties—to quell hunger.
Some people use meals as a way to keep on the schedules of their days:
It's six o'clock, so it must be dinnertime. Fast-food restaurants, for
all of their contributions to heart disease, succeed brilliantly in the
category of quelling hunger and keeping people on schedule.

My wife and I recently rented an apartment in the beautiful city
of Bruges, Belgium. The landlord and his wife, delightful people and
world travelers, had just returned to Bruges from our home city of
San Diego.

"How did you like it?" we asked, expecting the usual glowing response of the stunning scenery, weather, and activities.

"It was fine," they said. I thought I sensed hesitancy.

"What was wrong with it?"

Their response was adamant.

"It is just so difficult to *eat* there," they said. "When we wanted lunch or dinner, everywhere we went people were buying food to take away, and they ate as they walked or drove or did business."

I think they identified a serious flaw in our culture.

"When do you Americans just sit down and talk to each other?"

In some cultures, sharing a meal together is a symbol of peace, brotherhood, setting aside differences, trust, forgiveness, acceptance, even love. A dinner invitation means an invitation into another person's life. That's what Zacchaeus heard when Jesus announced that they were going to be at the same table.

Our friends in Belgium understood that there is another dimension of the shared meal that goes beyond the physical relief and sustenance it provides. "The mere act of eating together, quite apart from a banquet or some other festival occasion, is by its very nature a sign of friendship and of 'communion,'" Thomas Merton wrote.[2] Jesus reveals that dimension when he washes his disciples' feet before a meal. Meals are symbolic times of serving, sharing, and showing mercy. And when Jesus passed the bread and the cup for the disciples to share, saying, "This is my body," and "This is my blood," he is telling them that his very presence is revealed when they eat and drink together. One of the translations of the greeting "hello" in Mandarin is, "have you eaten?"

My grandparents knew the value of eating together. My parents, brothers, and I lived with them when I was very young. On Sundays in particular, my grandmother prepared more food than the family warranted, with the idea that she might find a visitor or lonely person at church that day and invite that person home. My mom continued the practice when we lived in our own house later. If she knew that someone was alone, or was going through a difficult time, or was from out of town studying at a local university, there was another place set at the table. We often drove to various parts of the city to bring the person to our house for that meal. Togetherness at mealtime was important. There was no agenda other than togetherness.

We experienced something around those tables. Sharing the food and drink, passing it to one another, serving it to one another, sometimes spilling it on one another, and in extreme cases, throwing it at one another, meant something. The shared experience meant that we were more than just our individual selves. Around that table we were something bigger. We were a collective group. We had hunger in common, and the food brought us together. The table was where we all presented ourselves to God and each other, and he presented himself to us. John Shea said that church is where we "Gather the folks, tell the stories, break the bread."[3] So I guess we had church around the table.

When my grandmother reached her nineties, she lived in a nursing home outside of Chicago. In those latter years, my grandmother lost her grip on the present. She didn't know any of us when we would visit. One of the last times I saw her was when I had a layover on a flight to the east coast. For years I had routed my flights through Chicago so that I could take a cab or have a relative pick me up and take me to the nursing home for a few hours.

On this particular trip she seemed to recognize me as someone from her past, but couldn't really muster my identity. Regardless of who I was, her first words were, "Have you eaten?" (She was Irish, not Chinese.) I assured her I had. She asked the same question maybe twenty more times while I was there. We visited for a while, and I got her singing some hymns. Her alto voice was still strong. At one point she stopped abruptly and said, "Do we have enough food for tonight?" I asked who she was expecting to come over. "Everyone!" she said.

"What will we need?" I asked.

"Make a list. We need hamburger, chips, buns, lettuce, tomatoes."

I humored her by nodding.

"You're not writing this down," she said.

I got a pen and paper and took notes. I figured her delusion would pass soon, so I stayed in the chair, and smiled at her.

"Why are you still here?"

"Well, I thought I'd talk to you for a while."

"GO!" She pointed to the door.

So, I got up and left the room. I walked around the floor of the nursing home for about ten minutes, got a drink of water, watched a little *Wheel of Fortune* in the lounge at a volume only the deaf could appreciate, then figured she had forgotten this piece of her past. So I returned to her room. She was sound asleep.

Even right up to the end, having a meal together was on her mind. It was what helped define her, because some of her best moments in life were experienced while sharing a meal with others.

What do we experience by eating together? We share the host's hospitality. And hospitality is at the core of our spiritual life. Most of our day is spent experiencing how we are different from one another—our race, our economic status, our education, our language, our heritage. Around the table, we experience what we have in common: hunger and need for renewal. "The bread of the Eucharist is called the 'host' after all, and for good reason," said Kathleen Norris.[4]

In the years prior to my kids' going to college, it was no easy task to have a meal where we were all together. We are similar to other American families in that the four of us had differing and competing schedules. When my son was still living at home, he and I ate breakfast together, but we didn't say much because we were both reading the morning newspaper. We might have commented on a story or a cartoon strip, but it was pretty quiet. My wife and daughter would wake up later, and they tended to eat on the run. I often don't eat lunch. My wife does if it's convenient. And I suspect that a lot of the lunches we hurriedly prepared for our kids in the morning got tossed or traded. The chaos I have witnessed during lunch time in public schools is anything but a time of renewal—it seems it is spent defending one's self. In other words, we spend our days being different from one another. I do my professor/writer thing, my wife does her accounting thing, my son does his student thing, and my daughter does her student thing. Everything we do shows how different we are from one another.

But we made a good deal of effort to have dinner together. It was one of the ways of acknowledging what we had in common, as opposed to what made us different. I'd be lying if I said it was an easy thing to accomplish. My son thought we were unreasonable when we didn't allow him to bring a book or magazine to the table. My daughter often wanted something different from what the rest of us were having, and usually asked if we could watch television while we ate, or if she could send text messages on her cell phone. I belong to organizations that think having a meeting during the dinner hour is efficient. But because my wife and I felt that it was crucial to share a meal together as regularly as possible, we did it. We unplugged the phone. Often we played a game that allowed for eating and playing. Usually the game created the opportunity to talk about our respective days. And we transcended the individual part of each of us, and became part of each other again. We saw what we had in common. Everyone served and got served. We were reminded of whose we were—each other's and God's. There was a Host. And we were the nourishment for each other.

Merton wrote, "In modern times we have lost sight of the fact that even the most ordinary actions of our every day life are invested, by their very nature, with a deep spiritual meaning. The table is in a certain sense the center of family life, the expression of family life."[5] Karl Rahner expands the concept beyond just traditional family members.

> What better way is there of symbolizing—or even actually bringing about—a loving, confiding unity among men than eating together, all sharing in common that bodily nourishment essential to their common existence, and all, in the course of this, opening their hearts to one another? But a meal can stand also as a sign for the final and perfect communion of humanity that will take place at the eternal banquet where the bread that will be eaten and the cup that will be drunk will be with the Lord himself. Then indeed will men be truly united to one another and to God.[6]

Mysterious Blessing

It's more than symbol. It's means. Harvey Cox, theologian and cultural analyst, told of going to a neighborhood Catholic church as a high school boy, even though he was raised Baptist. He was dating a Catholic girl who was a year older, and when she came home after a semester of college, he went to a Christmas Eve Mass with her. When it was time to receive the Eucharist, the girl whispered to him, "That's just a primitive totemic ritual, you know." She had just finished an introductory course in anthropology.

"A what?" he said.

"A primitive totemic ritual. Almost all premodern religious and tribal groups have them. They are ceremonies where worshipers bind themselves together and to the power of the sacred by a cannibalistic act of ingesting the mana of a dead god."

Communion, Cox said, was never the same after that. A symbol that is nothing more than a symbol is dead.[7] But when the symbol points us to something larger than ourselves, something eternal, the symbol has life. Tony Campolo doesn't remember thinking about the theological meaning of Communion when he was a young boy at church, but he remembers that "there was some kind of mysterious blessing in the air . . . I was aware that something special, something with inklings of the supernatural, was happening." He remembers a particular time when he was about six, and the minister quoted a verse condemning people if they took the Communion elements "unworthily." The plate with the small pieces of bread was passed to a crying woman sitting in front of the Campolo family. She waved the plate away and lowered her head, apparently out of shame.

Campolo's Sicilian father leaned over the woman's shoulder and, in his broken English, sternly said, "Take it, girl! It was meant for you. Do you hear me?" She nodded her head, took some bread and ate it. "I knew that at that moment some kind of heavy burden was lifted from her heart and mind," Campolo said. Since then, he said that he knew Communion was a special gift from God.[8]

Tony Hendra remembers taking Communion as a young man, just as he was beginning his relationship with Christ. He had been wrestling with whether the story of God was true—what could he believe about God and about himself?

As I took the host a few minutes later, all the conflicting and confusing thoughts and feelings I normally experienced, the usual objections and reservations and logical, sensible, commonsense hesitancies were swept aside, fused into a whole of certainty. It was all perfectly natural, it all made perfect sense—this was bread just as Christ had used bread, this was a meal just as the Last Supper had been; how else would you take your God into yourself but through your mouth, consuming him in this ordinary, mundane way? The ordinary *was* the divine, where common sense met mystery . . . What had always bothered and often panicked me—the wafer sticking to the roof of my mouth and having to be poked and peeled away sacrilegiously with the tip of my tongue—was welcome now, intended, a way to savor its nature before its material vehicle dissolved. The host practically burned my mouth with the presence of what it contained. I felt as if a shaft of light had pierced the top of my cranium and lit me up from the inside out.

Hendra said he ran out of the church dancing, whooping, doing pirouettes, hugging trees, happier than he could ever remember being. "Truth existed and so did I. I was real, me, a Me, not an idea or a possibility or someone else's incomplete theorem or a mutinous bundle of neurons."[9]

But perhaps the most startling account of the experience of Communion I've read is in Sara Miles' book, *Take This Bread*. It is a very personal and raw account—a spiritual memoir—where her entire life shifted with an experience of the bread and wine.

"I was, as the prophet said, hungering and thirsting for righteousness," she said. "I found it at the eternal and material core of Christianity: body, blood, bread, wine, poured out freely, shared by all. I discovered a religion rooted in the most ordinary yet subversive practice: a dinner table where everyone is welcome, where the despised and outcasts are honored."

Miles is a journalist, a civil rights activist, and, up until this Eucharist moment, had been an atheist.

"Eating Jesus, as I did that day to my great astonishment, led me against all my expectations to a faith I'd scorned and work I'd never imagined," she said. "The mysterious sacrament turned out to be not a symbolic wafer at all but actual food—indeed the bread of life. In that shocking moment of communion, filled with a deep desire to reach for and become part of a body, I realized that what I'd been doing with my life all along was what I was meant to do: feed people. . . . It took actually eating a piece of bread—a simple chunk of wheat and yeast and water—to pull those layers of meaning together: to make food both absolutely itself and a sign pointing to something bigger."[10] The bigger something it pointed to became a vocational call for her, and set her course for providing food to hungry people in poor neighborhoods of San Francisco. A bishop told her, "There's a hunger beyond food that's expressed in food, and that's why feeding is always a kind of miracle. It speaks to a bigger desire."[11] Communion evolved from bread and wine to groceries for everyone who needed them.

It's Always More

Is an average meal the Eucharist? Was the food bank started by Sara Miles eucharistic? Not in the official sense. Jesus's blood and body are not spoken of *per se*. Clergy aren't in charge. But do we experience the mystery and presence of God when we eat together and intentionally celebrate each other's day? I think so. Does it unify us the way the Lord's Supper unifies his church? It can. Thich Nhat Hanh said that a meal is a sacrament when we are aware of its sacramental possibilities. "When you eat your bread or your croissant in the morning, eat in such a way that the bread becomes life," he said. "Celebrate the Eucharist every morning while breaking the bread or biting into your croissant . . . If the piece of bread is the body of Jesus, it is also the body of the cosmos . . . When you eat like this, you are a new person."[12]

Meals aren't always means of grace, I know. They are obligations. They can be drudgery. They can even be scary. When I was in the Boy Scouts we spent two weeks of every summer camping in Northern Minnesota. It was the most obvious place to get most of our merit badges, including the Cooking Merit Badge. Not only did you have to prepare a meal for the entire troop (including appetizer, main course, dessert, and beverage—all cooked over a campfire) and clean it all up, it also had to pass the test of a judge from outside your troop. He had to eat everything you prepared, approve of your method and result, and not get sick. That was pressure! On him *and* the cook! One year our scoutmaster got the idea to bring live chickens with us on a canoe trip. If we wanted to eat, we each had to dispatch and prepare the bird the old-fashioned way. Several scouts became temporary vegetarians after that. My guess is that a lot of prayer went into those meals *after* they were eaten.

The word "grace," associated with a meal, usually means a prayer. It may or may not be heartfelt. Saying grace and experiencing grace can be two different things. And certainly, grace doesn't come with every meal. But it can when it is planned for. Or sought out. As if we were paying attention for its appearance. It is possible to use some mealtimes as means to see beyond ourselves and see the presence, love, mercy, and activity of God.

Sometimes meals are simply celebrations—birthdays, anniversaries, recitals, promotions, jobs well done. My kids get to pick a restaurant or a specific meal on their birthdays, and they know that eating somewhere or something they enjoy is one way we celebrate their presence in the world.

Sometimes meals reveal God's bigger purpose. The Sunday school class I am in used to work in a kitchen on Monday nights serving dinner to homeless people in San Diego. Usually there was tremendous gratitude on both sides of the counter. The homeless were often very kind to our children who went from table to table, refilling drinks. On the way home we had lively discussions about poverty, hunger, fairness, and taking care of others. It gave us a lot to talk about on the way home.

One of my undergraduate students taught me a lot about the sacramental nature of a shared meal. I had taken several students to a college media convention in Washington D.C. It was for both student journalists and their advisers, and the days were filled with professional development seminars. But since those sessions were geared for our very specific tasks and roles, and were conducted throughout the hotel where we were staying, I saw very little of the students during the convention. On our last night in Washington, we decided to have a meal together to talk about what we had been learning. We agreed on going to a Chinese restaurant about a mile from the hotel. We walked there in the early evening, and passed through an area called Dupont Circle. It is a Metro stop, but, at that time, it was also a gathering place for drug addicts, criminals, and homeless people. I filed it away in my mind that we would need to be careful and stay together on the return trip. Parents and college administrators don't appreciate it when you come back from a trip with just *most* of the students.

The restaurant gave us our food in large Styrofoam containers. None of us could finish what we had ordered, and none of us wanted to take the containers back to the hotels. The rooms did not have refrigerators, and we were leaving the next day anyway. When it was clear that we were not going to eat any more, one of the students gathered up the containers and closed them. I assumed she was being a servant-type, and was going to throw them away. Good upbringing, I thought. She got some plastic bags and utensils from an employee— all without our noticing. Then we headed back to the hotel.

When we got to Dupont Circle, it was very dark. I could see that the crowd had increased, and I became aware of my parental instincts to protect these students. Then I saw the student who had cleared our table approach some of the locals and hand them containers of food. They gathered around her and she patiently distributed food, utensils, and napkins. It all took maybe a minute. The rest of us stood in awe as we witnessed this act. Out of our excess, she provided some grace and mercy and relief through this food. I had been fearful because we were among hungry strangers. She saw it differently. The hungry needed what we were going to throw away. Give us this day our daily bread, some might have prayed. It was a holy moment. It belonged to God.

Airline Food

Several years ago I worked on a book project with Gary Morsch, the founder of a humanitarian organization called Heart To Heart International. I took my fourteen-year-old son with me to Kosovo where Gary and I conducted interviews with victims of the Serbian/ Armenian war. We went through villages that looked like they had just been bombed, even though the war had ended a year before. We spent a day with the family of Merita Shabiu, the eleven-year-old Kosovar girl who was raped and killed by an American soldier. We visited her grave. Then we visited a family whose father was mentally disturbed, the result, according to the family, of a Serbian gas attack.

The mother was in the last stages of life from breast cancer. Two of their six children bellowed in an adjoining room. We looked in—they were paralyzed from birth defects. The only motion one of them could muster was to slam his shoulders and head against the concrete wall behind him and moan at the top of his lungs. The other child just stared from under his blanket, motionless, like a wounded animal. His enormous brown eyes pleaded for something. Whatever it was, I knew I didn't have it. The mother died later that night.

As if that wasn't enough to put into the head of my about-to-enter-high-school son, as our plane ascended out of Macedonia, all of the lights went out and the plane lurched. The flight attendants were in the middle of serving beverages, but when that happened, they rushed the cart to the rear of the plane and fastened themselves in their seats. The pilot came over the loudspeaker and said that one of the two engines had died, and that we would need to make an emergency landing. He said he thought we had enough power to make it over the mountains and land in Sofia, Bulgaria. He didn't want to turn around for Macedonia, because that country was in the middle of a civil war, and we had taken off during a lull in the fighting.

I looked over at Blake, and he had his headphones on. I motioned for him to listen to me, and he pulled one earpiece off. "We lost an engine and have to make an emergency landing," I said, trying not to sound concerned. He simply nodded. The way teenagers nod when you're bothering them. I sat back in my own seat and watched us slowly fly just above the treetops, listening to what sounded like the one remaining engine moan "I think I can, I think I can." I thought about what Blake had seen in these two weeks: results of war, corruption and greed, pain, misery, poverty, disease, hopelessness. And now the possibility of a plane crash. I wondered if he was actually "getting" any of this, just months before he was going to enter the peak years of self-absorption. I looked at the passenger across the aisle from me. She was reading her Bible—the Psalm 23, with tears running down her cheeks. I watched another passenger lace up his shoes, in preparation to run from the burning wreckage, he told me later.

The plane landed safely in Sofia, amid emergency vehicles and fire-fighters in foil suits on the runway. The airline put us up in a beautiful, new hotel. Our rooms and meals were paid by the airline.

In the hotel restaurant there was a giddy euphoria buzzing throughout the room. Even the pilots and flight attendants were chatty and
cheery. It was as if we all knew what *could* have happened, but since it
didn't, it was time to celebrate life. And what better way to celebrate
than with a lot of eating and drinking! At an airline's expense!

We looked at the menu for a long time, and finally ordered the
seafood banquet. Soon our table was covered with platters of the
most beautiful lobster, crab, shrimp, fish, and vegetables I had ever
seen. Blake surveyed the scene and said, "How are we supposed to
eat this after all we have seen in the last two weeks?" All of us at
the table were struck silent. We prayed for those we had just been
with, thanked God for showing us the needs of the world, and asked
him to show us how we can live our lives so that we are agents of
hope and relief instead of pain and oppression. Then we ate slowly,
intentionally, aware of the sacred nature of that meal. It was both
a celebration of life and a reminder of the suffering we had seen. It
was a Lord's Supper kind of meal. It was filled with gratitude, and
a heavy dose of reality.

Still More

The celebration of life and acknowledgment of suffering is the reason why we celebrate the Lord's Supper, or Holy Communion, or
the Eucharist, in our churches. It is a statement that Christ has died
and that Christ has risen—suffering and hope. But in our churches
we often only get half of the message. The event is often a sad and
depressing time, with mournful music that reminds us of how much
God has done for us, and how unworthy we are.

Many of us grew up in traditions where Communion was designed to make us feel guilty about how we didn't measure up to
Christ—in other words, where the focus was on our sin, and our
distance from God. I think that's pretty much the opposite of the
point. At my church growing up we had Communion about twice
a year, and it seemed the purpose was to see how depressed we
could get. But that put the focus on us, not on God. For some, the
expectations that Communion would produce a radical change

built it up to something close to magic. Ron Hansen tells of his first Communion experience in church, wondering what changes would occur when he took the wafer and the cup. "Would I be a Superman, a holy man, a healer? Would homework now be easier? Would I be a wiz? Or would I be jailed in piety, condemned to sinlessness, obedience and no fun?"

What he discovered was, "I was still me; there would be no howls of objection, no immediate correction or condemnation, no hint that I was under new management, just the calming sense that whoever I was was fine with Jesus. It was a grace I hadn't imagined."[13]

No magic. Just a Presence. A burst of revelation.

It was a completely different experience for longtime newspaperman Jim Klobuchar, a writer whose columns and books I read growing up in Minneapolis. After being hospitalized and jailed for trying to combine driving with his alcoholism, he had an encounter with God that changed his life. In his book "Pursued By Grace," he describes the role of the Eucharist in his life since that conversion.

"It is a moment when my brokenness is healed, the evil in me is forgiven, the ugliness is wiped clean. If that is not God's grace, what else is it?"[14]

He described his first Eucharist in years, on a day he stumbled into church with a hangover. "I felt, for a moment, at least, the precious gift of reconciliation. If I didn't understand, even if I didn't believe, I felt the forgiveness of somebody, something."[15]

All of us come to the table with afflictions—some better hidden than others. But celebrating the Eucharist is a way to know "I am accepted and loved in the very condition I am in." When the focus is on God, we see the grace that has been there all along.

I believe we can experience that grace in everyday life, as well as in the prescribed events in our churches. The movie *Babette's Feast* is a prime example. Originally appearing in a magazine in the 1950s as a short story by Isak Dinesen, it was made into a movie in 1987 and won Best Foreign Language Film that year by the Academy of Motion Pictures Arts and Sciences. It is the story of a community of severely religious people in a cold, remote village in Denmark.

The founder of this Protestant sect has two beautiful daughters. One gives up the promise of a singing career and the other gives up the promise of marriage so that they can help perpetuate the ever-diminishing group.

After the father dies, the daughters try to maintain their group's separateness from "worldly ways," but it is clear that, despite their hymn singing, petty differences, gossip, and rumors are about to ruin whatever spiritual bond they have. Babette, a cook, appears to the sisters in a storm, escaping the civil war in France that has killed her husband and son. She works for no wages, preparing food for the sisters, the religious group, and the community's poor. Her presence and knowledge of how to make an average meal taste wonderful have a positive effect on the community, even to the point that they stop bickering when she enters the room.

When she tells the sisters that she has won a lottery, 10,000 francs, the sisters assume she will leave. But instead she spends the entire amount on an elaborate dinner for the group and prepares it herself. When the sisters protest, Babette tells them, "If you won't let me serve you, I will simply die." The most compelling part of the movie is seeing the skill and the devotion she commits to this meal, and, in contrast, the villagers' commitment to not enjoying it. The quail, the turtle soup, the wine and champagne, the dessert and coffee might make the world taste attractive, they fear. In fact, the sisters are so concerned about the worldly nature of what Babette is preparing that they call a special meeting of the group to warn them. They vow to lose their sense of taste for the night. What they unfortunately had already lost was the knowledge that the Creator of the world had also created taste and what tasted good.

The scene has very strong Last Supper overtones. It is served to twelve people, in memory of the death of the religious group's founder.

The food is so good that the villagers can't help but enjoy it, despite their words to the contrary. In the process of enjoying the meal, a slow transformation begins. Old wounds between the members are put aside. Confession takes place. So does forgiveness. The bickering is replaced by love.

Because of a meal.

Babette, the cook, is never summoned or even acknowledged by name.

A guest at the meal, a general, rises to speak, unable to contain his awe for the splendor they have just shared. He quotes from the founder's favorite scripture, Psalm 85, saying, "Mercy and truth have met together. Righteousness and bliss shall kiss one another." Then, as if testifying after a conversion experience he says, "We have all of us been told that grace is to be found in the universe. But in our human foolishness and shortsightedness we imagine grace to be finite. For this reason, we tremble before making our choice in life, and after having made it again tremble in fear of having chosen wrong. But the moment comes when our eyes are opened and we see and realize that grace is infinite. Grace, my friends, demands nothing from us but that we shall await it with confidence, and acknowledge it in gratitude."

The meal made him see things differently. Babette's feast connected him to something bigger than himself. He experienced the love Babette had for the villagers, and it changed him. It was a sacred moment for him and the villagers. They were different as a result of experiencing this meal. It was a Lord's Supper for them. It awakened them. All they could do was be grateful for what had been provided.

The opposite occurs in the movie, "One Flew Over the Cuckoo's Nest," when the oppressive nurses call the patients in the psychiatric hospital to come to the nurses' station for their medication. The patients line up in order to be drugged into submission. Some even open their mouths for the nurse to put the pills on their tongues, just as a priest would do. But a true eucharistic experience results in an awakening, not a dulling.

When two travelers on the road to Emmaus discussed the death of Jesus, and Jesus joined them, they did not recognize him. In fact, they were almost insulting to him, saying that he must be the only one in town who had not heard about the events of Jesus's death and the disappearance of his body after the third day. It is significant in the story that Jesus acted as if he were going to keep traveling, but they insisted he stay and eat with them—they showed him hospitality. It was when he asked God's blessing and broke the bread that they recognized him. Not until they had a meal together did they realize Jesus was in their midst.

Pass the Broccoli

Another purpose for sharing a meal together is to acknowledge that God is our provider. In her book, "Bread of Angels," Barbara Brown Taylor says that if we look at everything around us as coming from God, then there will always be manna, just the way it was provided to Moses and the Israelites in exile. A can of beans or grits can be manna. "It is not what it is that counts but who sent it, and the miracle is that God is always sending us something to eat."[16]

Which is another way of saying that God is constantly revealing his presence in the world. Are we paying attention? Are we seeing the order in the disorder? Sharing a meal together can be one way to see it.

It is no coincidence that Jesus called himself the Bread of Life, and that he told the woman at the well that he could provide her with water that will quench her thirst. It's no coincidence that he changed the nature of the wedding at Cana by turning water into wine, and that he fed five thousand with one basket of bread and fish. It is no coincidence that he insisted on *eating* with people whom the intellectuals called "unclean." It is no coincidence that he says the Kingdom of God is like a giant banquet table where *everyone* is invited. It is no coincidence that, in his last meal with his followers before his death, he is present as a servant, a sacrifice, a teacher and Lord. A Host. And it is no coincidence that, after his resurrection, he has breakfast with his disciples—he actually eats—and teaches them to feed and love others. He provides what we need and more, and we usually experience the "more" when we eat together. It's symbolism, of course, but it isn't *all* symbolism. Flannery O'Connor was asked about the symbolism of the Eucharist, and she said, "If it's symbolism, then the hell with it!" But the sacrament is experiencing a hunger beyond food that's expressed in food. It's a burst of revelation.

The expression "breaking bread together" is significant, Henri Nouwen said, because the breaking and the giving are one singular act. "Isn't a meal together the most beautiful expression of our desire to be given to each other in our brokenness?" he said. "The table, the food, the drinks, the words, the stories: are they not the most intimate ways in which we not only express the desire to give our lives to each other, but also to do this in actuality? . . . Don't you think that our desire to eat together is an expression of our even deeper desire to be food for one another?"[17]

There's something sacred about a meal together, as long as we're paying attention.

Michael Pitts, a colleague and friend at the university where I teach, discovered the presence of Christ as he attempted to feed a diseased man in Calcutta, India. He was in a center called the Home for Dying Destitutes run by Mother Teresa and the Sisters of Charity. This was where people were brought during their last days, when they had no one else to care for them. The man was too weak to feed himself, and his attempts ended up mostly smeared on his shirt. So Michael spooned tiny bites of rice, curry, and fish into the man's mouth. Soon the man became quite agitated and distorted his face as if he were in pain.

A fish bone was caught in the back of the man's throat, but his arms were too weak to reach up and remove it. He could only writhe and whimper. Michael figured out the problem, reached in the man's mouth and removed the bone. The man was still too agitated to want any more rice or fish after that. But dessert was half of a tangerine. Michael pulled the sections apart and brought them to the man's mouth. He ate those, and smiled.

While Michael fed him the last of the tangerine—virtually the only food the man actually swallowed—Michael noticed someone waving nearby. Two cots away, another emaciated man weakly motioned to Michael. He also had half of a tangerine, and he gestured that Michael could take it and feed the man he was helping.

The second man now serves as a role model for Michael.

"I will never, never, ever say again that I have nothing to give," he said. "If a dying man can offer a few sections of fruit to relieve the suffering of another dying man, then I will always have something to give."

It is the very ordinary nature of a meal together that makes the most profound point. Some tangerine slices, even. An ordinary meal, as Eugene Peterson said,

> A meat and potatoes meal, prepared and eaten by a family in their own kitchen. The emphasis is on ordinariness, the ordinariness of the place

(home), the ordinariness of the food (meat and bread), the ordinariness of those who eat (family members) . . . Not a meal accompanied by flowers and candles on the tables, music and dancing, and everyone dressed to the nines.

This is so characteristic of biblical spirituality: the ordinary and the miraculous are on a single continuum. Anything and everything that we believe about God finds grounding in what we do in the course of any and every ordinary day . . . 'Pass the broccoli' and 'Hear the Word of God' carry equal weight in conversations among the saved. The sacraments are served in kitchen and chancel alike.[18]

There is something about the presence of God revealed in food eaten together, if we're paying attention to the Host. Taste and see.

3

Finding the Current

The Sacrament of Confession

For all things sing you; at times we just hear them more clearly.

Philip Yancey[1]

I n the beautifully written and photographed movie *The Mission*, Robert DeNiro plays the part of Rodrigo Mendoza, a mercenary and slave trader in the 1700s in the mountains of South America. He stabs his brother to death over a woman they both love, and even though the killing was justifiable legally because it was a duel, Mendoza confines himself in a solitary cell in the local Jesuit monastery.

After six months of self-imposed confinement, he is visited by a missionary, Father Gabriel (played by Jeremy Irons), who ministers in the mountain villages where Mendoza has been trapping and selling the villagers for slavery. Mendoza is beside himself with grief and shame, and feels that no one could possibly know how black his heart truly is. Father Gabriel offers him a way out.

"You chose your crime," he tells Mendoza. "Do you dare to choose your penance?"

Mendoza snaps back: "Do you dare to see it fail?"

The scene then cuts to the missionaries canoeing upstream toward their mission, with Mendoza in their group. They are going to have Mendoza join the religious work among the very people the slave trader had been capturing and selling. The missionaries carry virtually nothing with them except for a Bible and a flute. But Mendoza has all of his armor with him—helmet, sword, breastplate—all evidences of his former self.

When the group begins its climb up a mountain next to a pounding waterfall, the missionaries make the difficult ascent in a gingerly, yet steady manner. But Mendoza barely slogs his way up, because he has tied all of his armor with a rope and drags the burden behind him. The armor causes him to slip on the muddy trail, and he slides backward violently. It catches on trees and rocks. But he collects himself, and his burden, and climbs again, caked with mud, miserable, while the missionaries wait for him at different ledges. The armor turns brown from being dragged through the mud, which only adds to its painful weight. These elements look like they are causing Mendoza so much strain that they—or his past—will ultimately drag him back down to the river and the falls and drown him.

At one point a fellow missionary says to Father Gabriel, "How long must he carry that stupid thing?"

"God knows," Father Gabriel replies.

In an attempt to set him free, a missionary cuts the rope, sending the burden down the mountain. Mendoza simply glares murderously at the priest, then climbs back down and retrieves it.

Finally, the missionaries reach the top, where they are greeted by the villagers. They all wait for the last of the party to ascend. Mendoza, barely recognizable because of the mud and scrapes he accumulated in the climb, inches his way up, still dragging the burden.

A priest says to Father Gabriel, "He's done this penance long enough—the others think so, too."

Father Gabriel says, "He doesn't think so, though."

When it dawns on the villagers who this straggler is, that he has been their enemy, there is animated discussion as to whether they should kill him. Mendoza, too exhausted to defend himself, simply awaits his fate. One of the local men pulls out a knife and yanks Mendoza's hair back, exposing his throat, and looks as if he is going to slice it open. The priests watch in nervous silence. Mendoza, strangely submissive, doesn't flinch. It's almost as if he wishes the man would kill him and put him out of his misery. After a few moments of discussion with the others, the man lets go of Mendoza's head and reaches behind him for the rope. He cuts the rope and pushes Mendoza's past over the cliff into the raging waterfall where it disappears.

But this time, rather than trying to hang onto it, Mendoza simply collapses in tears. They are tears of relief, fatigue, maybe even joy. The picture of this warrior, this monster, this threat to their very existence, covered with mud and tears, causes great chatter and laughter from the villagers. Then Father Gabriel goes to him, drops to his knees in the mud, pulls Mendoza's weeping head to his chest and proclaims, "Welcome home, brother." Mendoza's sobs turn to laughter.

This scene is one of the most profound examples of the place of confession, penance, forgiveness, and reconciliation I have encountered in film or literature.

Technically, the act of killing his brother was not a crime. But it was clear from previous encounters that there was murder in Mendoza's heart. He recognized it, and removed himself from all human contact. But a priest confronted him—even had the courage to call him a coward—and told him there was a way out of the solitary confinement of hate that Mendoza had created for himself. The escape was to serve the very people he had been oppressing.

But Mendoza was unable to move to a new place in his life without wanting a reminder of his past wrongdoing. His penance often nearly cost him his own life and the lives of the others trying to climb near him. The symbolism of his climb, while still holding on to the past, reminded me of my own self, and of others I know who feel that it is necessary to carry reminders of their past misdeeds, even if carrying the reminders nearly kills them and those close to them emotionally, spiritually, or physically.

The beauty of his being set free from his past by the very people Mendoza had been hunting still thrills me every time I watch that scene. He couldn't free himself. His spiritual leaders couldn't free him. His victims freed him. Then he was welcomed "home."

Set Free

Confession, penance, forgiveness, and reconciliation are part of the heartbeat—part of the order in our disorder—of what it means to be a whole human being. At various levels in our lives there is conflict, some which will never be completely resolved. But at those deep relational, spiritual, or even institutional levels, we make the climb out of the river difficult when we keep retrieving our past and carrying it with us. Usually we need someone's help in letting go of it, as was the case with DeNiro's character.

When his sobs became laughter, I remembered how Frederick Buechner described what led him to his own conversion experience. He described a minister who said that, when a person becomes a believer, "Jesus is crowned among confession and tears and great laughter, and at the phrase *great laughter*, for reasons that I have never satisfactorily understood, the great wall of China crumbled and Atlantis rose up out of the sea, and on Madison Avenue, at 73rd Street, tears leapt from my eyes as though I had been struck across the face."[2]

In my own life I have carried similar armor to Mendoza's in regard to the college I attended. As one of the few Democrats at this newly formed, Protestant, evangelical church-sponsored institution in the Midwest, created as a stay against the secularism and humanism the founders believed were blowing across the land faster than the area's legendary tornadoes, I immediately felt out of place when I saw that spiritual correctness and conservative political ideology were indistinguishable. If Jesus didn't say something about a topic, but Jerry Falwell or Richard Nixon did, well, then that was close enough. Whenever I thought differently from the dominant view of the administration and the vast majority of the students, it was forcefully made clear to me that I didn't just have a different point of view—I obviously had a spiritual problem. They weren't subtle about the fact that I didn't fit in. They looked for ways to drive the point home.

My response to this kind of pressure resulted in what psychologists would call "acting out." It involved, let's just say, some rule breaking. Passive in some regards, aggressive in others. One day, school officials searched my room in my absence. They were looking for evidence that I was part of an underground newspaper that was critical of the school. The newspaper was called Publick Occurrences, named after one of the first protest newspapers in the U.S. (a subtle point lost on the administrators, who were interested in only twisting history to support their religious zealotry). Instead of finding evidence of my being an agitator, they found something worse: a home winemaking kit fermenting in the windowsill. I even had my own label! The school had very strict rules regarding alcohol, so I was told to pack my bags—and leave the bottles with them. I tried to argue that, technically, it wasn't alcohol, since it hadn't finished fermenting. I offered to let them taste and see. They felt that I was missing their point.

What made matters worse to these administrators was that I was a monthly columnist for a youth magazine published by the Church of the Nazarene, and had a substantial following. To this point, the Dean of Students proclaimed, "I fear for the Church of the Nazarene if you ever have a voice of influence in it."

Curiously to me, though, I had an advocate or two on the faculty. They saw something other than a troublemaker, although I couldn't really see in myself what they were seeing. They approached the college president on my behalf, and I was eventually reinstated. Without the wine. Members of the very institution that was trying to get rid of me were also trying to save me.

Then, on graduation day, a different Dean of Students (who was later accused of embezzling from the university) tried to prevent me from marching in the commencement line with my classmates, and declared that I would never get a diploma from that institution. I thought my dad was either going to blow an aneurysm, or was going to kick the administrator right in the old testament. Eventually I did get my diploma in the mail from the school, after a few years of haranguing.

A person simply cannot forget experiences like those. Years of being told "You don't belong," and, "You can't be a Christian and think the way you do," created a great tension and conflict within me. While I secretly wondered if they were right, I also looked for opportunities to tell others what a joke that school was. When the school's current students would call as part of their fund-raising telethon, I could only shake my head and decline, while sending telepathic messages, "Get out while you still have a life!"

For years, that conflict blinded me to the good things that occurred as a result of attending that school. My closest friends today, decades later, are from there. I still go on spiritual retreats with them. They are deeply involved in my kids' lives, and I am in theirs. Professors there introduced me to writers who changed me and kept me sane—C. S. Lewis, Flannery O'Connor, William Shakespeare, Thomas Merton. I had no difficulty getting into the best journalism graduate programs in the country. Best of all, that school is where I met Marcia, who later became my wife. We met at a freshman mixer the first week of school, which has caused me all sorts of trouble in regard to the concept of predestination.

One of my former roommates was in town a few years ago, and we got to talking about school days. He sensed the hostility in my voice, and with a gentle rebuke, confronted me as Jeremy Irons's Father Gabriel confronted Robert DeNiro's Mendoza.

"Dean. That was decades ago. The rest of us have moved on," he said. "Even the school has."

What? You mean people weren't still as outraged as me over the bad treatment I got? I looked across the table at my roommate, who had been telling me about what a shock it was to discover that their new baby had Down syndrome. I felt ashamed of myself. But it started the unraveling of the rope that I had tied to myself, the thing that tied me to my past.

More recently, the school has asked for my help in establishing some journalism courses there. Then, in an act that parallels the South American villagers cutting Mendoza's rope, the school gave me its alumnus of the year award. When they first told me the news, I joked to Marcia and others that I must be one of the few graduates left who hadn't been involved in pedophilia or financial scandal. But my wife gently pointed out that none of the people who were players in my conflicted past at the college were even at the school any more. I was the only one carrying the burden of the past. I could hear one of those priests from *The Mission* asking, "How long must he carry that stupid thing?" Without actually saying it, my wife seemed to be asking me if it wasn't time to finally drop my armor into the river.

When I returned to the campus to receive the award, I sensed a reconciliation that I had not expected. The burden tumbled over the cliff to the falls below. The award is just a little statue. But the burden it lifted makes it seem on scale with the Statue of Liberty.

Rolling on the River

Why is the cycle of confession, penance, forgiveness, and reconciliation so important? Because it helps us live in community with one another. We drop our pretense of who we pretend to be, or who we try to be, and we simply are our true selves with one another. It is a basic human need to confess and be reconciled with ourselves, those around us, God, and creation. It is through this sacrament that we understand how we are responsible for the wounding and killing and breaking of each other as well as ourselves.

The practice of confession, penance, forgiveness, and reconciliation is not just for individuals. It's for institutions—universities, corporations, governments. One of the few examples of seeing this sacrament at work at a community/government level is the Truth and Reconciliation Commission in South Africa. The Commission was started when the brutal apartheid regime finally collapsed, and the victims of the white minority demanded justice. But instead of providing a tool for vengeance, the Commission created a forum for the victims to confront their oppressors and tell their stories. When the victims were finished, the oppressors could also tell their stories. It was like a confession booth, only for an entire nation. When something is wrong, we experience a transcendence when we name it, ask for forgiveness, and start down a different path. There is spiritual wisdom in the title of Bishop Desmond Tutu's book, *No Future Without Forgiveness*.

For the same reason we love to hear singing groups sing in harmony and wince when we hear someone missing the notes, we are not just appreciative, but are more alive when we sense that we are living in harmony, not discord. The act of getting from discord to harmony, which usually involves some type of confession, can take on a very sacred dimension because it is the means by which we experience wholeness with ourselves, with those around us, and with God.

Another way to think about this way of living is to consider canoeing on a river. Paddling in the middle of the stream usually takes the least work—sometimes all that is required is a little steering. The current is doing everything for you. But over on the edges of the river are rocks, fallen trees, low branches, and whirlpools that take much more effort to get through or around. Maneuvering through those impediments along the riverbank eventually uses all of our energy. If our journey on the river is going to actually take us somewhere, then the middle of the current is where we want to be. Otherwise we live from one impediment on the journey to another, and the current works against us. Confession that leads to reconciliation puts us back in the current. Makes us whole. Free. Confession allows us to experience God more fully. That's what makes it a sacrament.

"How easy is it to confess that my life is centered on me, my goals, my fears, my comfort?" asks newspaperman, alcoholic, and now Christian Jim Klobuchar. "Or to admit that what's killing my connection with God is my selfishness? That's where the needle was stuck for me for most of my life . . . I saw no vision and heard no voice. What I saw was truth, my shams and weaknesses and pretensions. What I felt was helplessness and remorse. What I received was acceptance . . . At that moment of wonder, I felt the embrace of something beyond me."[3]

Walter Wangerin Jr. tells of losing his temper at his eight-year-old son, Matthew, and saying some very hurtful things to him. I understand his description of losing control. I have done so with my children, students, and colleagues more than I care to remember. Guilt, embarrassment, and shame then set in, and the imposter grins back at me in the mirror like some sick clown from a low-budget Halloween movie.

After Wangerin's outburst, his son Matthew ran away from home. "Guilt is a very real pain, thick in the chest, sharp in the gut, and almost intolerable," Wangerin wrote. "The guilty man will hunch and cup his belly in order to hold the pain; but a broken posture does not ease it: there is no one to blame but himself."

Wangerin searched for his son, and found him already headed home, but only because there was someone in the park who had made him afraid. Home, Wangerin said, had only become the lesser of two fears.

"We went home in silence, he to his room, I to my study, where I sat in my chair and could not move. I faced the open door and grieved for the past and the future together. Earth stood still."

About a half-hour later, Matthew walked by his father's door and saw him.

"You okay?" Matthew asked.

"No," Wangerin said.

"Are you sick?"

"No. Yes."

Wangerin began to cry. Matthew came into the room and put a hand on his father's knee, and said, "Don't worry. I love you." He smiled, and left the room.

> That child! *That child had no right to forgive me so!* Where did he get the knowledge? Where did he get the maturity, the might of an age-less mercy, the transfiguring power to make me *his* son and to make his son *free*? . . .
>
> A door had opened in the universe, and through my son, and in my face . . . Matthew didn't speak the Christ; for an instant Matthew *was* the Christ—or rather, Christ abode in him, and I saw it; not with my eyes, for that was his own short-fingered hand on my knee, but with my soul, to which the Word had penetrated, changing it . . . I was forgiven indeed.[4]

He was whole again. Free. Reconciled to Matthew, to himself, and to God. Living in harmony. Riding in the current.

Formal and Informal

Grace, in the form of forgiveness and reconciliation, creates holy moments in us like the one with Wangerin and Matthew, or with the villager and his enemy Mendoza, or with my college and me. Even though there are times when we feel compelled to perform penance to "work away" our guilty consciences, those times satisfy only to a point. They still tie us to the idea that we must do something to be in the current of the river, or in the state of reconciliation. What really moves us back into the water or, in Wangerin's imagery, opens the door in the universe, is not how far we can carry our armor, or how much it costs us to do it. It is the acceptance of the word of mercy and forgiveness from others—from an institution, from a spouse (thanks be to Marcia, my wife), from a parent, from a child.

Confession is a means of opening our closed selves to one another. It is through this means that we "bear witness," or reveal, our hearts, our selves, to each other and to God. As Eastern Orthodox author and speaker Frederica Mathewes-Green says, it slows us down and opens our moments to the light of eternity.[5]

Some traditions make confession a formal practice as a way to acknowledge that the movement from the edge of the river to the center is a constant zigzag. That is simply another way of saying that we are in constant need of reconciling with our selves, those close to us, our communities, our world, and God. In Mathewes-Green's orthodox church, confession is a regularly celebrated sacrament.

> Preparing to go to confession can be stressful; one feels awkward and embarrassed to say some things aloud. But saying them, and then hearing them forgiven, turns out to be surprisingly liberating. It's freeing to have no secrets and to know that one's most shameful moments are seen, known and forgiven by God. Receiving this forgiveness through the priest, hearing the words aloud, contributes to a sense of permanency and reliability. It's not just you talking to the bedroom ceiling.[6]

But confession, penance, forgiveness, and reconciliation aren't just acts between the priest and members of the parish. In the Eastern Orthodox Church, they also take place among the members of the congregation. As a regularly scheduled part of their church year, members face each other and ask for each other's forgiveness.

> One at a time I bow to people I worship with every week, looking each one in the eye, men, women, children and aged. Each interchange is an intimate moment, and I feel on the wobbly border between embarrassment, laughter and tears. Just to pause and look at each fellow worshiper for a moment, to see the individual there, is itself a startling exercise.[7]

When she gets face to face with her eighteen-year-old daughter, it is even more intense.

> She has made it safely to adulthood past an adolescence that had its rocky places; yes, there are things to forgive here, too. I bow to her and manage to say, past the lump in my throat, "Megan, please forgive me for any way that I have offended you." I could think of a million mistakes I had made. She looks at me, her lashes wet, and says, "I forgive you, Mom." Then she bends to touch the floor and stands again and says to me, "Please forgive me, Mom, for everything." Can a mother do such a thing? You bet. A moment later we are in a marshmallowy embrace.[8]

Confession, writes Philip Yancey, establishes the proper positioning between creatures and their Creator. "I cannot receive healing unless I accept God's diagnosis of my wounded state," he writes. "God already knows who we are; *we* are the ones who must find a way to come to terms with our true selves. Psalm 139 cries out, 'Search me, O God . . . See if there is any offensive way in me.'" Besides being good religious practice, Yancey says, confession is good psychology. It is the fundamental activity of all sessions with a therapist. Buechner said that the questions God asked Adam and Eve are essentially the same questions that therapists ask today: "Who are you?" and "What is it that you have done?" The first question determines the present reality, and the second exposes the past. This is what's necessary to move into the future. This is "the result any good therapist hopes to accomplish," Yancey says.[9]

Lauren Winner writes of her own experience with confession as she struggled to make sense of healthy sexual behavior as described in the Bible and in church, contrasted with her own practice and that of her friends. She spoke of this struggle to a priest.

"Somewhere in the middle of that confession I came to the sexual sin, and my confessor said, gently but firmly (which are the two adverbs I now believe should apply to any Christian rebuke), 'Well, Lauren, that's sin.' And in that sacramental moment, kneeling with another Christian whose sole task was to convey Christ's grace and absolution to me, something sunk in . . . I knew that this priest had just told me something true."

Winner said that, even though she didn't understand intellectually what happens at confession, she accepted by faith that God's grace was uniquely present. "So it is fitting that in that moment full of grace I made a real beginning of chastity, because it is only God's grace—and not my intellectual apprehension of the whys and wherefores of Christian sexual ethics—that has tutored me in chastity."[10]

Part of the difficulty with confession is that we are never quite sure how it will be received. That is usually a good enough reason to keep things to ourselves. But keeping things to ourselves may result in our continuing to bump along the rocks, whirlpools, and branches near the shore of the river. NOT confessing keeps us from experiencing the whole life as it was meant to be lived. Healing is impeded.

"Confession puts us in the company of people who can speak truth in love to us, about our sin, about the need for amendment of life," Lauren Winner writes.[11]

But I am not limiting confession to a revelation of wrongdoing that needs forgiveness. Clearly that is a large part of leading us toward reconciliation. Sometimes, though, confession merely means revealing what is in our hearts at the time—good and bad.

I was at breakfast one day with a longtime friend. We hadn't seen each other for a while, and we were catching up on recent events in each other's lives. He had just adopted a daughter from another country and was animated in his description of how it all came about. Toward the end of our time together he said, "I have to tell you something. You look stressed. Are you all right?" He saw me bumping along the rocks and trees.

I had a decision to make. Something *was* weighing on me. It was private. I had agreed with Marcia that we would not discuss it with anyone. But here was a friend. A fellow canoer, peering into my heart and asking if everything was okay. I wouldn't have confessed my issue with just anyone. It wasn't Oprah-worthy. Lots of people are simply nosy and are not to be trusted with private information. Others want to cut the rope for you. I simply could not hide from him.

"No, things are not all right," I blurted, hands trembling around my coffee cup. Here goes, I thought. I told my friend that, since I had finished graduate school, my family was sinking financially because of trying to pay off school loans. Short-term needs led us to credit cards. We were in a fast downward spiral, and couldn't see a way out. Christmas was coming. Everything was past due. I would be pushing a panic button if I hadn't already pushed them all, invented new ones, and pushed those, too. My friend listened patiently, asked good, insightful questions, and, essentially, heard my confession. He wasn't the solution. He knew that, and so did I. He simply heard me.

As we walked from the restaurant (he did insist on picking up the tab, which was awkward), he said, "Hang on a second." Along one of the buildings we were passing was a cash machine. He went to it, punched a few keys, and came back.

"Here's $500. Make your kids happy at Christmas. Pay me back whenever."

First, I was embarrassed. My rant at breakfast about my money woes was not a hint for a loan. I was simply bearing witness to the state of my inner anxiety. Now I felt like a charity case, and it felt awful. To make matters worse, I knew that Marcia would be furious about my talking about this very private matter. Now friends were feeling obligated to bail us out of a jam we had gotten ourselves into. And it might be years before we could repay them. I felt like the self-doubting comedian Richard Lewis who paces the stage in concentric rings of comedic angst, each joke leading him further into Dante's joke hell until he is sure he has driven himself and the audience insane. It's funny when he does it. When I do it, it's pathetic.

"I can't accept this," I said.

"You don't have a choice. You would help me if I needed it. Let me be your friend."

I thanked him profusely, paced, covered my face like Lewis does, told my friend we would establish a payment plan (I was used to telling this to creditors), and, with great discomfort, put the money in my pocket. My friend hugged me. "Tell me if you need more money," he said. "That's all the ATM will give me today."

I dreaded the call to Marcia, but I called her right away, ready to plead that my friend had dragged it out of me—he was a master manipulator—honest, I didn't just tell him right off the bat, he tricked me, and maybe even hypnotized me. Her reaction caught me completely off guard. She burst into tears. Five hundred dollars wasn't going to make *that* much of a dent in our troubles. It would barely get us to the place where we could even *think* about Christmas. But it was a sign that we were being watched over, in her view, and that the rest would be okay. It was a signal that said, "Don't eat the horses—the Cavalry is on the way." It was the ravens feeding Elijah, one meal at a time. It was order in the disorder—a burst of revelation.

This would not have happened had a good friend not drawn a confession out of me. It wasn't forgiveness I needed, nor penance, but grace. Dispensed by a brother at an ATM.

Like Hanging Laundry

Anne Lamott tells of taking a giant step backward in her effort to become more disciplined and healthy when she binged, and then listened as the voices of self-loathing commenced. Eventually, she called some friends and told them what she had done. "I told them that I was lost, and fat, and had once again, in trying to give myself comfort, turned to the wrong thing . . . Telling helped a little. It felt as if maybe the worst was over." But the big question that loomed for her was *why didn't her faith protect her?*

Her friend on the phone said that it did. "You found your way out of danger—and disgust—through humility and even confession—to the love of safe people . . . You struggled through something really miserable. You told the truth, when it's so tempting to cover up and disguise it. You said, 'This is the mess of my life, and I need help.' And now you are being helped." Grace arrived, Lamott said, "like the big, loopy stitches with which a grandmotherly stranger might baste your hem temporarily."[12] Sometimes, she said, when we reveal our inner selves to someone safe, it's like doing laundry. "I'd been trying to wash and dry it inside myself, in my embarrassed mind, which doesn't really make much sense, laundry wise. When you hang things outside, they get air, warmth, light; and you see that even with the stains and frayed collar, the garment has kept you covered and warm for a long time."[13]

In the small group of guys I meet with, we experimented with the concept of confession. We didn't want that to be the central part of our gathering, and turn it into a contrived *True Confessions* time. Group confessions can get a little weird, or even lead to a "Can you top this?" phenomenon. I have witnessed these happen and, while they are entertaining in the way that passing a car wreck on the highway is entertaining, they aren't really very useful. It's like watching Reality TV, because, after a while, you're a little embarrassed not only to admit that you're watching it, but also that you are a member of the same species as the people on the screen.

But in our group, often someone would confess something from deep within himself just as a natural result of our discussion or the frequency of our gatherings. We had a context and a trust built up with each other, so speaking of private matters was normal. We tried for a while to be more intentional about it. We tried having each of us say, at the beginning of our time together, "I confess . . ." and then finish with whatever was really in our hearts at the time, the way theologian John Wesley's accountability groups were instructed to do. Sometimes the sentence would be, "I confess joy," and then the person would describe why he was joyful. Maybe the confession was fear. Or sin.

Confession, I learned, puts us on a plane toward bearing witness, which leads to wholeness, or reconciliation, whether we know it or not. In the collection of dialogues between rock star Bono and a rock journalist Michka Assayas, Bono says that even those dialogues were serving as a type of confession for him. "I have a room, which is my brain, and it's very, very, very . . . untidy! There is stuff fallen everywhere. There are some very important ideas next to some very silly ones. There is a bottle of wine that was opened five years ago, and there is some lunch I haven't eaten from last summer. There are faces of children who are going to die but don't have to. There's my father's face telling me to tidy up my room. So that's what I'm doing—tidying up my room."[14]

Deep conversation with each other, where we reveal the contents of our minds and hearts, is more important than we think. "Too often we think or say: 'I don't want to bother my friends with my problems. They have enough problems themselves,'" Henri Nouwen wrote. "The truth is that we honor our friends by entrusting our struggles to them. Don't we ourselves say to our friends who have hidden their feelings of fear and shame from us: 'Why didn't you tell me, why did you keep it secret so long?'"

We know that much of the suffering we endure and that we see all around us is the result of isolation and loneliness. People with serious addictions begin their road to recovery "when they can share their pain with others and discover that they are truly heard," Nouwen said. "When I discover that I am no longer alone in my struggle and when I start experiencing a new 'fellowship in weakness,' then my true joy can erupt, right in the middle of my sorrow."[15]

The very act of confession is what leads us to reconciliation. It is a sacred act, and can be part of our daily lives. It's really a matter of intent, and of noticing, as it is with all of the sacraments. After twenty-five years of marriage, Marcia and I started a practice intentionally that we had only experienced during crises in our relationship—we started regularly declaring what was in our hearts toward each other. Sometimes it is deep love and gratitude, and sometimes it is frustration and concern. Our confessions always lead to healing and wholeness.

"Confession and forgiveness are the concrete forms in which we sinful people love one another," wrote Henri Nouwen. But because we so desperately live in ways to keep us from being vulnerable with one another, seldom does reconciliation and healing occur. "There is so much fear, so much distance, so much generalization and so little real listening, speaking and absolving, that not much true sacramentality can be expected," he said.[16]

The ancient tradition of confession, penance, and forgiveness that leads to reconciliation has been part of civilization's social custom from the beginning. Restitutions, punishments, self-mutilations, disciplines, and other practices have all been part of society's effort to restore a covenant among its people. There were vast laws and rituals people needed to go through to attain reconciliation with their churches or communities, and it is not hard to imagine how these degenerated into legalism. The rich easily got around doing penance by hiring people to take abuse for them. If a broken law called for one hundred days of fasting for instance, a person could hire one hundred people for the day and not feed them. Penance achieved, reconciliation complete. When members of Gandhi's community were immoral with one another, instead of holding the offenders to the strict penance laws of the community, he felt that it would be better for the community to see him do the penance instead of the members. That way the community would see the seriousness of the offense. Christians see Christ's death on the cross as the price for taking on the sins of the world.

Much can be made of these acts by Gandhi, and especially of Jesus's sacrifice. But the cycle of living in harmony, disharmony, and harmony again is so much more a part of our everyday lives than we typically notice. Or at least it could be. There are opportunities every day—every moment?—for us to live in better relationship with one another. "When I go to my brother to confess," Dietrich Bonhoeffer wrote, "I am going to God . . . Confession is the renewal of the joy of baptism."[17]

Preserving the False Self

Why don't we live in this rhythm of confession and reconciliation more often? Sometimes it isn't just because we don't see it. Sometimes it is precisely because we *do* see it and it is too scary a proposition. Think about it—to be known, *really known*? All of the false constructs we have placed around ourselves to protect us from anyone really knowing us have taken a lifetime to develop. The illusion of our selves as we should be, and not as we really are, is easy to believe. The False Self dies hard. Donald Nicholl said that, after reflecting on the writings of St. John of the Cross, he formulated what he believes to be a spiritual law: "What you *are* always comes out; what you project rarely comes off . . . For almost a lifetime we may project an image of ourselves that enables us to get through, that deceives others and may even deceive ourselves. In the end, however, what we *are* always comes out; and it is for what we are that we are responsible." [18]

The reason we project a different image to others is that we are trying to be who others think we should be, Buechner said. "We wear masks, and with practice we do it better and better, and they serve us well—except that it gets very lonely inside the mask, because inside the mask that each of us wears there is a person who both longs to be known and fears to be known . . . Deep in you is a self that longs above all to be known and accepted."[19]

In his book *Father Joe: The Man Who Saved My Soul*, Tony Hendra described his first encounter with this particular priest, to whom Hendra had been sent as a teenager because of his involvement with a married woman.

"Gentleness bubbled out from the funny figure in the scruffy black robes like clear water from solid rock . . . I felt on the brink of learning an entirely new set of possible responses to the world." With a few words from Father Joe, Hendra said he could see this married woman in a different light, as a tragic, tortured woman. "I felt toward her something like love, or at least the gentleness I owed her. How had he done that?" By simply hearing Hendra's confession, Father Joe had changed the way Hendra saw his life and the world around him. "I'd never felt so safe and secure with anyone in my life. I wanted to tell him everything that had ever happened in my few years." When Father Joe left the room, Hendra said he heard the squeak of the priest's sandals on the linoleum. "Then silence. And peace."[20]

There are times when, because of my job as a journalist or as adviser to a university newspaper, news stories that tell how things "really are" accomplish the very opposite of reconciliation. They divide and possibly create hard feelings or hostility. When I write a story about someone's wrongdoing, as I did in an investigative magazine story on San Diego city politics, healing and reconciliation are not in the air. By definition, the journalist's job is, at times, to hold people in power accountable. When a U.S. Border Patrol supervisor on the San Diego/Tijuana border took offense to my line of questioning about a border patrol agent standing on the U.S. side shooting an eleven-year-old boy on the Mexico side, the supervisor leaped across his desk at me, knocked his chair into the wall behind him, picked up a glass ash tray in mid-lunge, and took a swing at my face. We still haven't reconciled that one.

When the university newspaper does a story about a male professor who is sexually harassing female students, and the university knows about the harassment but does nothing about it, that professor (and, perhaps, much of the campus community) doesn't see the value in telling that story. Pretending something didn't happen so that the community can live with a false sense of "everyone is getting along just fine, thank you," is a sick habit, but one that Christian organizations continue to cling to. Church history, up to the present day, has never delighted in the harsh spotlight of public scrutiny and accountability, especially when it comes to sex. How, I am asked, can we live in community and reconciliation when we do stories like that? My answer is simplistic, I know, but I reply, how can we live in community and reconciliation when we *don't* talk about those things, where there is no accountability? Reconciliation is tied to confession and openness, not to pretending that there isn't a problem. Otherwise it's all a charade, even though we haven't really fooled anyone.

Still Searching

It is difficult to see a harsh story appear in the campus newspaper, and then go to faculty meeting or to a chapel service with the object of that story. I have had countless private conversations with those colleagues, some where grace abounded, and some where it did not.

Even in the movie *The Mission*, harmony was not the final act, as the mission was ultimately destroyed by, of all things, the Church.

Brennan Manning told a group of us about an incident years ago that still brings him considerable self-reproach. It was in the days when he was a Catholic priest, and had just finished a retreat of solitude and fasting. Some wealthy and influential friends called him and asked if he'd like to come to New York to see a Broadway show with them. He jumped at the chance. During the intermission, Manning and his friends stood out on the sidewalk, impressing one another with their knowledge of theater. A homeless woman selling newspapers approached them. Without interrupting his conversation, which Manning said he was sure was impressing his influential friends, he reached in his pocket and handed the woman a quarter. She offered him his newspaper, but he waved her away, not missing a beat of the spirited discussion.

The woman noticed that Manning was wearing a priest's collar, and softly broke into the conversation. "Father, could I talk to you for a moment?" Manning said he turned on her with all of his fury, and said, "Can't you see I'm talking with someone? Do you make it a habit of interrupting people? No wonder you're in the condition you're in. Wait over by the wall, and I'll be there when I'm finished."

The woman backed up, and, as Manning turned back to his friends, she softly stammered, "Jesus would not have talked to Mary Magdalene that way."

In the moment it took for the comment to register with Manning, he turned back to her, but she was gone. He frantically searched the streets and alleys around the theater.

"I've been looking for her ever since," he said. "I made it difficult for her to believe that God, whom she hadn't seen, loved her, when the priest, whom she had seen, did not."

Harmony, wholeness, reconciliation are the goals—not just within our families, our faith communities, and our places of work, but in all of creation.

By intentionally looking for ways to seek bridges to one another, we realize how the grace to do so arrives when we bear witness to what is in our hearts. We need each other to confess to, to receive forgiveness from, if we are going to live in freedom and reconciliation, as the Mendoza character did when he reached the top of the mountain.

When my wife and I first moved into the house we live in now, our next-door neighbors had their own business and worked out of their house. That meant they were home all day. They made fishing lures and they also took groups out on sport fishing expeditions. We had a German Shepherd dog that loved to run along the fence between our houses and bark at them as they worked in their driveway. The neighbors seemed nice enough, although they had a rough edge or two. They were suspicious of everyone, especially the government, and weren't too sure about Marcia and me, either. The combination of academia *and* journalism made me just a little shady in their eyes (especially when I wore my "Trust Me—I'm a Journalist" T-shirt). To top it off, we drove a Volvo. It was the trifecta of anti-Americanism, in their view.

When Marcia became pregnant with Blake, we shared our good news with our neighbors. Always able to find the shadow in sunlight, they said, "Ugh. I hope your baby doesn't cry all the time like the baby that was in your house before you. Those parents left him in his bedroom [which was right across from the neighbors' work area in their driveway] with the window open and let him cry all day and night. Drove us crazy."

Obviously, we didn't expect them to host the neighborhood baby shower.

One day when we got home from work, Marcia and I started going through the day's mail. One item was a letter from our next-door neighbors. It had a stamp on it and had gone through the post office, even though our houses were within steps of each other.

"How odd," I said, as I opened it and began reading it out loud.

The letter was a litany of their complaints about us as their neighbors. Our dog barked too much and left deposits along the fence that made it difficult for them to work in their driveway. I played my music too loudly with the windows open. We had friends over who were loud when they got back in their cars late at night. On windy days our eucalyptus trees shed leaves into their boat on the other side of the fence. Someday those trees were going to blow over altogether onto that boat and then we'd have a real problem on our hands, the letter said.

As I read this out loud, I took on a German accent and clicked my heels for emphasis. Marcia was not amused. The letter finally ended with demands that we do something about these offenses.

"I'll do something, all right," I said, feeling the testosterone filling my being.

"What are you going to do?" Marcia said, her eyes filled with tears of hurt and humiliation.

"They want to get into a war of words with a writer? Bring it on!" And I headed for my computer.

Marcia headed for the kitchen. I heard activity in there, and momentarily left my words-as-weapons outpost to check on her.

"What are you doing?"

"I'm baking bread."

"At a time like this? Who can eat when we've been insulted? I'm not hungry."

"It isn't for you. It's for our neighbors."

I thought about this for a moment, then caught her drift, feeling a John Cleese/Basil Fawlty character coming on.

"Right, dear. You bake the bread, and I'll get the crushed glass and needles to put in it. Halloween in Detroit wasn't *that* long ago!"

Marcia turned to me. This time she was really crying.

"If we are going to live here for a long time, we are going to have to find a way to be neighbors with these people. This is the only way I know how."

I headed back to my computer, grumbling, "Well excuse me, Mother Teresa."

Both of us agreed that my letter was brilliant, witty, cutting, and justifiably vicious, but when the bread was ready, that's all we brought next door. Just before I rang the doorbell, I noticed a sign they had put just above it. It was a laminated definition of the word "soliciting" from the dictionary, just above a larger sign that said "No Soliciting. That Means You!"

Certain that we weren't soliciting, I rang the bell. The lady of the house came to the door and opened it. When she saw it was us, her eyes got big and she took a step back. I didn't know if she thought we were going to let the dog loose on her, or club her with a eucalyptus branch. In one hand I had a loaf of fresh bread. In the other was the letter they wrote. I extended the bread.

"We baked you some bread," Marcia said. "Can we talk about this letter?"

They invited us in, and the awkwardness of the moment disappeared almost immediately.

"We're really sorry about the dog," Marcia said as we sat down on the couch. "I don't know what we can do about the trees, but we'll do what we can."

The neighbors were quiet for a moment, still staring at the warm bread.

"Oh, it's not that big of a deal," the lady finally said. "We just don't see you that often, and thought maybe a letter would be the best way to communicate."

The conversation warmed up, and soon they were offering us drinks, snacks, and a game of cards.

After spending most of the evening there, we were at their door, telling our new best friends thanks for a fun time. The husband hemmed and hawed a little, clearly wanting to say something else. He kept looking at Marcia's stomach, visible because of the baby inside.

"We've never had kids," he finally stammered. "Do you think that your little one, when he or she is about ten, would like to go fishing with us?"

"As long as you don't use him for bait," I blurted. Another tender moment peed on by the author.

But it was an incredibly sweet offer. Our evening together had been a reconciling moment. And even though we felt like we were the ones who were offended, the bigger issue that Marcia recognized was that what we *really* needed was to live at peace with our neighbors. The bread was a symbol, and more.

When my friend Dana Walling died, Michael Pitts, another close friend of Dan's and mine, wrote a song about living through the tragedy. In the midst of our grief, our sense of injustice about his premature death from a brain tumor, all we could do was speak to one another about what was in our hearts—our gratitude for knowing Dana, and our confusion regarding his senseless departure. On our own we were bumping along the bank of the river. But with the help of the community, we headed back to the current. Michael concluded that there is only one way to experience grace through an experience like this. Here are the lyrics, his confession:

> (Chorus)
> By grace and together
> That's how we live every day of our lives
> It's by grace and together
> That's how the Father's compassion arrives
> It's by grace and together we live.
>
> That is how we will make it through this very hour
> And how we will know of his love and his power
> Not knowing today what tomorrow may bring
> Is cause to remember and reason to sing.
>
> (Chorus)
>
> When more than we have is what our life demands
> That's when we will feel the great strength of his hands
> And the breath of our God will feel much like your voice
> And his comfort through you will be cause to rejoice.
>
> (Chorus)
>
> In moments of joy and in moments of pain
> He comes in a way that we cannot explain
> And the brush of his hand will feel much like your touch
> And there we receive what is needed so much.
>
> (Chorus)

4

Leaving the Porch

The Sacrament of Confirmation

Look again. There's a great deal more. I know that narrow world
by heart and I can tell you from here a few things you may not have
noticed.

Walker Percy[1]

One December night while I was in graduate school in southern Ohio, our elderly next-door neighbor knocked on our
door and asked if we wanted to see how she and her husband had
decorated their house for Christmas.

"My husband made all of the ornaments for our Christmas tree.
He carved a lot of other decorations, too, like a little pond with ice
skaters on it. It's very pretty. I think the kids will really like it."

We practically leapt to our feet in assent.

The reason we were so excited was that we were bored out of our
minds. At Ohio University, where I was attending, classes for the fall
term had been out since before Thanksgiving. That gave me lots of
concentrated time in the library for work on my dissertation, but for

the rest of the family, it was anything but fun. It was cold and snowy, with a stainless-steel hue to the sky that made it seem like it was nearly night all day long. Plus, with school out of session, this already-slow college town crept to a crawl.

Blake was three and Vanessa seven months. With kids that age, in dreary weather, a little cabin fever sets in on everyone. A highlight for Marcia and the kids was to walk to the city bus stop, catch the bus, and ride it to the end of its route, which was at a shopping mall at the edge of town. The mall was deserted, by and large, from the day it opened. Only about one-third of its available space had been leased to stores. The rest of it sat empty, like much of the town that month. When the bus driver was done with his lunch, he would turn the bus around and drive back. Often, Marcia and the kids were its only passengers.

So a chance to go to the neighbor's house and see some craftsmanship? Woo-hoo! Maybe even stay for a cup of hot chocolate? Does it get any better than this? Get the nitro pills, dear—we're going next door!

Marcia got Blake bundled up in his borrowed snowsuit, hat, mittens, scarf, and boots. I put heavy clothes on baby Vanessa and zipped her into the heavy wool, hooded papoose we had gotten at a baby shower. Her arms and legs were inside the cocoon, so all that you could see of her was this tiny oval where her face peeked out. Held upside-down she looked like a large, plaid raindrop with a face. Then Marcia and I quickly got on our heavy coats, hats, and boots and headed out for the twenty-step walk from our house to our neighbors'. We crunched through the snow and talked to the kids about how wonderful this was going to be. People in Athens had the time and talent to really do Christmas right, we told the kids. It wasn't like lame San Diego, where they string lights on sailboat masts and parade around in the bay in eighty-degree weather smugly singing "I'm Dreaming of a White Christmas."

Within a few seconds we were at the neighbors' house. We knocked on the door of the front porch, and the woman who had invited us over came out to greet us. We stood, shivering, as she pointed out their Christmas tree through the window. The tree and the decorations were inside the house. We were on the porch.

"See those lights on the tree? Each one lights up one of the ornaments my husband made," she said.

We leaned forward to see. I could tell that they had a roaring fire in the fireplace. In our drafty, rented house next door there was no fireplace.

"I can't see, Mom," Blake said.

I handed Vanessa to Marcia and picked up Blake, who weighed at least fifteen pounds more wearing all of his winter gear.

"Can you see the skating rink on the table? My husband made it and the skaters."

"Where are they, Mom?" Blake said.

Vanessa was a little young to realize how odd this all was. But one of the great things about kids who have recently learned to talk is that they don't know how to sugarcoat things.

"Why aren't we going inside, Mom?" Blake asked, as he leaned practically out of my arms, trying to see the decorations. "Aren't we going to have some hot chocolate, Mom?"

We all stood on the porch for a while longer. Freezing. We waited for what we were sure would be an invitation inside the house.

"Well, thanks for coming over," our neighbor said. "I thought the kids would enjoy this."

"Thanks so much for inviting us," Marcia said. "It was fun."

I was speechless. We spent more time putting winter clothes on the kids than we did on our neighbors' icebox porch, straining to see some carve-by-number figurines safe in the confines of a warm house? We couldn't go inside at least to thaw?

After an awkward moment of silence, Marcia said, "Well, thanks again. Merry Christmas," and we left.

"Why are we leaving, Mom?" Blake said. "We didn't go inside and see the decorations."

When we got back inside our house, Marcia and I looked at each other and said, "What was that about?"

"Where's the hot chocolate, Mom?" Blake said.

So I went out to the garage, got in the car, drove to the grocery store and bought some hot chocolate for us all, shivering the entire way.

Later, I came to two insights about this experience. One had to do with how strange our neighbors were. More about them later.

The other was that this illustrated the spiritual journeys of many of us. A lot of the time it seems that we know there is something special, wonderful, meaningful, inside. So we get outfitted for the trip to the interior—our personal Great Interior. We walk through some difficult elements to get there. We get a college degree in philosophy or theology, maybe. We get on the porch, catch glimpses of what life is like in the interior rooms, but for whatever reason, we remain on the porch bundled up in our shallow, shivering lives.

All the while there is a voice, like my son's, that keeps saying, "Aren't you (we) going in?"

Know Me Better

"Superficiality is the curse of our age," said Richard Foster in the opening sentence of his book, *Celebration of Discipline.* "The desperate need today is not for a greater number of intelligent people, or gifted people, but for deep people."[2]

There are moments, or maybe even longer periods, of our lives where we become deeper, more mature people in our understanding of the spiritual dimension of our lives. They are times when we evaluate, critique, question, discard, gain, internalize, recognize, and confront realities and myths about our faith. We are given the choice to decide whether it's worth taking the next step, which is a move toward something deeper than what we had previously known. When we step forward, the result is a more authentic faith, one that is not inherited or assumed, but internalized as one's own. It is less prone to being knocked off center by circumstances or charlatans who claim to have it all figured out. These deeper times lead us off the porch so we can explore the great interior rooms. They are, as is the case with all of the traditional sacraments, a time of great awareness, or *intensification* of awareness. This depth is a burst of revelation. But unlike some of the other sacraments, the experience is more about the path itself than the events that occur along the path.

In the ancient traditions, depending on who is explaining them, this time of spiritual deepening is considered the sacrament of confirmation. It is a time when we realize there is so much more, and consent to exploring spiritual depth as it beckons us. Some faith traditions tie confirmation directly to further education, resulting in stating a creed. Some traditions, like the one I grew up in, would call it a sanctifying experience.

When I was sixteen, I was part of a group of young people from all over North America that gathered in the mountains of Colorado for a time of discipleship, spiritual training, and celebration. After I had been there a few days, I noticed the leaders of this gathering, and I remember seeing a quality to their character—a depth—that I didn't have. I had already started my journey with Christ, but I sensed in these leaders that there was something more. One early morning while I was on a walk through a beautiful part of the camp, during what our schedules called "Solo time: Walk and talk with God," I realized that I desired this additional dimension to my life that I had seen in the others. As clearly as if it were spoken out loud to me, an inner voice said, "It is time you got to know me better."

It was deep calling to deep. It didn't seem to need a reply. But it was a moment where I was confronted with heading into a room that I had only recently realized even existed. The porch was no longer satisfactory. I moved toward yes. My decision set me on a different journey, of trying to separate out what seemed true about my faith, of what I should pursue, of what I should let slip away. It was a call to be a spiritually deep person.

This journey didn't occur all at once, of course. And there have been other confirming, or sanctifying, moments that have turned me down other hallways into even more interior rooms. More revelation. But they all point to something that is both beyond me and within me, further into a Presence that is there, but seems to be ever more of a Mystery. They bring me to a point where I say, "I know and I don't know. I know only in part." Now I am less prone to being sucked into believing whatever the latest "new thing" is, because I know that this kind of depth is beyond a faith that can be described with a bumper sticker or a book series on end times.

Recently I attended a conference in Barcelona that gathered Christian journalists from around the world. It was a challenging, thrilling, enlightening, and encouraging thing to see people of faith who work at the BBC, CNN, ABC News, the *New York Times*, National Public

Radio, newspapers in Sudan, Zimbabwe, Hong Kong, television stations in Canada, Colombia, and Venezuela, and international news services. Our meeting focused on staying committed as truth-tellers in all that we did. I was delighted that it wasn't a meeting that promoted stealth Christianity, propaganda, or trying to sneak subliminal Christian messages into broadcasts or publications. No one talked about "infiltrating the godless media." No one said there was only one way to look at certain issues. Instead, the conference focused on integrity, fairness, balance, telling complete stories, seeing other elements of stories that many journalists miss (such as a faith dimension), seeing stories that no one else sees, and giving a voice to the voiceless.

During a social time before a dinner, though, I had a conversation with one participant that made me shudder. He had seen in the conference program that I was both an educator and a journalist.

"I teach journalism in the U.S. also," said the man, who was from a country in a different part of the world.

"Great! Where?" I said.

He mentioned an institution that I was vaguely aware of.

"I've never actually done journalism, though," he said.

"So what do you teach?"

"I still teach journalism courses, but I don't teach them anything about writing."

Now I was completely confused. And I know I am not good at hiding my skepticism.

"You teach journalism classes with no journalism background, and you don't teach writing. What is it that you teach these aspiring journalists?"

"I teach worldview," he said. "I teach students what to think."

How convenient, I thought to myself as I backed away from this scary person in case he was contagious, to have someone come into a class, having never practiced the craft he was supposedly teaching, and pour his certainty into the students' empty skulls. Why bother thinking for yourself when you can pay somebody else a handsome wage to do it for you? Why bother exploring the inner rooms when you can see the ornaments just fine from the porch, and listen to the description from a swaggering tour guide? Isn't that close enough?

No.

The world needs more deep people who won't accept simple-minded statements that explain atrocities such as the September 11, 2001, attacks as the result of feminism, abortion, homosexuality, and the lack of formal Christian prayers in U.S. schools. "The past should teach us caution," said Philip Yancey. "Theologians in Europe debated for *four centuries* God's message in the Great Plague, yet in the end a little rat poison silenced all their speculation."[3]

The sacrament of confirmation can be experienced when we are confronted with the sense that there is something more, that there is sacred space we can move into. But this intensification is unlike the way most of our lives work, where we set a goal, then take the necessary steps to achieve it. This isn't like going to school in hopes of getting a degree. Or deciding how much money you want to make by a certain age, and setting goals for yourself every five years. Or going to a seminar and "visualizing your success." This isn't about making a team, or getting down to your ideal weight. This is about giving your life over to a Presence that says "It is time to get to know me better," and takes you on a journey into rooms you didn't even know existed. It's an invitation to abandon certainty and follow Mystery, wherever it leads. The word "confirmation" may seem a contradictory one here, but what this sacrament is "confirming" is not information that we might have committed to memory. It is confirming that we are no longer satisfied living out on the fringes, and that we are headed to the great interior. It is as if God comes closer, but in reality is only increasing our awareness that he has already been with us. "Since God is always present, it might be better to say he turns up the voltage in our interior world," said Thomas Keating.[4]

There is no formula for experiencing this inner dimension. The Presence "is not a quality which we can set out to acquire like big muscles or a sun tan," said Donald Nicholl. "The truth is rather that we sometimes catch glimpses of holiness in the world about us." Those glimpses, then, "leave us longing to be at one with the Source of the holiness we have glimpsed, that is, the Holy One."[5]

While there is no formula, there are at least two elements that aid us greatly in our quest to explore these inner rooms, as I believe God is continuously beckoning us to do. They seem contradictory at first, but they are really complementary. Silence is one of them.

The other involves the presence of a spiritual guide. They both function as means to help us "cleanse the lens," as Richard Rohr would
describe it, and see things more clearly, more accurately, with more
maturity and depth.

Language of Silence

I think it is impossible to enjoin the rite of intensification if there
is constant noise in our lives—whether the noise comes from the
television, car radio, headphones, or chatter from people around
us. The deep people I know are those who have found a way to tune
all of that out for a period of time. They disengage from all of the
inputs, and then re-engage in a purer, more compassionate manner.
They are not dependent on their senses and outside stimulation for
their knowledge of the sacred and holy. Crisis does not throw them.
It deepens them. "Silence is God's first language; everything else is a
poor translation," said Thomas Keating.[6] Unless the noise stops on
occasion, we do not have a chance at experiencing the sacrament of
spiritual depth.

Every great spiritual thinker and writer practices silence and solitude on a regular basis. Jesus did it, even in the midst of the crush
of hungry, hurting, fearful people in need of a healing touch. Before
he started his ministry he went to the wilderness (both a physical
place and a wonderful metaphor) for a considerable time. But even
during his ministry he would get away to a lonely place to pray, away
from the demands, away from the temptation to over-identify himself
with what he was *doing*. Intentional silence is where we sift out the
accurate from the absurd, the real from the imaginary, the need from
the desire, the useful from the distracting, the substantive from the
emotional, the true self from the false self. It is where we experience
this Presence for ourselves, not vicariously through another's experience. It is where we don't take ourselves quite so seriously. It is where
we are "voluntarily understimulated," Rohr said, with no feedback
and no data.[7]

As we travel on this inner pilgrimage, Thomas Keating says we
"begin to discover that our identity is deeper than just the surface

of our psychological awareness."[8] This journey is also an exercise in letting go of our preconceived notions—about ourselves, God, others, how the world works, nature, all of creation, things that we think offend us and energize us—and allowing them to be confronted, maybe even redirected. "Our preconceived ideas and prepackaged value systems are obstacles to grace," Keating said.[9]

I came from a culture that approached God as one would approach a benevolent parent, a policeman, a rich retired person, a judge or a vending machine. What that meant was that you approached God when you had something to say. It could be a demand, a request, an agenda, an attempt to justify an action. But you initiated contact with God when you needed something. Other than that, you kept your distance. Occasionally you might approach God the way Anne Lamott described someone she knew. At the beginning of the day her friend's prayer was "Whatever." At the end of the day her prayer was, "Oh well."

What would happen to that relationship—*any* relationship—if the purpose for interaction was not based on needing something? What if the only desire was togetherness?

On a recent backpacking trip in Yosemite, the group I was with decided to take it easy one day. We had talked about taking a day hike from our campsite to a peak called Cloud's Rest, one of the highest points in the national park. From Cloud's Rest you could look *down* on Half Dome. But most of the guys decided they were too tired. I ended up going early that day with one other guy, a friend from high school days. Scott and I did the nearly ten-mile hike mostly in silence. Were we angry with each other? Uncomfortable? Out of things to say? Were our vocal chords damaged? Not at all. We simply were enjoying the presence of one another on the journey. We didn't need anything from each other, except to be a companion. And because of the silence, deer were unafraid of us and walked nearby, birds called out, the sounds of the forest provided background music. We weren't distracted from the beauty of the hike by having to respond to one another or fill the silence with noise. We saw and heard things we otherwise would not have seen or heard. And I believe we knew each other better at the end of the hike, despite the fact that we said almost nothing.

Times of silence don't always work that well. When they are forced, they may not be useful at all. In college I took a course from one of my professor heroes on Native American History. The professor was Native American; his insights came from more than a textbook. He told the class about a tradition in some Indian tribes, called a vision quest. Young braves would go out into the wilderness, sworn to silence, meditation, and fasting, to seek a vision for their future. The Great Spirit would then reveal some kind of insight to the brave, and the boy would return a man.

It sounded like an attractive idea. In addition, since I was a borderline student, I saw the opportunity for some extra credit in the class. "Dr. Reed, I would like to attempt my own vision quest this weekend," I told him. "I will camp out in a tent, fast the entire weekend, take a vow of silence, and bring a journal to record my vision. And I'd like to take Randy with me." Randy was another borderline student. Dr. Reed hid his skepticism, gave his blessing, and that weekend Randy and I were in a tent on a field outside of town in search of a vision. And a better grade.

Our intentions could not have been clearer. We tried to re-create all of the conditions we could to usher in the vision. We even brought cigars to smoke in lieu of a traditional native pipe or peyote buttons. But I was not prepared for the discomfort of fasting for a weekend. I got a vicious headache from not being able to feed my caffeine addiction. I was too hungry to study. I slept a lot. The only vision I got—and I am serious here—was during a dream: the Golden Arches of McDonald's were lowered on angels' wings from the sky. All Randy got was a stomachache, and a serious lust problem for the donut shop near our campus. We had the quest, but no vision. We got the higher grade, though. The first time for something like this is bound to be difficult and full of mixed messages. We should have eased our way into it. But now that I've done this kind of thing a few times it is easier to be in the proper frame of mind for the deepening to occur.

A few years ago I was assigned a story by a newspaper, and the person I needed to interview lived about an hour's drive north of my office. I got about five minutes into my trip, and the car radio went out. I flipped through some different channels, hoping I had just lost connection with that particular one, but I wasn't getting anything.

Not even static. Keep in mind, I love listening to news programs on the radio. I like call-in programs when the topic is something I wonder about. I like listening to the blues and to jazz. No radio or CD player on a one-hour trip? And the iPod hadn't been invented yet? I couldn't stand the thought. It seemed like a cruel, cosmic joke.

I pulled the car onto the highway's shoulder and checked under the dashboard for loose wires. I made sure the antenna was still attached. I checked the speaker wires. Everything seemed fine.

For most of the trip to my interview I fumed. Part of the fun of driving that far away was that I got to listen to something worthwhile. When that was taken away, I was lost.

But an interesting thing happened on my way home later that day. I got used to the silence. I started thinking about people I hadn't thought of in a long time. I started praying for them. I thought about things that had been bugging me lately, and I sensed God's desire to purify them. I let the Presence overtake them. Something else happened. The story I had gone to cover was a confusing one. As I was interviewing the people I needed for the story, I knew I would have a difficult time coming up with an interesting way to tell it. That, too, fell into place in my mind as I drove in the silence. It didn't take the stimulants I usually needed, which involved a heavily caffeinated beverage and fear from a never-satisfied editor. Both were historically part of what jump-started me into productivity. In the silence, the story came together as if it were a giant jigsaw puzzle being assembled in my mind by an outside hand.

"There are no limits to what the Creator can do with those creatures who are ready to stop, be still and silent, to empty themselves, to cease their hurry," said Donald Nicholl.[10]

When I got home that night I told my wife about the radio. She offered to go with me to get it fixed that night, because she knew how dependent I was on it. I told her that we could wait awhile. For the next several weeks she kept asking when I was going to get it fixed. I never did fix that radio. I had something better.

Thomas Keating said, "This Presence is immense, yet so humble; awe-inspiring, yet so gentle; limitless, yet so intimate, tender and personal. I *know* that I am *known* . . . It is like coming home to a place I should never have left . . . A door opens within me, but from the other side . . . It is both emptiness and fullness at once."[11]

The door that opens from the inside is the door we approach when we want to experience more than just the shallow, hurried, frustrating, unfulfilling life of a porch dweller, when we want to intensify the awareness of the presence of God. It is a Presence that has been there all along. "We cannot attain the presence of God," Richard Rohr said. "We're already totally in the presence of God. What's absent is awareness."[12]

More recently, I was on a hiking and exploring trip in Tibet with two friends. We had been staying in Buddhist monasteries, chanting with monks, seeing mountains and lakes unlike anything we had ever experienced, and we decided that, in one little village, we would split up from one another for the rest of the day and be silent. We'd get back together whenever we were done, we agreed.

I hiked along a furious-paced river, and climbed for an hour or so until I was well above the village. On a bluff, under a tree, I sat watching the river turn a perpetual prayer wheel that was the size of a grain silo. As long as water rushed down the mountain, the wheel turned. The wheel inside my head kept spinning as well—was this the best possible vantage point? Did Rick or Gary get a prettier spot? Am I getting as much out of this trip as I can? Did it end up costing more than it should have? Would I get a good magazine story out of it? Will I ever get my book published? Will anyone really believe me that I was a decent writer at one time? Will I ever play hockey again? How long have I been up here? I wonder if the other guys will be done sooner than me. What if I make them wait? What if they make me wait?

You get the picture.

I had purposely put my watch in my pocket so I wouldn't be checking to see if I had been up there "long enough." But I estimate that it took a couple of hours for my mind to finally quit racing and just watch the river. You can't force yourself to stop thinking. You can only create the conditions to let your mind stop on its own. And once that happened, something else occurred. The emptying of my mind became a filling of my heart. Sitting, gazing, being, I realized that tears were streaming down my face. The feeling that was causing them was as clear as could be—the feeling was gratitude. I sensed the presence of my wife, my son and daughter, and the deep, deep love we have for each other. And that sensation led to gratitude. The rest of my time on the hill, watching the prayer wheel turn, was drenched with gratitude.

Later that night the three of us tried to describe our afternoon. We couldn't.

Letting the mind slow down so that we can enter the Great Interior can be scary. Many of us do everything we can to avoid it. It's simply not very comfortable. But it's the only way to grow. And the growth becomes part of the holy quest.

"Why would anyone want to embark on the daunting inner journey?" Parker Palmer asks. "Because there is no way out of one's inner life, so one had better get into it. On the inward and downward spiritual journey, the only way is in and through."[13]

Follow Me

This rite of intensification, or sanctification, or spiritual maturity and depth, or confirmation, is also made clearer with the help of someone else. Some call this person a spiritual director, or guide, or mentor. All I know is that the path to the interior rooms, or the process of cleaning the lens, is difficult to do alone.

Several years ago I taught a writing class at a small university in Switzerland. Before I left the United States for this assignment, I had heard that this university was not technically in Switzerland, even though it was surrounded by Swiss borders. It was actually in an enclave of Germany, but the enclave was within Switzerland. I had never heard of such a thing.

"There are stone markers that surround the enclave," my vision-quest friend, Randy, told me. "They're out in the woods."

I found this very intriguing.

Sure enough, when I got close to the university, after I had crossed into Switzerland, the road signs announced that I was in the town of Busingen, Germany. The post office sold only German stamps. The bank dealt only in deutschmarks. The phone numbers in the town carried Germany's country code. There is no border guard or passport inspection as you enter the town. But the people in the town are German. Those outside are Swiss.

This wasn't a pretend town, like Solvang, California, where tourists are made to *feel* as if they are in Scandinavia; or Greenfield Village in Dearborn, Michigan, where people act *as if* they are in Henry Ford's neighborhood; or Monticello, Virginia, where the *fantasy* is that Tom Jefferson might be right around the corner inventing something or flirting with a slave. This was as if there was a Canadian province inside Wyoming.

The reason for this arrangement goes clear back to the Reformation, where an Austrian baron vowed to never sell his town to the Swiss, who were buying up the surrounding land. He commanded that stone markers be placed around Busingen's perimeter. That much information can be found in history books. What I was interested in, for whatever reason, was whether those markers still existed.

Whenever I had a free afternoon, I tromped off into the woods looking for them. Sometimes I convinced Marcia, Blake, and Vanessa to come with me. The kids were nine and six. One afternoon I endured the derisive comparison from my wife that these markers had become my search for Noah's Ark, Bigfoot, and the Snow Leopard all in one. Only this was no solitary odyssey, she pointed out. I was dragging them along. She started calling me Homer. My literature-challenged children assumed she meant Homer Simpson.

I began to wonder if I had fallen for a practical joke by my friend in the U.S. Maybe there were no stones surrounding Busingen. Randy and I had gone to great lengths over the years to tweak one another. Was he capable of getting me this bamboozled from a completely different continent? Was he that good?

On my last afternoon in Busingen, the university had a reception for its departing faculty. During the get-together, Dan, a theology professor, approached me.

"I hear you're looking for the stone markers," he said.

It was as if he had started singing a Wagner opera. I melted.

"You've seen them?" I asked, barely able to contain my excitement.

"Let me change my shoes. I'll take you to them."

I convinced Marcia and the kids that, at long last, we were going to see the stone markers. They reluctantly came along. We followed

Dan down an asphalt path that turned to dirt and emptied into a farmer's field full of yellow flowers. On the other side of the field was the forest.

"I saw them in there a long time ago," Dan said, pointing to the barely visible forest above the chest-high flowers. While rain clouds swelled, we worked our way through the field, occasionally losing sight of the kids. They hopped so they could see us ahead.

"Try not to think about Hansel and Gretel," I said to them at the forest edge.

Marcia, scratching at chigger bites on her ankles, was losing patience.

"It's our last day in Europe," she hissed. "Do we have to be spending it like this?"

Yes, as a matter of fact, we did. I wasn't ready to say that if we didn't find them, then our overseas experience would be a waste, but I thought it.

It began raining, but the canopy at the treetops kept us from getting drenched. It was damp and cold, though, and after about an hour of searching, the weather matched our spirits.

"What should my confidence level be about now, Dan?"

"I think we're pretty close," was all he'd say. It was about the twelfth time he had uttered that very statement. Blake began rolling his eyes after about the fifth time. The stones were slowly becoming folklore and a waste of our last day in the country. Then I heard the words I had been waiting for.

"Here's one!"

We ran to Dan. The stone was about two feet tall, gray, rounded at the top, similar to a small tombstone.

It was at an angle, adding to the feeling that we were in an old, haunted cemetery. I didn't really know if this was what I was looking for. I rarely do. We cleared some brush away from the top and saw a perfectly chiseled straight line in it.

"The boundary continues along the line," Dan said. "So there should be another one in this same direction."

Deeper into the forest, following a sight line continuing from the marker, we found another one. And another. Outside a different edge of the forest, we found more.

It wasn't exactly the Emerald City, or even Stonehenge, but we were all thrilled with the discovery. Well, I was thrilled. My family seemed relieved. We took pictures of the kids with a foot in each country, oblivious to the rain that was coming down hard now. There were pastures in the near foreground and a rising cloud coming off the Rhine River a mile away. Dan just smiled, rain running off his face.

"I never doubted you for a moment," I lied on the way back.

The truth is, I suspected that the existence of markers was more than just a fable or a practical joke. But I couldn't get much verification on my own. I needed some help. I needed someone who had been in this forest before, who had seen the markers and could help me see evidence that the story was true. This is what spiritual guides, mentors, and directors do for us as well.

Christians, in recent history, have not been comfortable with this concept of having a spiritual director or mentor. Some might attempt some spiritual training and call it discipleship, but it's not the same thing. For Westerners, the real problem with the concept of a spiritual director is that we don't like to admit that we need help. Vulnerability is not a virtue. Submission is the devil. The American Revolution was about not wanting to submit. Over the years we have replaced our fundamental need for guidance with the gods of independence and self-sufficiency. Those idols are two of the reasons we never leave the porch, and never experience the *more* that beckons us.

When we experience the guidance of someone familiar with the interior rooms, we see beyond our personal agendas and pettiness and get a cleaner lens for our intensified awareness.

Thomas Keating got advice from his spiritual director that seemed at first to be counterintuitive. He was preparing for Lent in the monastery where he lived. Fasting was held in high honor, and he wanted to be a good example to the other monks. But Keating was in fragile health, and fasting for him usually resulted in his having to stop his fast, causing him to feel like a second-class citizen. At this particular Lent season, Keating approached his director about beginning a fast, even though both of them knew he always had to drop out of it after a few weeks.

"Do you want to know the penance that God wants you to do this Lent?" his director asked. Keating said yes.

"Gain twenty pounds."

To drive the point home, the director told him to eat two Hershey bars and drink a glass of cream between meals.

Keating writes: "My first thought was, 'Has the abbot gone mad? Does he think this is a country club?'"

Reluctantly Keating began this unusual observance, fearful that the other monks would find out and lose confidence in him.

"I had to throw all self-respect to the winds," he said. "They fasted and I did not." He faithfully ate the Hershey bars and drank the cream between meals every day and gained ten pounds.

"The great gift the abbot gave me was not the ten pounds, but his insightful perception that I was attached to the observance of fasting in a way that was not wholesome. The peculiar penance that he imposed freed me from my over-identification with what I had interiorized as the proper way to be a monk and especially a monastic superior."[14]

We all have myths about ourselves, about God, about each other, about creation, that prevent us from going deeper. It helps to have a person who knows us and loves us to point these things out. It's risky, though. It doesn't feel right to open ourselves to the wisdom of someone else. It feels too cultish, too much like Jim Jones telling us to drink the Kool-Aid, or too Heaven's Gate-ish, telling us to eat the applesauce and hop on the comet. But this allowing someone to advise us as we endeavor to grow spiritually isn't the same as following a flawed person blindly to our own destruction or bankruptcy. It is allowing a flawed, but trustworthy person, to help us see more clearly.

I remember complaining about all of the things in my life that were keeping me from being a writer to the small group I meet with regularly. My classes had too many students. My department chair scheduled my classes throughout the day so that I didn't have any big blocks of time to write. For that matter, I simply had too many classes. It was a great job except for the students. Other writer/professors I knew didn't have near the workload I had. My home life wasn't helping, either. My kids were very little, which meant they needed lots of attention. My wise wife felt that it was important that I share in their upbringing. That meant I had to limit the number of conferences I attended, and writing projects I accepted. Besides, even when I could write, I didn't have a separate room to do it in. Our house is too small for a study. My desk is in the bedroom, which means if someone wants to change clothes or go to bed, the solitude I feel necessary for my creative juices to flow gets disrupted. Philip Yancey has a cabin in the mountains to write. My journalism school mentor has a writing shed on the other side of his spacious property. I have a desk in a crowded bedroom. My school didn't respect my need to write. Neither did my family, I whined.

One of the guys in this group asked a couple of gentle questions, then said, "*Are* you a writer, or are you *wanting* to be a writer?" I had to think about that one. I had written some stuff, gotten it published. But I knew he was asking something deeper than that.

"I am a writer," I said.

"Then you should start acting like one," he said. "You have listed all of the reasons for not writing. Real writers write anyway."

Only a person I trusted could have said that without it being offensive. He said it in love. He cleansed the lens so that I could see more clearly. He helped me stop complaining about what I couldn't have out there on the porch, and showed me that the door to the inside was open, waiting for me to walk through. I could wallow in my ego's needs out on the fringes, or I could respond to the beckoning inner truth. I just needed a little help seeing it.

The man in my small group is not my spiritual director in a formal sense. But each man in the group functions as such for each other in many ways. Sometimes we need each other's help to see what we aren't seeing.

One time in my own vocational confusion, a spiritual guide sought me out instead of the other way around. I had grown increasingly frustrated in my job at a particular university. In part, my dissatisfaction was stemmed from the lack of writing time that I felt entitled to (no ego issues there!), but I was also getting seriously criticized for the job that I was doing. As adviser to the campus newspaper, I knew that criticism came with the territory. But it was getting vicious, and my own competence in leading a group of journalistic crusaders was called into question. I had some colleagues who believed I wasn't spiritual enough. I began to doubt whether the university was a good fit. What I really wanted to do was get away from the people whom I had grown to intensely dislike. They obviously didn't appreciate my many gifts and depth and insight.

I wrote to a highly prestigious university and asked them if they would be interested in me. To my surprise, they wrote back immediately and said yes. I filled out the forms they sent, and they sent me a plane ticket to come out for an interview. It was very enticing.

But in the middle of this process, my pastor in San Diego called me. "Do we need to talk?" he said. The academic world is a small one, and he had heard about my interview.

My pastor and I have a long history together. In two different cities I have gone to churches where he was involved. He was one of the people whose spiritual depth so impressed me in Colorado when I was a teenager.

"Let me take you to lunch," he said.

We met that week, and I told him the whole story.

"It sounds like you want to remove yourself from a bad situation," he said.

Exactly. I knew he would get it.

"I will tell you from my own experience, that moving to a different job doesn't always solve the problem," he said. He told me of decisions he had made when he was younger where, because things had gotten difficult and people had become critical of him, he uprooted his family and moved. Then moved again. Then again.

"My family paid a price for my trying to find the perfect job," he said.

He was cleaning my lens so that I could see the situation more clearly. He was helping me examine my motives, my egocentricity, my willingness to sacrifice my family for the potential of a little less criticism. He had been down this road.

The inner Presence was beckoning me to let go of my ego trips and power agendas and addiction to affirmation. I saw this more clearly with the help of a guide. I ended my pursuit of employment at the other university.

When my son was fourteen he began meeting with a student from my university every week for the purpose of becoming a deeper Christian. They got together at In-N-Out Burger on Thursdays for one hour, and worked chapter by chapter through C. S. Lewis's *Mere Christianity* and *The Screwtape Letters*, before reading Brennan Manning's *The Ragamuffin Gospel*. Sometimes they talked about the chapters, and sometimes they just talked about life. The student had lived through a lot of difficulty, and understood the concept of grace better than most people his age. My son is a richer person as a result of this kind of contact. He sees that the faith walk is something more than youth camp altar calls and shallow emotionalism. In a scrapbook Blake made of his junior high years, he wrote about these times with his mentor: "To get to meet with someone closer to my age who doesn't always know the answers to my questions (not that my parents always do), and someone who isn't also influenced with the responsibility of being my parent, was such an outlet for me. I do not know what I would do without it. His wisdom made up for the fact that, for some journeys I am on, he had reached the destination, and [for] others we are traveling together, often pretty close together . . . I am where I am today spiritually because of him."

If finding a spiritual guide simply isn't practical, it is at least possible to trust someone of spiritual depth in a time of crisis, as a type of intercessor. Sometimes Marcia and I go to a retired colleague, Reuben Welch, who was our university chaplain for many years. Because he has known his own share of difficult times, and because of his spiritual maturity, he points the Way into the Mystery and Depth more clearly than anyone I know. When Blake was little and broke his left, then right femurs within the same year, and the emergency room workers at the hospital began an investigation with Child Protective Services to see if we were abusing him, Marcia and I experienced some of the darkest days of our lives. We could just envision the government coming to our house, taking our body-casted three-year-old son away, until it all got sorted out, like some sort of Kafka novel. We had the double whammy of worrying if he had bone cancer and if he would be taken from us.

At that point we did not know how to pray. We were too terrified and angry. But we had confidence in someone who did, so we called Reuben and told him what was happening. This was not like calling a lawyer and asking him or her to get to work, or a bail bondsman for a way out. We weren't asking for advice or a free pass. We were asking someone to go before God on our behalf because we simply didn't have what it took to do it ourselves. Reuben calmly prayed for us over the phone. He called every now and then. He told us "When nothing is happening, Something is happening." He told us to trust. He made no promises.

Blake didn't have cancer. The hospital gave Blake a whole-body X-ray to see if there were other unreported fractures (there were not). He was able to come home after spending a couple of nights in the hospital. And Reuben interceded for us.

Finding an authentic spiritual mentor must be done prayerfully and carefully. Otherwise you could end up with misguided people on a power trip who get their spiritual jollies by telling other people what to do. It's also possible to find a sincere person who is sincerely wrong, like the tour guide I was with in Washington, DC, several years ago. As we passed the Lincoln Memorial, the guide pointed out some holes near the roof. "Those are bullet holes shot by Confederate soldiers during the Civil War," the guide intoned. No one seemed to pick up on the fact that Lincoln was president during the Civil War. How could a memorial to him have already been built, and shot at, while he was still president? Discernment in choosing spiritual directors, as well as tour guides, is important.

Those Wacky Neighbors

Earlier in this chapter I mentioned our strange next-door neighbors. Something happened between us a few months later that shows why I need both more silence and spiritual direction in my life. One or the other could have helped me avoid something that is every writer's nightmare. It was a humid evening in June, and I was in the final, desperate throes of my doctoral dissertation. Panic, fear, self-doubt, fatigue, and madness were my friends. Marcia was out in the front yard with the kids, and I was upstairs in the bedroom typing and sweating in our unair-conditioned house. I heard our neighbor lady in our yard chatting with Marcia, but I couldn't pick out what was being said. Later on, when the kids were in bed and I was finished for the night, Marcia said, "Our neighbor came over tonight with the strangest question. She said she had just read a devotional magazine with several of the articles written by someone named Dean Nelson from San Diego, and wondered if it could be a relative."

I felt the color begin to drain from my face.

"What did you tell her?" I reached for my wrist. My pulse was up to about 180.

"I told her that it probably was you, since you write for a lot of Christian magazines."

"What did she say then?" Now I was shivering. Freezing. Hot sweat became cold sweat.

"She said that she was going to go home and re-read the articles since now she knew who wrote them. And why do you look so sick?"

I was struck dumb. My throat had sealed shut. I needed to give myself a tracheotomy.

"Don't tell me you wrote something mean about her. Please tell me you didn't."

What were the chances of writing unkind words about someone whom you barely knew, in a little esoteric prayer publication, and have the person you wrote about actually read it? Really—what are the odds?

"What did you say about her? And when are you going to learn your lesson?"

I have a bad history of saying the wrong thing at the wrong time. After a shark attack off the coast of our campus, I said something insensitive in class about the person who had been eaten. A young lady took offense.

"What are you—her roommate?" I said, continuing my insensitivity.

A matter of fact, she was.

A friend once told me he was going to northern California and would work his way down the coast, surfing all the good spots along the way for the next several months, but I saw him in a coffee shop a couple of weeks later.

"What happened, Greg? Did you get lost? All you had to do once you got on shore was turn right. How hard can that be?"

I wasn't as witty as I thought. His father had been killed in a plane crash, and he had had to cut his surfing trip short.

And when I wrote about how much it annoyed me that my next door neighbor picked up pinecones out of her front lawn and threw them into mine, all in the context of writing a devotional on loving your neighbor even when your neighbor bugs you, I never dreamed she would be on this prayer journal's mailing list. Honestly, I didn't think *anyone* read that magazine!

I would stand in my kitchen window and watch as she methodically picked up those cones (they weren't the cute little Vacation Bible School cones, either. These were the dense, green pine ones that weighed a couple of pounds each and either shot out of the power mower like a missile, or stopped the mower dead in its tracks) and tossed them a few feet into my yard. Perfect illustration, I thought, to write about loving your neighbor despite her annoyances.

I told Marcia what I had written.

"You're on your own for this one," she said, as she headed for bed.

I avoided that side of our house for as many days as possible. But one Saturday I was outside playing with the kids in the yard.

"Hello neighbor," I heard behind me.

"Oh, hello!"

"I assume you were writing about me."

I was dead meat.

"What are you talking about?" All people busted in this manner believe that if they can stall a little, an earthquake or a nuclear blast or a massive heart attack might occur and end the conversation before its resolution.

"In that prayer journal. You wrote about your neighbor who throws pinecones in your yard."

I just stood there, looking dumb, squinting in her general direction, pretending to not understand English.

"I do that, you know. The pinecones are from your tree. I shouldn't have to clean up after your tree. You were writing about me, weren't you?"

"Well," I felt a lie forming in my mouth before my mind could choke it, "writers tend to form composites of people they've known over the years. I wrote that a long time ago, and I'm sure I was just combining the traits of several neighbors I've had. Have a nice day!"

I rushed the kids into the house. That didn't go as well as I would have liked. Maybe I am Homer Simpson after all. We moved back to San Diego within a few weeks. Someone is probably reading this chapter to her in a nursing home this very moment. On the porch.

5

Weaving the Family Web

The Sacrament of Marriage

There is only one thing you have to do. You must have the freedom to recognize me where you didn't expect me; otherwise you aren't free.

Richard Rohr[1]

After a hard-fought ice hockey game (is there another kind?) at the Metropolitan Ice Arena outside of Minneapolis, I climbed into my dad's station wagon, exhausted but exuberant. The high school team I played on had just beaten a cross-town rival. I was giving our goaltender a ride home, and for the first several minutes in the car all we could talk about was the game.

It was a January night in Minnesota, which meant that it was very dark and very cold. I eased the car onto the freeway, and we continued our recap of the game's highlights.

Suddenly the goaltender said, "Have you noticed that all of the headlights up there are coming toward us?"

I quickly focused on the road, and realized I had pulled the car onto the highway going the wrong way. I yanked on the steering wheel and swerved into the median separating eastbound traffic from westbound. The car then sank in the deep snow.

My teammate and I crawled out, and headed for an exit so we could call for help. The car was hopelessly stuck.

The highway patrol officer who came to the site berated me for my carelessness, and continued to marvel in a not-very-convincing tone that we had not been drinking. The tow truck operator did not hide his irritation at having to crawl into the snow under the car to attach the towing cable to the frame.

But these comments from authority figures did not concern me nearly as much as what I anticipated my dad would say. He was at a dinner party, and I needed to call him from the highway patrolman's car. He arrived just as the car was being pulled out of the snow and pointed in the right direction.

"Are you okay?"

"Yes."

"The car looks okay."

"Yes."

We stood, silent in the middle of the cold highway. The goaltender, wisely, stood a ways off, shivering.

"How am I going to get home?" I asked my dad as I handed him the keys.

"You're driving. You got on the wrong side of the highway. It's not very clearly marked. I'm surprised more people haven't done it."

We stood for a while longer.

"See you at the house. I'm glad you're both okay."

I didn't care about the hockey victory anymore. This was a new level of exuberance. In spite of the ditched car, my dad saw something. The value of another chance? A grace moment from his own past? All I could feel was acceptance, love, and gratitude.

This is how God sees his creation. He likes what he sees. He sees himself in it. And the delight that God takes in his creation draws us back to him. When we experience this kind of love, and know it for what it is, we realize it is sacred.

Families can be ideal places for us to experience the sacred and the holy. Because we have those moments with our own intimate relationships and creations, we have a clearer sense of what God desires in the way we experience him. Families can be microcosms of our relationship with God. Parents take part in the creation of life and they delight in it. They view creation as a means of grace. They see sacraments in little things. They see themselves acting in mercy, forgiveness, and justice for the sake of their creation. They will take on pain and even death in order to save their children. Or at least they can. I find my greatest understanding of the nature of God in my life as a husband, father, and son.

Rabbi Michael Lerner wrote, "Ideally, families provide our first and most enduring experiences with love, caring, and well-being. In the family, we are loved for who we are, not what we have achieved or how much money we make. Families offer us refuge from the world of work and competition, and they allow us our first taste of the deep joy that comes from sustained intimacy."[2]

When my son was two, I was in graduate school in Athens, Ohio, a rural town in Appalachia. My wife would try to get over to the university at lunchtime so we could spend a little time together before I returned to classes. She and Blake came over one day, and the three of us played on the hill outside the journalism building. After I went back in the building for class, Blake decided he wanted to run down the steep, grassy hill. Unfortunately, the grass was wet, and one foot slipped forward as he fell backward. The fall gave him a spiral fracture in his femur. I cannot adequately describe the pit of my stomach when the doctor showed me the X-ray of the fracture. Why didn't we protect him? We were both Sweeney Todd to this helpless child.

The doctor put him in a cast that started at about mid-torso and continued down to his foot on one side, and to his knee on the other. Seeing half of your child's tiny body covered in plaster is a disturbing enough sight. Watching him try to fall asleep like that was something else altogether. When we would finally get him settled down in his bed, and his body finally started to relax, the muscles in his leg would begin to release their tension, which allowed the broken bone to slightly move. The nerve endings of the two broken ends would then brush each other, filling Blake with excruciating pain. He would scream, which would wake him up for a while longer; then we would get him calmed down again, and almost asleep, when it would happen again, as if he were jolted by touching a car battery. This went on several times for the first few nights he was home from the hospital.

I remember one night standing by his bed, stroking his hair, singing softly to him, trying to get him past that crisis point, then watching the pain sear his body, and thinking, "I would gladly take that pain on myself if I could spare him." I knew what I was saying. As a youngster, I got my upper jaw broken and front teeth snapped off at the gum line playing ice hockey. The exposed nerves led to abscesses, and one of the corrective surgeries was done without anesthetic because my mouth was too swollen. You don't forget pain like that, no matter how many years have passed. PTSD? It runs through my veins. Still, I desperately sought for a way to take Blake's pain onto myself so that he wouldn't have to suffer. I suspect my parents felt the same way about my ordeal with my teeth.

In that moment, which I consider a holy, sacred moment, I was ushered into the Presence of God. It was a fleeting thing, because I was occupied with trying to help my son. But the message I sensed from God was, "I know what you mean."

It was in the context of being a dad—a part of a family—that I understood something about the purpose and presence of God. We live out the life of the created creator in the sphere called family. Families mirror God's creation story in us.

A Different Definition

But what, exactly, *is* a family? I know what religious leaders on television and radio say it is, and I know what politicians say it is during election years, despite the way they ignore their own. But since those groups haven't instilled much confidence in me before, I wasn't satisfied with a definition based on fear, myth, rhetoric, or reelection hopes. So I asked some kids—five-year-olds from the school in our neighborhood, representing various ethnic and economic groups.

What Is a Family?

"The people who love you and take care of you."

"People who are together and love each other."

"Who you live with."

"People that are related to each other and love each other and sometimes have a pet."

"A group of people that love and care for each other."

"People in a group and they're living in a home. It's some people who you know."

"People who buy you presents."

"A family is someone who can take care of you so you have someone to live with, so you don't live alone. They need to love you. In my family, on Friday, I get to Rollerblade. Thursday I have dance."

"God is a family."

"Where there's a lot of people in your house."

"A mom, a dad, and a dog."

"All the people in my house is a family."

"A mom, a grandma, a grandpa, and an aunt."

"A family is where people live."

"A family is whoever sits around your table at supper."

That's what five-year-olds think.

Robert Frost defined it pretty well in his poem, "Death of a Hired Man," only he substituted the word "home" for the way I am using the word "family": "Home is the place where, when you have to go there, they have to take you in." Families love irrationally. What other group, club, or association allows a membership regardless of intellect, appearance, or achievement?

Jesus had his own view on what a family was. Interestingly, it does not coincide well with recent attempts by political and religious leaders to define it. Mark 3:35 describes a scene where Jesus is teaching in a very crowded house, when his mother and brothers arrived and asked to see him. "Who is my mother? Who are my brothers?" he asked. "Looking round at those who were sitting in the circle about him he said, 'Here are my mother and my brothers. Whoever does the will of God is my brother, my sister, my mother." That's a big family. A redefined family. In Matthew 23:9 Jesus says, "Do not call any man on earth 'father'; for you have one Father, and he is in heaven." When Jesus called James and John to follow him, they were mending fishing nets with their father, Zebedee. "He called them, and at once they left the boat and their father, and followed him" (Matt. 4:22). As a young boy, when his parents couldn't find him, he was in the Temple. Worried, they asked him why he wasn't with them on their journey. His answer may sound precocious, but it is consistent with what Jesus believed was truly central to the revelation of God in the world. "Why are you surprised to find me in my Father's house?" he said (Luke 2:49).

Perhaps one of the most compelling ways Jesus addressed the family issue was from the cross. As he looked down, "Jesus saw his mother, with the disciple whom he loved standing beside her. He said to her, 'Mother, there is your son'; and to the disciple, 'There is your mother'; and from that moment the disciple took her into his home" (John 19:26–27). With that, Jesus redefined what a family is. He is telling us, "Wherever I am in the center, you have a family." It isn't our blood that binds us—it's Presence.

Within the family web, however it is defined, is plenty of opportunity to experience God's presence. It is as if all of the attributes of God can be lived out in this context. In my own growing up I remember lots of forgiveness in my home. Perhaps the most obvious example is another incident involving my teenage driving and my dad's car. I passed a group of cheerleaders having a car wash one day. They wore swimsuits and waved signs about the money going to a good cause—I can't remember what it was, but I remember who it was extorting the passersby. Immediately sensing the filth of my dad's car, and knowing he would appreciate my bringing it home clean, I pulled into the parking lot and did my part for altruism. As I drove home, I sensed that my mom's car was probably dirty, too. So I pulled the car into our driveway, waved to my dad who was grilling hamburgers, and ran into the garage to get in my mom's car.

Once I started the engine, I adjusted the radio and out blasted one of my favorite bands, Commander Cody and the Lost Planet Airmen, playing "Beat Me Daddy, Eight to the Bar." The title is a reference to rhythm, not family violence. I pumped up the volume and, filled with adrenaline, testosterone, and faint hope for a date with one of the cheerleaders, threw the car in reverse and sped out of the garage.

With my dad just a few feet away as a witness, I crashed my mom's car into my dad's, which I had just parked in the driveway. I slinked out of the car, looked at the damage of the two, and looked at my dad. He said, "Aw, Dean." He helped me clean up the mess, then he finished grilling the burgers.

Unexplainably, I was not punished for this act. Stupidity, sometimes, is all the punishment one needs.

Who Are You People?

One of God's attributes is that he takes delight in us, as he does in all of his creation. We can experience this, too, in our family structures. It is easy for me to delight in my kids most of the time. It was a struggle, for a while, to face the fact that neither of my kids was interested in playing sports. All I did as a kid was play sports. I didn't know seasons according to spring, summer, fall, and winter. I knew them as baseball, tennis, football, and hockey. And as indoor hockey rinks began multiplying, it became just one season year-round.

But neither of my two children showed much interest in any of this. My wife and I wanted them to at least know how to play these games, though, if for no other reason than playground literacy. For a few years Blake played soccer, basketball, and baseball. Vanessa played soccer, softball, and negotiated a deal to include dance. At the end of their contractual obligations, they announced that they did not intend to continue. I was stunned. Were these my children? The line in Richard Russo's novel *Straight Man* seemed to apply to my kids and me: "It's not an easy time for any parent, this moment when the realization dawns that you've given birth to something that will never see things the way you do, despite the fact that it is your living legacy, that it bears your name."[3]

What I discovered is that, for me to fulfill what a co-creator must be, I had to lose my expectations for who my kids were becoming, and instead find ways I could interact with them at their levels, and try to provide as many tools for their development as I could. It's a little like sculpting, the way it was described in Irving Stone's book, *The Agony and the Ecstasy*, about Michelangelo. (That would make a great parenting book title, too!) When the great sculptor would go to the quarries to pick out pieces of marble, he often didn't have an image in his mind as to what he would create. He would pick out a slab, take it to his studio, and begin to chip away at the rock. Only when he began removing parts of the rock did the image within begin to present itself to his artistic imagination. The sculptor's task was to remove the impediments that were keeping the real, hidden image from becoming known. It wasn't the sculptor saying, "This is what you are," and forcing his idea, or will, onto the stone. It was the sculptor asking, "Who are you?" and taking away the hindrances so that the image could emerge. This is what parenting is like.

We have all seen families where parents try to fill the emptiness of their own lives with their children, as if children are put here to meet their parents' needs. In those cases, the parents dictate to the children with a sick ferocity. When the children disappoint, or eventually leave, what is left? Parents who haven't done their own inner work to find out who they are. A parent whose son or daughter declares, "I want to be exactly like you—I want to grow up serving you," hasn't done a very good job of helping that child discover his or her own unique self. A family is a community organized around developing each other.

In *Zorba the Greek*, Nikos Kazantzakis tells a story that I think best applies to parenting.

> One morning . . . I discovered a cocoon in the bark of a tree, just as the butterfly was making a hole in the case preparing to come out. I waited a while, but it was too long appearing and I was impatient. I bent over it and breathed on it to warm it. I warmed it as quickly as I could and the miracle began to happen before my eyes, faster than life. The case opened, the butterfly started slowly crawling out and I shall never forget my horror when I saw how its wings were folded back and crumpled; the wretched butterfly tried with its whole body to unfold them. Bending over it I tried to help it with my breath. In vain.
>
> It needed to be hatched out patiently and the unfolding of the wings should be a gradual process in the sun. Now it was too late. My breath had forced the butterfly to appear all crumpled, before its time. It struggled desperately and, a few seconds later, died in the palm of my hand. That little body is, I do believe, the greatest weight I have on my conscience.[4]

Now I am relieved my kids don't want to be just like their mom or me. Their individuality helps me understand God's ways better. We all have so many variables woven into our DNA that, rather than God prescribing only one path for us to follow, there is ample provision for us to develop into individuals. We are even given the choice as to whether we want to acknowledge the activity of God in our life. And always, when we look back, we see how God was present, providing, ahead of us, the whole way, providing order to the disorder.

Just as we never sense God saying to us, "Why can't you be more like the kid across the street," parents who pay attention realize that their own kids are theirs for only a while, and that the job of a family is to guide each other into experiencing God's unconditional love.

Being a parent is like being a good host to a stranger, Henri Nouwen said. We don't really own them. They are on loan. "This is good news. We don't need to blame ourselves for all their problems, nor should we claim for ourselves their successes. Children are gifts from God . . . They are like strangers who ask for hospitality, become good friends, and then leave again to continue their journey."[5]

The hard part of parenting is in giving our children freedom. What if they don't turn out the way we want them to turn out? What if they don't fulfill their potential (which is another way of saying, what if they don't fulfill their parents' expectations?). Thomas Keating said the parents' task is to model God's love. "The vocation of parents is to manifest in daily life the kind of love that God has for their children. That is surely one of the principal graces of the sacrament of matrimony."[6] That's what my father showed me when I piled the family car into the snow. Or when I piled it into the other car. I'll stop with the examples there. I have so many to draw from.

Walter Wangerin Jr., tells of his attempt to be a stay-at-home dad, and also be a full-time writer. This worked fine during the school year, but became complicated when his kids were home during the summer. "Three times my children slew the book in me," he wrote. "Three times!" When he finally chose to put his children ahead of his own interests, something happened.

"Then I discovered my mother's mothering and the astonishing quality of her love. Then: when I chose. When I sacrificed the writer-self and consciously renounced my book and offered my children, completely, a parent. I had to do the former to allow the latter. These were the same act after all. I had to let the core of me die—for a while at least—that they might properly live."[7]

Tell Me A Story

Families can do a lot to factor the sacred and holy into their collective lives. Whether it is a family connected by faith, agreement, arrangement, or biology, we can pay attention to how God is working within it. The means for experiencing God's work are similar to some of those adopted by the people of God in the Old Testament.

One means is the practice of telling stories about the past. When my daughter was very young, at bedtime she would ask my wife or me to tell her stories about when she was a baby. With the lights out, one of us would sit on the edge of her bed and tell about how, when it was time for her to be born, we drove the seventy-mile stretch on a two-lane road from Athens to Columbus, Ohio, and how I watched for both a highway patrolman (because I was speeding) and for a place to pull off the road in case we didn't make it to the hospital before she arrived. I had helped deliver babies before, but never at a highway rest stop. We would tell about how her three-year-old brother introduced himself when she was just a few hours old, how he asked, "Would you like to pick up a toy?" We told her about how he sneezed right in her face, causing Mom to nearly end one life just as she had brought a new life to earth. We told about how our German Shepherd slept under her crib to protect her, and how it nearly bit the head off of Uncle Darrell's dog when it came too close to her. We told her how we decorated a room for her, how her great-grandmother crocheted a blanket for her, how I wrote a poem for her, how we worried about her when she was sick, how we laughed with her when she learned something new. We told those stories to her over and over.

Now that our kids are teenagers, we still bring out the old videos now and then. They love to watch them. What strikes me is how fierce and primal my love was for my kids. And how much more fierce and primal my love for them is now that they are young adults and don't need me to provide for them. I wonder if that's how God feels. Through the storytelling of the past, I sense that they are soothed by seeing and knowing that they were wanted, anticipated, and are the source of such joy. When we pay attention to our own past, we see that God has done these very kinds of things for us. When we tell our stories, and realize their ability to transcend the moment, they become more than stories. They connect us to our beginnings, sometimes all the way back to the heart of God.

When I was young I loved hearing my Grandmother Cunningham speak of how my grandfather left her after just a few years of marriage for a life of gambling, drinking, and womanizing. She never divorced him, but continued to pray for him. He was gone for more than a year when he had a conversion, a true turning-around experience, and he asked my grandmother if he could come home. She said yes, and told her parents that she was going to the train station in Chicago to meet him. Her parents insisted that they go along, including brothers and sisters, to greet him as a family. The parents made everyone dress in their Sunday best to meet this loathsome creature at the train to welcome him home. My grandmother's brother loved to insert how angry he was that he had to go do this. He wanted to spit on this person who had caused his sister so much pain. But the family gathered, hugged my grandfather and kissed him, and welcomed him home.

My grandmother would take hours to tell this story. It was always interrupted by tears, and verses of scripture or hymns that had helped sustain her. I didn't know it at the time, but one of the reasons I think I loved that story so much was that it was such a bigger story. It was the Prodigal Son story. It was *everyone's* story at some level. But it was our family's story, too. Everything in my family for the following generations was different because of that story.

Still, storytelling is a way to acknowledge how we have had fun, how we have gotten through difficult times, and how we are connected to our past. We experience those significant times again and again in the context of our families, and we see, through stories, God has been present in our lives.

The night before my fortieth birthday, my mom called.

"I know it's not quite your birthday, but I also know you don't like to talk on the phone first thing in the morning," she said.

I was glad she had picked up on that preference.

"I also know that it has been a long time since I have been able to tell you what to do," she continued. She was right again. "But just this once, obey your mother. When the phone rings tomorrow morning, answer it. Obey me."

She really knew how to make it attractive!

The next morning the phone rang early. I remembered her order and considered whether I wanted to be bothered. Finally, I picked up the phone.

"Is this Dean?"

"Yes."

"Happy birthday, Dean!"

"Who's this?"

"Jim Bouton!"

I was struck dumb. The former New York Yankees pitcher calling me? Then I went into denial, thinking it was one of my friends calling as a prank. So I put him to the test.

"Are you calling from Texas?" I said that because Mickey Mantle had just died, and there had been controversy as to whether Bouton would be welcome at the funeral, given the details about Mantle that had been in Bouton's book, *Ball Four*. The caller talked to me a little about the funeral, proving his legitimacy.

Bouton had recently been in Minneapolis on a book-signing tour, promoting a new edition of *Ball Four*. Our family lore is that this is the only book I read in high school. I quoted it constantly and even tried to pattern my own writing style after Bouton's sarcasm. My mom saw an ad in the newspaper about Bouton's appearance, and she and my dad headed right for the store. She told Bouton about my severely limited canon, then gave him a copy of the first book I had written, called *New Father's Survival Guide*. He loved being part of a family legend, and my mom wangled a promise out of him to call me on my birthday. On the phone we talked about baseball, about writing, about Mantle for a while, then he had to go. I don't know if I breathed during the entire conversation. In the mail were several books with notes to me from him, including a statement about how he had enjoyed my fatherhood book.

Why did my mom go to the effort to do this for me? She took delight in her creation and wanted to make me happy. There is a lesson about God in this. He takes delight in us throughout each of our lives. What's my response? Gratitude, and a desire to do something similar for my own kids.

A young lady who has been our kids' babysitter for years came to our house for dinner recently. She's a college graduate now, and is headed off to Europe for graduate school. Our goodbye meal wasn't sad at all. We got to talking about her strength of character, how she had worked through her parents' divorce, how she paid her own way through college, how she had gotten through many personal crises. The recurring theme was how God had been part of her journey throughout. At the end of dinner, my junior high daughter brought her subject notebooks out of her school binder and said, "What are some Bible verses I can put on my notebooks to remind me that God is always with me?" We spent the next hour or so finding promises of God's presence that Vanessa wrote on the *outside cover* of each notebook. Despite her being in junior high, where appearances are everything, she was not afraid to be known as a believer.

Had her mom and I told her that this would be a good idea, that would have killed it. If a youth worker at church would have said it, that would have been a little extreme. Instead, hearing the stories told around the table drew something out of her. It was a sacred time of acknowledging the presence of Christ in our friend's life, which made our daughter want that same presence at school.

There are other means through which grace is experienced through our families. Richard Louv wrote a newspaper column about a woman who hated Christmas shopping and all of the materialism associated with the season so, instead of giving presents, she decided that her family members should write letters to each other, stating twenty-five reasons why that person is loved or valued. Some reasons were tender. A brother wrote to another brother, "You rode me on your handlebars to school when I was in junior high." Some were revealing. A teenage son wrote to his dad, "You would bribe me to go get ice cream late at night after Mom went to bed."

Louv tried the idea out on his own family. It gave him a chance to articulate the little things—the little graces he experiences with each member. People wrote to him after the column appeared and told their stories of how meaningful this exercise was. One family even read the notes they had written to their father as a eulogy at his funeral.[8] These are intentional things that connect us to something bigger. They're sacraments.

Family Lessons

In addition to storytelling, parents can establish traditions that can allow for sacred and holy moments to occur. Parents can't create the moments themselves—that would be contrived and hollow. But they can do things to help their children pay attention. My daughter and I had a couple of traditions as she was growing up. We Rollerbladed to the neighborhood coffee shop on Saturday mornings as often as possible. Sometimes we took the dog, and when the server brought us our pastry and drinks to the sidewalk table, he'd bring a bowl of cold water for the dog. Neighbors stopped by the restaurant, and our table. Other dog owners brought their dogs by to say hello. And I got to hear about events in my daughter's life that I would otherwise never have heard about. She might not say ten words to me in the house. At the coffee shop she barely stopped for a breath.

She and I also go clothes shopping once a year. The clothes, for me, are just an excuse for me to let her be the focus of everything that day. We get to the stores when they open, eat all of our meals at malls, and, by 8 p.m., start making the hard decisions. By that point we have put dozens of items on hold at various stores. When we decide which items we're actually going to buy, the last hour or so becomes a bit frenzied. But it's all fun. What I find interesting is that these traditions usually aren't the sacred moments themselves. They create space for the sacred moments to occur later, like when she came home early from a sleepover at a friend's house, very upset. She felt free to tell me what had happened. Would she have felt that free if we hadn't had these times of openness before? I doubt it. The way can be prepared.

One of the things my wife and I learned as parents was that sometimes the kids have better instincts than us. It seems that often parents, because of their age and life experience, assume they are the only ones capable of speaking with any authority. But occasionally, at least in our family, the most reasonable—even prophetic—voice came from one of the kids.

When our daughter was six, someone had recommended that she attend a modeling agency's call for talent. She had Shirley Temple hair and a Disney voice. We didn't see the harm in trying it out. In fact, I hoped modeling might become the means for paying college tuition down the road. Since she wasn't going to deliver on the athletic scholarship, a modeling contract would suffice. The agency was very professional and had her picture taken with several different outfits. Then they had her read some lines in front of a video camera. As the evening went on, Vanessa and the agency scouts got more and more energized. And Blake, who was nine, got more and more surly. I finally told him to straighten up, because he was making us all miserable with his foul mood. I assumed he was just jealous of all the attention his cute younger sister was getting. He burst into tears.

"Don't you see what's happening?" he pleaded softly.

I had no idea what he was talking about.

"If you already think people pay too much attention to their bodies and hair and clothes, what do you think this is going to do to Vanessa?"

He could hardly speak because of how hard he was crying.

I just stared at him. He was absolutely right. He was speaking the truth clearly. He was warning us of trouble ahead if we pursued this idea. He was *so* right. Darn him.

"Let me talk to Mom about this," I said.

Late that night I told Marcia what had happened. It was unmistakable in our minds what we should do. We called the agency the next day and said we were no longer interested. They persisted, called for several days, then finally gave up. The voice of Truth came out of a fourth grader that day.

"Go to your cell, and your cell will teach you everything," wrote Abba Moses of Scete, a fourth-century desert father in Egypt. I would modify the statement this way: "Go to your family, and your family will teach you everything."

Marriage is a sacrament, according to the ancient traditions, because, as two people visibly live with the other's interests as more important than his or her own, the relationship reveals self-emptying love. Marriage bears witness to that love because it points to something bigger than just the two participants. That's what a sacrament does. When Christ refers to himself as a bridegroom, and Paul speaks of Christ and the fellowship of believers in a marriage context, then we understand our own marriage relationship better. It is to be filled with humility, selflessness, compassion, mercy, and forgiveness. The very attributes of Christ are supposed to be manifest in how spouses treat each other. Marriage lived out this way ushers in the presence of God. And the world sees it. But this purpose is often missed, which can lead to unreasonable expectations in a marriage, which can then lead to disillusionment or worse.

"Loving one another is not clinging to one another so as to be safe in a hostile world," Nouwen wrote, "but living together in such a way that everyone will recognize us as people who make God's love visible to the world."[9]

One of the most profound scenes I have witnessed at a wedding is when the groom led the bride to a chair, removed her shoes, knelt before her and then washed her feet. She then washed his feet. It was a slow, methodical, somewhat messy portion of the ceremony. Not a bad metaphor for marriage right there. Maybe the scene was so moving to me because I knew the couple. The young man was born to a prostitute. Her only reason for not aborting him was that her doctor told her that she had had too many abortions already—her body might not survive another. So this boy was brought into the world by default. A father was never identified. It could have been anyone. The baby was unwanted, and finally raised by another prostitute who wanted to change her line of work. She became a waitress at an all-night restaurant. She was introduced to Jesus. She wanted to raise the boy in a Christian home.

As a university student, the young man became a mentor to my teenaged son. The bride worked in the junior high group at our church, and was mentoring our daughter.

It struck me, as I watched the foot washing, that it was probably as hard, if not harder, to accept a foot washing as it was to give one. I suspected that it felt awkward for each of them to have their feet washed. But selfless love gives and receives. "By marrying the right person, we reconstruct the image of the incarnate God, and that's what marriage is," wrote the philosopher Joseph Campbell.[10] The Franciscan poet and musician John Michael Talbot wrote that marriage means something is happening on earth that reaches across the cosmos to the heart of God. "In marriage, the material meets the mystical, flesh and blood mix with spirit and soul."[11]

It is one thing to say you will love. It is another to show it as a sacrament as Christ did for his followers—his friends. What we do and say matters.

Reuben Welch, a professor, speaker, writer, and friend, said that in marriage, we are commanded to love, not to own or control or dominate. He describes coming home from leading a spiritual retreat where he spoke about love. In his absence his wife was father, mother, chauffeur, referee.

> When I go home, she'll say to me, "How did it go?" And I ought to say, "Fantastic. I wish you had been there. How did your weekend go?" And then I need to just be quiet for half an hour or more and just listen. You see, her words can come into my ears while I'm looking around waiting to tell her about this and that. But I just need to lay my words aside and look and listen and bring all of my attention to her—as a person. Isn't that what love means? All of me is here—at attention to care and to will your good . . . Love says I'll put the paper down, I'll turn the knob off, I will look and I will listen and all of me is present here to listen and to look at you.[12]

My friends Jack and Barbara have been married for more than thirty years. When she was diagnosed with breast cancer and started the radiation treatments, her hair started falling out in bunches. Each stroke of a hairbrush caused Barbara great emotional grief. Finally, they set a chair in the middle of their kitchen, wrapped a sheet around Barbara's neck and shoulders, and Jack shaved her head.

"Each handful of hair produced more tears," Jack said. "Sometimes there was some laughter. But mostly it was tears because we were so afraid. But we knew we wanted to go through this together."

Tears, laughter, fears, and hope are ingredients of everyone's life. It's when we share those ingredients that they become sacraments. And families are in a better position to share them than any other group.

Early in Marcia's and my marriage, I had a job in Detroit that wasn't a good match for me (see chapter on vocation), and I was contacted by an old friend about a new opportunity that would employ both Marcia and me. I thought it sounded perfect! When I got home that night and told her about it, she thought it sounded terrible!

What was wrong with her? We had a dilemma. Who was right? I was absolutely convinced that this was the answer to my prayers of needing an escape from a rapidly deteriorating situation at work. She was convinced that this was the kind of assignment that would make her miserable. It may be a good match for my gifts, but it wasn't for hers, she said. We were stuck.

We decided to take a few days to think and pray about it, and ask for direction from God. At first I prayed that Marcia would see the light and stop being so stubborn and see things the right way, which of course was my way. I was the male, after all. And since God is obviously "all man," as Stephen Colbert says, we have a special bond. I can't tell you how Marcia prayed. Eventually, my prayer shifted a little. It was no longer a prayer of pleading so that she would give in, but it became a prayer of direction for what would be the best thing for the two of us. The prayer evolved into *what would make Marcia and me the best people, and what would be the best for our marriage?* Within a few days my priority shifted from what would be best for me, to what would be best for *her* and *us*. I felt that God was showing me that I was being selfish. I needed to put Marcia first. Taking this new opportunity was not in her best interests. She didn't think it was right. I needed to honor that and keep looking for something where both of us had confidence.

We had a meeting at our kitchen table. She went first. "God showed me that I was putting my own priorities first," she began. "I was being selfish. I want God to use you in the best way possible, and if that means I need to set my own wishes aside, I am willing to do that. I think we should take the new job."

At first I was confused. What? She pretty much stole everything I was about to say. Is it plagiarism if someone says something as her own words, if you were about to say the same thing? Eventually I said virtually the same thing she had said to me, which made me sound lame because she had already pretty much said it. So we had a new dilemma. Now what do we do?

We didn't go. And that was the right decision. I recommended someone else for the job, and it actually was perfect for him and his wife.

Years later in Minneapolis, when I was in another job that was a bad match for my gifts (are you seeing the pattern here?), an opportunity came up where I was being recognized for my abilities with an offer that seemed almost too good to be true. It was a huge promotion, with loads more money. The only downside was that I would need to spend one week per month in Los Angeles. I penciled it out. On the one hand, it seemed pretty good—I'd be home seventy-five percent of the month, and bring home a lot more money. Job-wise it was a no-brainer. Marriage-wise, it was not so clear. Would that much time away be good for our life as husband and wife? The money just didn't seem to be worth losing part of our shared life together. It didn't take us nearly as long to figure that one out. I didn't do it. I'd rather be with Marcia more and make less money than have it the other way around.

In his book *Tuesdays With Morrie*, Mitch Albom told of his visits with his college professor, who was dying. Mitch asked Morrie many of life's most difficult questions, including how to know if a marriage is going to work.

"There are a few rules I know to be true about love and marriage," Morrie tells him. "If you don't respect the other person, you're gonna have a lot of trouble. If you don't know how to compromise, you're gonna have a lot of trouble. If you can't talk openly about what goes on between you, you're gonna have a lot of trouble. And if you don't have a common set of values in life, you're gonna have a lot of trouble."

And the biggest value, according to Morrie?

"Your belief in the *importance* of your marriage," he said.[13]

Whether the married couple has children or not, the commitment of the spouses must be primarily to each other. "When you make the sacrifice in marriage, you're sacrificing not to each other but to unity in a relationship," Joseph Campbell said. "You're no longer this one alone; your identity is in a relationship. Marriage is not a simple love affair, it's an ordeal, and the ordeal is the sacrifice of ego to a relationship in which two have become one."[14]

Life Together

One of the aspects of God's love revealed in marriage is faithfulness. This is so much more, though, than just staying together simply because you have taken a vow. That's endurance. "Faithfulness means that every decision we make in our lives together is guided by the deep awareness that we are called to be living signs of God's faithful presence among us," Nouwen said. "And this requires an attentiveness to one another that goes far beyond any formal obligation."[15] God became human to make his love more tangible. Marriage continues that incarnation. Families mirror God's creation story in us. Marriage mirrors Christ's selfless love.

That's not to say, though, that marriage means we lose our personal identities. Frederick Buechner says that within marriage, the husband and wife still have their lives apart as well as together. "They both still have their separate ways to find," he said. "But a marriage made in Heaven is one where a man and a woman become more richly themselves together than the chances are either of them could ever have managed to become alone. When Jesus changed the water into wine at the wedding in Cana, perhaps it was a way of saying more or less the same thing."[16] Buechner goes on to say that it is within the fragile and formidable walls of our own families that we learn, or do not learn, what it means to part of the broader Human Family.[17]

But it would be crazy to assume that just because the sacrament of marriage might have been made in heaven, there is a magic potion that keeps the relationships out of trouble. The wisdom of my son at four, when Marcia was pleading for quiet, and he said, "Mom. You have kids. You're gonna have noise," can be restated to say about living life together: "You've got people living in close proximity. You're gonna have trouble." It is the very certainty of trouble, though, that allows the truth of the sacrament to come through. Conflict within families allows each member to experience and accept the others' unappealing attributes, and have his or her own unappealing attributes received by the others. Difficulties within a marriage, for instance, are evidence that the marriage is succeeding. "Love makes you vulnerable," said Thomas Keating. "When you feel loved by God or another person, you do not have to be self-protective. Your defenses relax and the dark side of your personality arises . . . One purpose of the sacrament of marriage is to provide the grace to process each other's dark side."[18] When a couple bears with the failures, weaknesses, or dark sides of each other, they manifest the love of God to each other.

In her book *The Practice of Prayer*, Margaret Guenther acknowl-edges that the kind of love demanded in a family does not come easily.

> "Sometimes we are tempted to walk out on a house full of small chil-dren who depend on us or a spouse who no longer enchants us after fifteen years of marriage or an aged and sick parent who needs our care. The idea of a clean sweep and a fresh start can be very attractive, especially if we can blame God for our apparent dereliction . . . It is not easy to sustain our passion for following God's call in the face of the down-to-earth realities of ordinary family life. Nor is it easy to live into the question *where is God in the nitty-gritty?*
>
> Gandhi—who did not have a good track record as a family man—is reported to have said, 'If you don't find God in the very next person you meet, it is a waste of time looking for him further.' I would add, 'If you don't find God in the person who forgets to put the toilet seat down or brings home a disastrous report card or violates the 11:00 p.m. curfew, it is a waste of time looking for God further.' Families are social entities, but more importantly they are spiritual communities."[19]

One of the clearest examples of this between Marcia and me oc-curred just as it looked like I had destroyed our twenty-fifth wedding anniversary celebration. We had been planning for a couple of years, in great anticipation. We had rented an apartment for just the two of us in Bruges, Belgium, a year in advance. I had gotten flights by using frequent flier miles. Marcia's mom was coming to town to take care of our kids. Everything came together for this significant event. Previously we have celebrated anniversaries at Stratford, Ontario, the Ozarks, Palm Springs, San Francisco, Laguna, or other places within driving distance from where we were living at the time. We were always just a babysitter's phone call away from returning in case of an emergency. But a quarter-century of life together was worth something more substantial, we figured.

On the Friday before our Wednesday departure, my wife, ever the planner, wanted us to revise our wills, in case something happened to us while we were gone. Then she wanted the wills notarized. "Please pick up the passports at the safety deposit box and meet me at the notary's office," she said on the phone. I was glad she had suggested

this, because I couldn't find my passport anywhere in my desk or
briefcase or garage.

While waiting for the notary to ask for my signature, I began
looking at my passport, starting at the back, admiring the beautiful
stamps some countries put on those pages. India's is colorful. The visa
from China brought back lots of memories. Tanzania, Macedonia,
Spain, Austria, the Netherlands—all magnificent reminders of what
an eventful few years it had been.

When I got to the front of the passport, my eyes wandered down
the information lines. That's when the volume of voices in the room
went silent, the walls went white, the orbit of the earth slowed to a
stop, and the temperature dropped fifty degrees.

"Did you hear me?"

I recognized the voice. It sounded like my wife's. She was looking
at me funny.

"When does your passport expire?" I could have sworn that cold
air came out of her mouth, just like Bruce Willis's wife at the end of
the movie *The Sixth Sense*. Suddenly I could see dead people. They
all looked like me.

I handed her my passport and put my head in my hands. She handed
the document to the notary. No one spoke.

"There's a place in L.A. where you can stand in line all day and get
it renewed," the notary finally said. I nodded, walked to the parking
lot and slowly drove home. I called L.A. Yes, they have a same-day
service, but they do it by appointment only. Their first appointment
is Wednesday afternoon. Our flights were for Wednesday morning.
No, it won't do any good to show up on Monday morning and crash
the line. We won't take you.

I called the airline. Any chance we could book those frequent flier
tickets for a day later? They were back to their usual tricks of nonco-
operation. The cost of buying tickets at this late a date was prohibitive.
The apartment was booked through the rest of the year. I thought of
the first chapter of Job. There really IS a conspiracy. We are merely
the pawns of the spiritual powers.

While contemplating whether my life and/or my marriage was
ending, I looked at the back of my passport. The service I had used
to get visas for China and Tanzania had put its stamp and phone

number on the passport's plastic casing. I called them and explained my situation.

"This happens all the time," the bored voice in Washington, D.C., told me. "We'll fax you some documents now; fill them out, sign them, and send the papers and your expired passport to us by FedEx right away."

I did what I was told, feeling like I was talking to hostage takers telling me where to drop off the money if I wanted to see my baby again. Name the time. Name your price. Add some zeroes to it. I won't call the authorities. Just give me back my trip, I beg you!

True to their word, they sent the forms immediately. I filled them out in the FedEx parking lot, stuffed them in an envelope with the passport, wished them Godspeed, and slowly drove home. Things seemed okay between my wife and me on the surface. We told the kids about it. My daughter would pass me in the house, pause, and hug me unsolicited, as if it were my last cigarette before the execution. I caught my son staring at me from another room. "What?" I asked. He slowly shook his head. "You are so screwed," he said.

The earth didn't start spinning again until Monday morning, when I called Washington. Yes, they had my passport, and yes it was already at the U.S. State Department being rushed through. I should have it by tomorrow, they said. That was one day before we were leaving. A little tight, but a livable margin.

They called Monday afternoon. Bad news. I had forgotten to sign the back of one of the forms. I signed one. Not the other. Passport rejected.

My wife saw my body language and stood behind the chair I was sitting in while I discussed my options on the phone. She reached down and began to massage my shoulders. I tucked my chin at first, hoping she wasn't actually feeling for my windpipe, but when I realized she was getting the picture that our anniversary trip was not going to happen because of me, after two years of planning, and she was still willing to share this shameful moment with me, I understood the concept of grace.

"There's still a chance this will work," the emotionless voice in Washington said. "Sign the form now, fax it to me, and we'll take it in first thing Tuesday. We'll get it on the earliest overnight and you might have it by 8 a.m. Wednesday."

The airport shuttle was coming at 9:30 a.m. It was the only option left.

My phone rang Tuesday afternoon.

"The courier is on his way to the airport right now," he told me.

That night I woke up at 3 a.m. and turned on the television to see if there were any storms or accidents on the east coast. I woke up again at 5 and saw that Marcia was already up, staring out the kitchen window into the darkness.

At 7:30 a.m. a van pulled in front of the house. The driver had an envelope. I signed for it before he was completely out of his vehicle. Two hours later another van arrived and took us to the airport.

Within a day we were riding bikes along canals in Bruges, playing in the North Sea, enjoying the art and sights during the day, and the jazz clubs at night. I massaged Marcia's shoulders a lot.

I remember the trip. I remember the tension I caused. But what I remember most was, at my lowest point, I did not get condemnation. I got a neck rub. I got a massage that said, "We're in this together, regardless of how badly you screwed this up."

Bringing our flaws to our loved ones can be the very means that moves the relationship forward. How else do we remain in our deep relationships? How else do we grow? With God or anyone else? It is within the framework of families that we learn how to become advocates for one another.

Family life in general is a series of small surrenders that move us downward, but actually lead us upward. It's about giving away power and rights. It's about being unselfish. It's about feeling the way God feels—where we take delight in letting someone else's life be more important than our own. Married life, Anne Lamott says, is one spouse secretly thinking he or she got the better deal.[20]

In his book *Sacred Thirst*, Craig Barnes says that marriage is a great place to practice and experience what he calls "two-handed giving," where we don't hide or withhold anything. It is like the love we receive from God. He tells newly married couples that he knows how their marriages will end, if they are blessed with this kind of activity. They will end like the marriage of two elderly Dutch people in his congregation. The husband, Mr. Huijssoon, was dying at home, and Barnes went to visit him for the last time.

Barnes writes "I did what pastors do in such a situation: I embraced the family, sat down and listened to them, reminded them of the resurrection, prayed, and quoted a few Scripture verses. But the most powerful message in that room came from Mrs. Huijssoon. After forty-nine years of accompanying her husband around the globe, she had spent the last years focusing all of her attention on the overwhelming demands created by one stroke after another. Eventually the strokes robbed her beloved husband of his mind."

In the smelly, exhausting experience of watching someone die, Mrs. Huijssoon caressed her husband, moistened his dry lips with a cloth, and whispered comforting words in his ear. "She withheld nothing from him," Barnes wrote. She told Barnes that doing this wasn't easy, but it was never a burden. "It was just love," she told him.

"Who doesn't want to spend life giving and receiving this kind of love?" he wrote. "The problem is that we have been hurt so many times that we close our hands around our hearts . . . But when you are clutching at something, you can neither give nor receive love, which always requires two open hands."[21]

Marriage and parenting are activities that are best conducted with both hands open. This is how we then can begin to fathom how we are the beloved of God—it's here on earth, in our families, as it is in heaven. Healthy families can provide us bursts of revelation, as they did for Barnes.

As our kids have gotten older, my wife and I have realized that our family is much bigger—and needs to be much bigger—than just the four of us. Our family web includes our church relationships, neighbors, school friends, and colleagues from my wife's and my jobs. As our kids grew, they needed more physical space. But they needed more family space, too, that extended beyond just who lived under our roof. Parents are weavers of the web. If they're not attentive, a web will be woven for them. And they never stop weaving, because the family doesn't remain constant. It is in motion continually because relationships are dynamic and not stagnant. Of course, things will happen that are out of parents' control. But as much as possible, weaving the bigger family web takes prayer, effort, imagination, and attention. When our kids no longer felt as if they could talk to their mom and dad, we wanted the web to include good advisors, guides, even spiritual directors. That doesn't just happen on its own. There's some intentional weaving going on.

We tried to weave our own home into a broader web for others, as well. Over the years we have kept kids of bipolar parents who were simply not able to manage their families, kids of abusive parents, pregnant teenagers, friends of our kids who didn't feel safe in their own homes, kids with eating disorders. There are a lot of keys to our house floating around out there.

"A family web is so delicately woven that it takes almost nothing to set the whole thing shuddering or even to tear it to pieces," Frederick Buechner said. "Yet the thread it's woven of is as strong as anything on earth."[22]

I had a dream the week before Blake went to junior high school. He had gone to a small neighborhood elementary school, where he had the same teacher all day. It was supportive and safe. Now he was heading toward a school with nearly one thousand students from all over the city, and would have to navigate multiple classes from multiple teachers who may or may not remember his name or even care about him. Earlier that year, I had been in China to work on a book, and spent a day walking along the Great Wall. My dream, as most dreams are, was somewhat convoluted, and put pieces of different things together. But here's what I remember. In the dream I was at the Great Wall again, but this time I was there with Blake. I was holding him upside-down by his ankles over the edge of the wall, on the Mongolia side, and I could not see the ground below. It was simply black space below us. I let go of his ankles. Then I woke up.

I had this dream several times.

In the years since, the web has shuddered a few times, but it has held.

6

Getting Drenched

The Sacrament of Baptism

This is the first, wildest and wisest thing I know, that the soul exists, and that it is built entirely out of attentiveness.

Mary Oliver[1]

Standing around the giant campfire, my fellow Boy Scouts and I were trying to be serious because the scoutmaster had demanded it. But you know how it is when you've got dozens of boys together out in the woods around a campfire. We were as serious as a whoopee cushion. Boys around a campfire aren't about seriousness. They like to start fires and they like to put them out with water that has passed through their kidneys first. They are about throwing sticks, leaves, gum wrappers, articles of clothing, each other, anything that is loose, into the fire. One boy would say something dumb that, under other circumstances would not be remotely funny, and we would laugh until we were gasping. Why is it that when the pressure is on to be serious, the stupidest stuff becomes rich comedy—Pee Wee Herman becomes Robin Williams?

We were in northern Minnesota, deep in the woods, and had been for nearly two weeks. It was our annual summer camp. Toward the end of the experience was the climactic point: seeing who in the troop was considered the best camper. Every year the troop inducts a selected scout into an elite group called the Order of the Arrow. Heavy on Native American tradition, mythology, and symbolism, the selection ceremony calls for having the scouts stand in a circle, forming a ring around the fire. Then members of the Order, usually outfitted in Native American ceremonial costume, would visit the campsite and take the new inductee with them for a night of silence in the woods. Our group, though fully versed in the solemn nature of the ceremony, acted more like the campfire scene in the Mel Brooks movie *Blazing Saddles*.

Then one of our adult leaders hissed, "Listen!"

In the distance we could hear a slight "ching . . . ching . . . ching . . ." approaching.

"It's Santa Claus," I yelled, cracking up everyone in the ring under twenty-one.

The sound got louder, and we got quieter. Soon, two painted, muscular Indian braves came out of the woods to the edge of our campsite. Now everyone under twenty-one was terrified. One of the braves had an ankle bell that chinged when he walked. They both walked slowly, deliberately, toward our circle. The one with the ankle bell moved inside our circle, between the fire and us, and began to walk slowly, sizing up each scout with a look of disdain. The other brave paralleled him, but walked behind each of us, on the outside of the ring.

The inside warrior made a complete circle, then slowed down even more and began again. He was clearly looking for something. Or someone. When he got in front of me, a tiny, shivering fourteen-year-old with an overbite, he pushed his terrifying face close to mine and sniffed ferociously. I could smell him, too. He was mostly animal. His eyes were dots that revealed only blackness—like a falcon's—and I trembled like his hamster meal. Then he moved on. I reminded myself to breathe. He got two campers past me, then whirled back and screamed at the top of his lungs (or maybe that was me screaming?), and he leaped through the air, knocking me into the warrior stationed behind me. Instinctively I struggled at first, but realized the futility and gave up. When I did, they picked me up, produced an arrow, and put my hand around it tightly. Then they thrust my arm toward the fire so the wooden shaft of the arrow would be blackened slightly. I pulled the flaming arrow back and blew out the small fire. Then they turned me toward the forest, one warrior walking in front of me, the other behind me, and marched me out, making me hold the arrow high above my head in triumph.

It started dawning on me what this meant. I was chosen—"tapped out"—for membership in the Order of the Arrow. I was no longer just a scout. Either that, or it was the most sensational child-abduction incident in our camp's history!

I knew that I was in for a long night. The tradition is that the newly selected member is initiated by a night of silence alone in the forest. That didn't bother me. The woods didn't frighten me, even though it was so dark at night that you couldn't see your hand held centimeters in front of your face. My concern was for the predators that lurked in the forest. There were bears up there. Timber wolves. Bobcats. Snakes. I feared the mosquitoes the most. They swarm until you're in tears. They're big enough to be the Minnesota state bird. They've been known to suck the badges right off of a scout's shirt. Holy men don't levitate in Minnesota. They are carried on the backs of mosquitoes. You could spray graffiti on these insects' wings.

After the first couple of hours of being deposited in the forest, I got in tune with the sounds of my surroundings, including my own breathing. Leaves rustling a little meant mice, I supposed. There were some sounds in the air—bats, I figured. The high-pitched whirring sound in my ear was from mosquitoes. I thought about wood ticks, which you can't hear, and wondered if they were silently invading my clothing, giving me Lyme disease that wouldn't be diagnosed until I was in my thirties. I wondered if I was sitting in poison ivy. I was trying to be Siddhartha—silent, emptying myself of expectations and fears, excited about my new calling. Still, I knew the night was just beginning, and wondered if I would sleep.

Before long I heard another sound. Something walking. It sounded too steady to be a wild animal. Soon it made a sound that I recognized. No one clears phlegm like our assistant scoutmaster, who was also my dad.

"Dean?"

I thought about how to respond without breaking my vow of silence. But you can't *not* respond to your dad.

"Over here." I stood up.

"Come on. You can sleep in my tent tonight." I never saw him. I only followed his footsteps back to the campsite, where I went inside his tent, laid down and immediately fell asleep. This was a father who could not stand the thought of his creation spending one night in the darkness. Rules are one thing. Fatherhood is another. We never told anyone we had violated the rules. If the organization's elders are reading this now, I will send back my sash.

Stephen King Gets It

Initiations like the Order of the Arrow's are part of the experience of becoming something in addition to who you already are. They are steeped in tradition, and are usually well thought out. (Initiations into fraternities and sororities, which often involve hazing, take these traditions to a level of cruelty and stupidity.) The traditions are a means by which we experience a larger world than the one we previously knew. Sometimes they involve a symbol for turning away from who we were before the initiation and toward who we are now becoming. That's why I held the arrow over my head as I was marched into the woods. It was a proclamation that I was different from the boy who left the circle around the fire. I was a member of Something Else. I was baptized.

In the Christian tradition, baptism is a means by which God uses the symbol of water to show that our old self is washed away and we accept our new self as a member of a spiritual family. It is a means by which we recognize ourselves as new creatures. It's a type of initiation. I have seen many baptism services in the church I attend. They are very moving experiences, as the person in the pool publicly declares his or her faith, and is then gently placed under water by the pastor. There is always a nervous moment in the congregation as we hope the person won't get dropped and the pastor won't get electrocuted by the nearby microphone, and then relief when the new creature stands again. Baptism is a way of saying "I accept the grace of God freely given to me, and I want it to wash over me, and I acknowledge that it changes me."

But it's more than just initiation. It's a statement that the past is the past.

The best example of baptism I have seen was not in my church or in a church setting at all. It was in the movie *Shawshank Redemption*. Based on a Stephen King story, the movie shows a man (played by Tim Robbins) who is serving a life sentence in jail for a crime he did not commit. Even though the prison life is brutal, and he receives severe beatings, he maintains his hope. He is assigned to assist the church-going, hymn-whistling, Bible-quoting warden who is also a vicious, vengeful megalomaniac embezzling millions of dollars from the state.

The Robbins character stands up for justice, stands up for his fellow inmates, and embodies hope despite his seemingly hopeless circumstances. It soon becomes clear why he has hope. For years he has been working on an escape plan. The night he breaks out there is a terrifying electrical storm outside. At specific moments when thunder crashes through the prison, Robbins pounds his way into the prison's sewer system. He crawls through the pipe that carries the human waste from the inmates and guards to a river outside, stopping frequently to vomit. Finally he makes it to the outfall and collapses in the river. He staggers to his feet, and in the deafening downpour, lightning flashing around him, he stumbles through the water from the earth and the sky, taking off his prison clothing, heading toward freedom.

When I first saw that scene, all I could think of was the word baptism. He had just crawled through some of the worst muck imaginable. He had just lived through the worst life imaginable. And now he's in the water, being born again, shedding his old self. Just as when Christ waded into the Jordan River to be baptized by his forerunner John and a spirit descended and a voice proclaimed him as God in the flesh, a similar scene played out in this movie. Heaven and earth came together in a unique moment to say, "You're free now." Free from what? From false accusations, from hypocrisy, from bondage. From your past.

Contrast that baptism scene with the staged baptism scene in the movie *There Will Be Blood*. The Daniel Day Lewis character is a driven, despicable oilman who agrees to be baptized only to get the rights to build a pipeline on a rancher's property. The preacher, who is not much more honorable than the Lewis character, demands that Lewis tell the congregation that he is a sinner and that he has abandoned his son. Lewis does so, but the preacher demands he say it louder, and repeat it again, even louder. The whole thing is a sham. The preacher knows it and the person getting baptized knows it. And no one is different as a result of it.

Baptism is always better when it comes as a surprise.

Writer Anne Lamott says that Christianity is the wettest religion there is. It's about tears falling on parched ground, drinking living water so we'll never thirst again.[2] In her book *Traveling Mercies* she writes, "Most of what we do in worldly life is geared toward our staying dry, looking good, not going under. But in baptism, in lakes and rain and tanks and fonts, you agree to something that's a little sloppy because at the same time it's also holy, and absurd." It's about getting drenched, then coming out maybe a little disoriented, but with the knowledge that a new day is upon you, she said.[3]

Baptism, Eugene Peterson wrote, is the Genesis account of creation all over again. "As Jesus is lifted out of the water, God breathes life into him."[4] In the Jordan River, Jesus emerges knowing full well who he is. Buechner said that the sacrament became part of the Christian movement in the earliest stages as a symbol of dying to the old self and rising to the new self.[5]

When I go backpacking during the summer in Yosemite National Park, the guys I go with have a tradition. After a hard day of climbing, at elevations above nine thousand feet, with packs weighing about fifty pounds, a few things are unmistakably true: we are exhausted, we are soaked with sweat, we are overheating, and we are filthy. On one day I was filthier than normal because of the tumble I took on the trail where I unintentionally cartwheeled and then came to rest on my back, feeling very much like a flipped-over turtle. You could have drawn pictures in the dirt that covered me. But at the end of any given day, even without falling, everyone is caked with dirt. The campsites where we spend the night are often near a lake. Those lakes are fed by snow. They're ice cold. Tradition is tradition, though, and tradition says that when we get to a particular site, we take off our sweaty, disgusting, Pepé le Pew clothes, put on swimsuits, and jump in the lake. As much as my body resists the initial plunge, and as much as I remember the movie scene where Butch Cassidy and the Sundance Kid are about to leap from a cliff into a river, and Sundance confesses that he can't swim, and Butch tells him that it doesn't matter because the fall will probably kill him first, I realize that it doesn't matter how tired my muscles are. I'm probably going to drown, but maybe the cold shock will kill me first. I count down from ten with everyone and follow the gang in and head for the big rock in the middle of the lake. The water is always colder than I remembered from the last time. I can't tell if I am on fire or freezing. My arms and legs are saying, "Are you nuts? They can't drag for your body up here. You'll be preserved in ice for future archeological explorations. They'll think they found Lucy when they discover you at the bottom." And yet, when I get to the rock and sit down, the dirt is gone and I am more awake than I have ever been in my life. All that I had collected on my self on the trail is now settling at the bottom of the aptly named Cathedral Lake, and I am clean. New. Baptized.

Something else besides our past gets washed away in baptism. The sacrament is a means by which God washes away the illusion of who we think we are. Baptism is what Thomas Merton calls "the sacrament of illumination."[6] It is a means by which we discover who we *really* are.

We all know people—and probably *are* these people—who are lost unless they have their costumes on. The costumes may be their professions, their military ranks, their education, their roles in life, or their physical attributes. But they are costumes nonetheless. When university professors can't even sign a handwritten note about a meeting announcement without adding "PhD" after their names, you know they don't know who they are without that title. Who are you really without the "Lieutenant Colonel, retired" after your name? Who are you without your biceps or your augmented breasts or your children or grandchildren? Who are you without the fancy car? The word hypocrisy means "playing a part." Who are we really without our actor's equipment—our costumes and our masks?

A friend of mine is a high-profile criminal defense attorney in San Diego. He has won some of the most amazing cases—against police departments, the Hare Krishnas, the U.S. Navy—I have ever seen. Yet, when I typically see him at his house or at our church, he looks like one of the homeless wanderers off the streets of Ocean Beach. Baggy tank top, baggier shorts that don't match. At the parking lot of his law office, I almost expect to see a shopping cart with a ratty sleeping bag wadded in it instead of his car. When he's in court, though, he is the snappiest dresser in the building. Tailored, expensive suits with suspenders and silk ties, calf leather shoes. I asked him why he never wore those cool clothes anywhere else. "That's my gunslinger's costume," he said. "I only wear it when I'm in a battle." He knows who he is with his costume on or off.

Secret Identity

Sometimes the illusion of who we are is a little subtler. Several years ago my cousin's college-age daughter was nearly killed in a head-on car accident in Kansas City. She had severe brain damage, and it was not certain whether she would survive. If she did survive, the brain damage would perhaps leave her in a coma the rest of her life. My cousins, John and Linda Seaman, were missionaries in the Ivory Coast in Africa at the time. They returned to the United States, not knowing if they were coming home for a funeral or a long recovery. Their daughter survived the crash and became conscious, but had months of rehabilitation ahead of her. I talked to John on the phone, and he was clearly hurting. Still, he recounted several examples of God's activity amid the tragedy. I told him I wanted to spend some time with him and the family.

"I'll bring my notebook," I said.

"I want you to come, but leave the notebook at home," he said. "Come as my brother, not as a journalist."

At first I was wounded by his statement. Eventually I got it. Sometimes I play the role of reporter at the expense of my true calling, which is to be a person of compassion. John saw me putting on the robe of journalism before I did, and told me to leave it in my closet.

Baptism is what occurs when we are shown who we are apart from our roles, our masks, our attachments, and our created selves. It is the means by which we take on the most real roles in our lives. It is when we hear a voice from heaven or indirectly through a cousin, "This is my child, in whom I am well pleased." Baptism doesn't minimize those other identities we have. It just makes them not so important. For the work that I do—writing and teaching—it was important that I get a PhD from a good university. The degree educated me further about my area of expertise, it usually garners initial respect from students, along with legitimacy among colleagues, tenure from my university, and better treatment from flight attendants who think I am a *real* doctor (as my kids call MDs). I don't minimize the work it took to procure it, although I do understand columnist Dave Barry's point that there are about as many PhDs in the U.S. as there are air molecules, and that anyone can get one if they have enough time and money. Still, I had better know who I am apart from that degree. And apart from my role as a journalist. And apart from my role as a father and a husband and a son and a brother.

As a journalist I fall into the identity trap very easily. I want to tell a good story when I write, but deep down what I really want to do is please my editors. I suppose that reveals all sorts of unresolved father and mother issues, but the reality is that I want the heavens to open up when I publish something and have the world hear the voice of my editor saying, "Dean Nelson is one of ours, in whom we are well pleased."

One morning the national editor of the Boston Globe newspaper called and asked me to cover a story about forest fires in northern California and file the story by the end of the day. I didn't know if I could do it, but I agreed to the assignment. I immediately headed for the airport, flew to San Jose, rented a car, found the forest firefighters' base camp, followed a group of them to fight a fire, flew in a National Guard helicopter to get the big picture, hand-wrote my story, and dictated it over the phone (this was before the age of laptop computers) before their deadline. I gladly received the praise of my editors. I wore the cloak of "reporter" with pride. Later that year, when I wrote a story for their sports section about the parade in San Diego for the America's Cup yacht race winners, the sports editor told me I had "made chicken salad out of chicken s—." That made my day.

But this passion in my role as a journalist cuts both ways. When I get a rejection from a publisher who says, "I have no idea what to do with this book proposal," or I overhear another editor of a national newspaper say, "call Dean Nelson as a last resort," I am as low as can be. If all that I am is a reporter, then I am at the mercy of editors who are very busy people, whose goals in life involve publishing news, not salving writers' self esteems. I had better know who *else* I am in addition to a writer.

When I see other dads teaching their kids how to surf, my stock as a father takes a hit.

When I see husbands treating their wives better than I treat Marcia, my role as a husband takes a hit.

When I see adult sons and daughters pay more attention to their parents than I do to mine, my role as a son takes a hit.

All of those things can motivate me to be a better dad, spouse, and son, but they can also be traps. The roles we play are clearly *part* of who we are. The messages we receive from others about how well we are doing in those roles can determine our entire self image. But at the core we are not those roles or the messages we receive about them. Baptism clarifies this.

"What Genesis suggests is that this original self, with the print of God's thumb still upon it, is the most essential part of who we are and is buried deep in all of us," Buechner said. But the world does its work on that self, he said. The world shows us that we need to become someone else if we are going to survive, and so we assume we can create a better self than the one we were given. "That is the story of all our lives . . . and in the process of living out that story, the original, shimmering self gets buried so deep that most of us end up hardly living out of it at all," he said. "Instead we live out all the other selves which we are constantly putting on and taking off like coats and hats against the world's weather."[7]

Rabbi Zusya, one of the revered teachers of Hebrew wisdom, once said, "In the world to come I shall not be asked 'Why were you not Moses?' I shall be asked, 'Why were you not Zusya?'"[8]

Baptism takes the myth of who we think we are and holds it under the bright spotlight of who we *really* are.

There is a homeless man who lives on the streets of downtown San Diego, and his "territory" is near a tourist trap along the San Diego bay called Seaport Village. The man's name is Ricky. He has a cart that is filled with his belongings, which include some clothes, a blanket, and a broom. He's heavyset, looks about 60, and is missing three fingers from his right hand. Even though he is homeless, he feels like he needs to earn his keep each night, so early each morning he takes his broom and sweeps the parking lot near Seaport Village. No one pays him to do this, nor has anyone asked him to. It's his gift to the city. Or maybe a way to mark his territory. My friends from church, Jack and Aileen, walked past him one morning, and Ricky shouted to them, "Happy Honeymoon!" They stopped to talk with him. When they asked him where he lived, he said, "This world is not my home." Jack and Aileen said they knew an old church song that had that line in it. They agreed to bring him a copy of the song next time they saw him.

After a few more encounters with Ricky, Jack and Aileen learned that Ricky had been married, but lost his wife and baby in a car accident. He had struggled with drug addiction ever since. The conversation eventually turned to faith. Ricky told them he had tried to follow Christ over the years, and then blurted out this declaration: "I want to be baptized." He said he felt incomplete as a Christian because he hadn't had this experience. Jack and Aileen talked to the pastor of our church, who agreed to have Ricky baptized at one of the regularly scheduled baptism times at the end of a worship service.

Twice they went to pick up Ricky to bring him to a service. They couldn't find him either time. One Monday morning, Jack walked through Ricky's territory, and there he was. Ricky was sad and tearful that he had missed his chance. But while the church baptistery was closed and dry, the hot tub in Jack and Aileen's yard had water in it. Jack called our pastor. Friends called friends. By that evening, twenty-four people gathered in the yard to witness the baptism of Ricky.

"He said he needed to do this," Jack said. "He said he needed to have the experience to signify who he really was."

Who Are You Really?

How do we know who we are, *really*? In her commencement speech at the University of California at Berkeley, Anne Lamott addressed the tension students feel between following their own creative identities and fulfilling the expectations of their parents and professors.

"Your problem is how you are going to spend this one odd and precious life you have been issued," she said. "Whether you're going to spend it trying to look good and creating the illusion that you have power over people and circumstances, or whether you are going to taste it, enjoy it, and find out the truth about who you are."

After achieving some acclaim in her own life as a writer, she said she expected that the anxiety deep inside her would dissipate, and that she would be whole and fulfilled. "The culture says these things will save you, as long as you also manage to keep your weight down. But the culture lies," she told the students.

When she finally started getting published regularly, which was her whole reason for being, she said it was like a greyhound catching the mechanical rabbit that it had been chasing its whole life. "It wasn't alive; it had no spirit," she said.

> It was fake. Fake doesn't feed anything. Only spirit feeds spirit, in the same way only your own blood type can sustain you. . . . In the Christian tradition, they say the soul rejoices in hearing what it already knows. And so you pay attention when that Dr. Seuss creature inside you sits up and says, "Yo!" . . .
>
> It's magic to see spirit largely because it's so rare. Mostly you see the masks and the holograms that the culture presents as real. You see how you're doing in the world's eyes, or your family's or—worst of all—yours, or in the eyes of people who are doing better than you— much better than you—or worse. But you are not your bank account, or your ambitiousness. You're not the cold clay lump with a big belly you leave behind when you die. You're not your collection of walking personality disorders. You are spirit, you are love, and . . . you're here to love, and be loved freely.[9]

Loving and being loved freely are results of baptism, because we become part of a larger community of others who are also trying to live as *their* true selves. Vincent Donovan wrote, "Is baptism a call to individual salvation and self-fulfillment, or a joining of an orga- nization? Or is it not an incorporation into a community, a community called to the salvation of the human race?"[10]

Baptism confronts me with who I really am—someone created by and loved by God. When the water, or the experience, washes the illusion off of me and the real soaks in, the illusion is exposed and is made powerless. Baptism gives me solid ground to stake my identity on instead of on the constantly sinking sand of whatever the culture at the time has deemed important. In *Traveling Mercies* Anne Lamott writes about Mary, a member of her congregation who was baptized in the Mississippi River in Louisiana as a young girl. When Mary got to the river, she saw that there was a ring of poles sticking out of the water. Early that morning, the deacons had gone into the river and found a solid place to stand amid the muddy, shifting river bottom. They stuck the poles to show where Mary would not lose her footing in the river's current. The titles, the masks, the illusive identities, the roles all shift. There is a place in the river that doesn't.[11] That's where we have to stand.

Baptism is a series of small births out of water or other symbolic amniotic fluid, from which we emerge from our petty security systems and walk in a new relationship with the world.

There are historical arguments about baptism that say it isn't a legitimate means to God's grace in your life unless you are immersed, or sprinkled, or poured over. That's the same kind of argument as whether prayer is legitimate if our hands are turned palms up, showing that we're receiving what God has for us, or our hands are turned palms down, showing that we let go of everything we cling to that keeps us from God. It's also the same kind of argument about whether legitimate worship is possible if the congregation sings a chorus from the Psalms fifteen times with guitars and drums, or if it can only happen with a hundred-year-old hymn, with a tune that used to be a drinking song, accompanied by a pipe organ. At the church I attend, we sing Charles Wesley's hymn "And Can It Be?" as if it were our congregation's fight song. The older generations hate it that way because the drums and guitars drown out the organ. The younger generations tolerate it, but it doesn't sound enough like the "Jesus is my prom date" songs they like to sing. But these arguments about music styles exist simply to avoid looking at the real. In baptism we experience moments when it seems that heaven and earth come together in a unique way, and that we are different as a result of those moments. Baptism is a dividing line. A gate. A bridge. It is a symbol that shows we affirm our true identity. It is a means God uses so that we can point to it and say, "That's when all things became new." And since God is continuously making all things new in every moment, those moments of baptism happen all the time. The rituals we follow in church matter because they connect us to the larger tradition and practice of our forefathers. But they aren't the only way to experience God. Sometimes there's a burst of revelation, like the screen in a Monty Python program that says, "And Now For Something Completely Different."

Baptisms occur in church, obviously, but not only there. You can't script the moments, unless you are making a movie, and you can't force them into occurring. The spirit of God descends, a door opens in the universe, darkness is pierced by light, and you're led to conclude that there is so much more to the activity of God than you originally thought. You're initiated again. All you have to do is notice.

Sometimes this experience of More can occur through something as simple as a song. I have heard the song Amazing Grace so many times that it risks losing its meaning. I have sung it even more. I remember hearing Judy Collins sing it a cappella at the Minneapolis Auditorium. I watched on public television, mesmerized, as Bill Moyers explained the song's history and interviewed people about the significance of it; I gave videotapes of the program as Christmas presents that year. The 2007 Hollywood movie *Amazing Grace* was a marvelous portrayal of the life of William Wilberforce, who paid the price to pressure England to end its slave trade.

I have contributed to the cheapening of the song by leading groups of young people to sing "Amazing Grace" to the tune of "Gilligan's Island," or "The Addams Family" theme song, or "The House of the Rising Sun," while I accompanied on the banjo.

But there have been other times when I have heard it that I had a clearer sense of who I am in the big picture as a result. Arlo Guthrie, son of legendary Woody Guthrie, gave a wonderful concert when I was a graduate student at the University of Missouri. He played excerpts of his hilarious "Alice's Restaurant" album, along with many of his irreverent protest songs, and some from his dad's epic collection. For his encore he played "Amazing Grace" seated at his piano without his band. The concert hall took on a church-like aura. Those in the audience who weren't softly singing along, affirming the truth of the lyrics, were silent. No one shouted requests for songs he hadn't played. No one screamed to get his attention. It was as if this hush was an agreed-upon moment that we all sensed was holy. All of the variables of the individuals in the audience, all of the decades of songs Arlo is known for, and all of the depth of that great hymn became focused into one beam of illumination and clarity. Everything that had happened earlier was a set-up for that moment. My wife and I could only be struck with wonder and tears. The world thirsts for grace, Philip Yancey says, and "when grace descends, the world falls silent before it."[12]

Diane Schurr is a jazz piano player and singer. Whether she is playing in a concert hall or a jazz club, I try to see her when she is in town. She also ended a concert I attended with "Amazing Grace." But she emphasized something different from Arlo Guthrie, because of her own personal context. She is blind. "I once was lost, but now am found," she sang, building up to a climactic point. "Was blind, but now I see." She sang that phrase forcefully. With certainty. Over and over. Each time she repeated it the crowd roared even louder. It was a different expression of affirmation from the Arlo Guthrie experience. This was an audience saying, "We know you do. There is a sight other than our eyes. We know you see something." We longed to see what she saw. She fed off of that response, and the moment transcended the music, the concert hall, optic nerves. It redefined "sight."

When Aretha Franklin sings it on her live "Amazing Grace" album, she emphasizes a completely different element because of *her* context. The song takes twelve minutes on the recording, because there are some specific things she doesn't want the crowd to miss. When she sings the line, "Through many dangers, toils, and snares I have already come," she sings the word "Through," and stops. She sings it again. And again. And again. She adds syllables to that one-syllable word. She adds vowels. She covers octaves with it. The organist in the background plays louder with each repetition, and the crowd responds with its own increased assent. She is making a point. We don't get around danger, toils, and snares. We don't avoid them. We don't have a choice in this life. We must go *through* them. The crowd audibly gets it. A light of truth shines through and pierces the darkness. An inaudible voice speaks within the audible, tells us whose we are, and that grace will carry us. Through.

There was another time that I heard this song—and tried to sing along but couldn't. The church I attended in Minnesota was a small, evangelical community church. It was a narrow-minded congregation, at least in regard to worshipping a white Republican Jesus. The war in Vietnam had just ended, and refugees from Southeast Asia were streaming into communities throughout the U.S. One winter Sunday night, during a time in the service when people gave testimonies about the activity of God in their lives, a lady stood and told about how her neighborhood was becoming filled with Cambodians. I braced myself for an insensitive remark. Instead, I heard, "I was watching the children on my block waiting for the school bus, and they had no shoes. They were standing in the snow, barefoot. I don't think they had even seen snow before now. So I wonder if some of us could gather the extra shoes and socks we have in our houses, and I will give them to these children so they won't freeze here."

The church responded with bags and boxes and car trunks full of our excess, and she distributed them. Soon some of those Cambodian neighbors began attending our church. Soon we found a pastor who knew their language. Soon the Cambodian congregation became larger than our exclusively Anglo congregation.

One Sunday morning, when both the English-speaking and the Cambodian-speaking congregations were worshipping together in a joint service, we sang "Amazing Grace." They sang a verse in Cambodian. We sang a verse in English. When we got to "When we've been there ten thousand years, bright shining as the sun," we sang it together, each in our own languages. Of course you know what happened. Heaven opened and the Spirit of God descended and gave us a glimpse of the world to come. It was illumination. The American mask and the Cambodian mask, the resident mask and the refugee mask, the alien mask, the rich mask and the poor mask, shattered. Heaven and earth came together for the moment and reminded us of who we really were. It was a glimpse of the real.

When Jesus teaches us to pray by saying, "Your kingdom come . . . on earth as it is in heaven," he is telling us that the Kingdom of God is continuously visiting, interrupting, invading, disrupting, what we *perceive* to be the world. We step into the Jordan River throughout our day. When we let it wash the chatter around us, we hear the voice that says "you are more than your job, your role, your mask. You are mine. And I am pleased." When we step out of the river, we are initiated, illumined, and clean.

7

Reaching Match Point

The Sacrament of Last Rites

I have found what I was searching for without ever having discovered
what it was.

Peter Matthiessen[1]

*D*ean—
  *I promised a letter. Here goes. You anticipate well. Words
from your letter: Ambiguity. Uncertainty. Faith. Fragile. Absurd. In-
comprehensible. Mythology. Nursery-rhyme theology. You wanted
to know, you said in your letter, what is left when the myths have
fallen away. The words from your letter tell where I am. More than
I would like to admit, I am afraid. I'm afraid of the little things, the
big things.*

  *In my entire life I think I have been in touch with God no more than
eight or ten times. One of those moments occurred two or three days
before my May surgery. I was answering a letter from a former student
and she asked what she should call me once she becomes a teacher
in our department. I said to her in my response, "Call me Ishmael."*

Then I added, "Of course, you are to call me Larry." Being a poor speller and a terribly insecure person, I went to the dictionary to make sure I had spelled Ishmael right. In checking the spelling I happened to notice what the word Ishmael means: "God hears." As it turned out, the words were perfect for the time in my life. The surgery was not successful. The tumor I still have with me. So, better that I saw in the dictionary "God hears" than "God answers prayer." God doesn't always give us what we want. But he does hear. We bet our lives on that. That moment before surgery, the dictionary, not the Bible, tells me that God hears. Coincidence? It just happened? Pay no attention to it? Or, God speaks to Larry? God speaking to Larry??? The God of the universe says something to me??? However presumptuous, however absurd some may think it, I'll take it as at least a wink from God. I'll take it to the bank.

Enough of this. You're a busy man. But this is, I think, a fair, a fairly accurate statement as to where I am.

And yes, I would like to see your Fawlty Towers *tapes.*

Through the experiences of working for hospitals and ambulance crews, and then the loss of close friends, I have come to appreciate the ancient tradition of trying to be sacramental in the approach to death—of looking for holy moments during the transition, of allowing the Presence of God to fill those moments. Seeing the grace in dying is not an act of magic, where we believe that there is something in the anointing oil that we otherwise put in our salad that will make the difference between heaven and hell. It is a way of facing the final moments, not pretending that they really aren't there, but finding freedom in them, and recognizing that God is in them. Here. Now. It is a way of celebrating the life that has been lived, and the unknown life that is ahead, and giving it all to God. It's saying that Mayday isn't the last word. It's wishing someone bon voyage, traveling mercies, and thanks for coming.

But the end of a person's life is laden with grief on our part, and maybe some fear on the dying person's part. That's unavoidable. We grieve because we can't imagine life without the dying person. We grieve for ourselves, for the loved-one-shaped hole that is left in us. We grieve because separation by death seems so vast and permanent.

And while we can't avoid or ignore the grief and the fear, sometimes those very things distract us from seeing grace and Presence in the moments leading up to someone's death. They keep us from being fully awake to the moments, and we miss their message to us. There is so much we don't know about what is beyond this life—so why not concentrate more of our energy on what we do know in the here and now?

Larry Finger, the man who wrote the letter above, was my friend. Is my friend. We played a lot of tennis together, having both been on our respective college teams long ago. He was about fifteen years older than me, but he still won virtually every game. He didn't like to compete as much as try to keep the ball in play. That's how our conversations were, too. Sometimes we talked about how hard it was to be believers. We embraced the doubts—gave each other permission to wonder out loud if it was all true, and hoped together that it was. We taught in the same university literature department. Sometimes our tennis matches took place during the chapel hour or faculty meetings. We had our priorities. In addition to tennis, we shared a love for certain writers: William Faulkner, Garrison Keillor, Frederick Buechner, Flannery O'Connor. We also loved Monty Python, particularly the comedian John Cleese in his hilarious role as a hotel operator Basil Fawlty in the show *Fawlty Towers*. I have the whole series on video.

When Larry was diagnosed with cancer, none of us took it too seriously because he was the healthiest one in our department. While everyone else was eating donuts in department meetings, he was eating carrot and celery sticks. He limited his coffee intake. He weighed the same at sixty—about one hundred and fifty pounds — as he did when he was in college. So we figured that this was just a hiccup along the way to his living until he was one hundred. But he got worse, and the doctors became pessimistic. Exploratory surgery showed that he had taken a turn down a road from which there was no likely recovery.

When that happens to a friend, I think a lot of us simply don't know what to do or say. None of us wanted to believe it. Since we had a faith, we held out hope that Larry would be healed. But he kept getting worse. Faith and doubt became brothers.

I began writing Larry letters. We lived eight miles from one another, yet there are some things that are hard to say when looking into a dying person's face. Still harder, perhaps, are the responses from that person, in person. So I wrote, and tried to explain why I was writing instead of talking face to face. At first they were letters that told him how important he was to me. But Larry and I had had enough deep conversations over the healthy years that I also felt safe asking him to articulate what he was thinking during this part of his life. Was he afraid? Did his faith matter at this point? Could he separate out what Anne Lamott calls the "colo-rectal theology" that seems to dominate airwaves and pulpits from the Truth about himself, about life, about love, about God? What did he understand, in these circumstances, that he didn't understand before? Did he have clarity on anything, or was it all gray? Did he believe anymore? *What* did he believe? Why? His answer to my first letter is above.

"Life always carries a fatal dimension and some hint of having fallen into a trap," said Ortega y Gasset. "Except that this trap does not strangle us, but leaves to life a margin of decision and always permits us, out of the imposed situation, to achieve an elegant solution and to forge for ourselves a beautiful life."[2]

Larry's sentence, "Call me Ishmael," of course is the first sentence of Moby Dick, an account of a search for a great, terrifying beast of the sea. The Ishmael of scripture is a young boy, born of Abraham and his concubine Hagar. When Ishmael and his mother are banished from their home, it appears they are going to die. Ishmael cries. God hears his cry and an angel tells them to not be afraid. He makes them a promise about their future. When they open their eyes, they see a well, and, for the moment, they are saved.

Watching It Happen

I'll never forget the first time I saw someone die. Prior to this experience, I had never seen anything die, except for insects. Even my dog, when she got old and frail, was put to sleep while I was away at camp.

In high school, I signed up for a course called Medical Biology. It was a combination of class instruction as well as one night a week volunteering as an orderly in the not-so-orderly Hennepin County

General Hospital in downtown Minneapolis. It sounded like a perfect class for me, because ever since my first conscious memory about careers, I wanted to be a medical doctor. I was even named after a family friend who was a doctor. Thinking of Christmas presents for me was no problem, since everyone knew I just wanted medical stuff. As a little kid I got the plastic doctor's bag, complete with toy stethoscope and hammer for checking reflexes. Duchess, our dog, was very patient as I tried out everything on her except for the toy thermometer. Soon I graduated to the real stuff—real stethoscope, real dissecting kit, real microscope. I never did get those real defibrillating paddles I kept asking for, though. Imagine the damage to my psyche whenever I had to rub two frozen waffles together and yell "CLEAR!" before attaching them to my bare-chested dad trying to take a nap. I grew up in the television era of programs that contrasted the soft tenderness of Dr. Kildare with the primal animalism of Ben Casey, MD. Remember, I was also a hockey player. So I leaned toward Ben Casey.

Being an orderly in an urban general hospital meant I got to see everything. I got to break up fights between drunks and drug addicts, pick glass and gunshot fragments out of people's faces, restrain combative patients who didn't want stitches, clean out wounds and orifices that made me gag, help deliver babies, talk someone down from a bad acid trip, soothe frazzled nerves of a child getting a cast put on an arm, see heroic measures taken by doctors and nurses every night in a manner that will never be matched by a television program. And the first week on the job, as a sheltered seventeen-year-old boy, I got to see someone die.

He was a middle-aged man brought in by ambulance after suffering a heart attack at home. The nurses told me to get the stabilization room ready while they paged the hospital for the code blue crew. I set out instrument packets, arranged IV poles and trays, then went to the driveway doors to wait for the ambulance. When it came, everything happened in a blink. He was rushed in on the gurney, through the doors I had propped open. The crowd of doctors and nurses descended on him like gulls on a sandwich at the beach. Shirt and pants cut off. IVs inserted. Electrodes attached. It was all noise and controlled confusion. Over the din I heard "He's not responding," and watched as a muscular doctor jumped onto the gurney and straddled the man, and pounded on his chest with his fist. That lasted about 20 seconds. Then silence. The doctor climbed down, electrodes came off, needles were tossed in a bucket. The only sound was of gloves coming off of skilled, but unsuccessful, hands. The medical team dropped their masks, caps, scrubs, bandages, and towels on the floor, and walked out without a word, like athletes leaving a locker room after a tough loss. I stood in the corner, now alone with a body. He was a mess. The room was a mess. I was a mess. Where was the dramatic orchestra music? Where was the lone, mournful violin during this man's last, tender moments with his family? The reality was that there were no tender last moments. Instead, he'd been with violent, cursing strangers who were violating him in order to try to save him.

I slowly backed out of the room's double doors, my eyes locked on this horrifying centerpiece. Then I heard, "Doctor, how is he?"

His wife and children had just arrived. No one had given them the bad news yet. They looked at me, a child myself, Doogie Howser, wearing a scrub suit and a stethoscope around my neck, with hope. I stammered, "We're doing the best we can." Then I walked past them, past the driveway where the ambulance had delivered their husband and father, to the bushes, and threw up. My body, my whole self, was rejecting all of the things I had been taught about death. It wasn't like what I had seen on TV. It wasn't like the deathbed conversion stories I had heard in church. In this case it was brutal, violent, painful, and wrong. It shouldn't have happened this way, my stomach said, as it emptied into the hedge.

I worked in emergency rooms in Minneapolis and Kansas City for three more years, and for one summer on an ambulance crew in Oregon. Sometimes I saw death come peacefully. Most times it was a struggle or a surprise. A bike accident, a hang glider collapse, a car wreck, a drowning, a shooting, a suicide. Even when I wasn't working in this kind of context, when I wasn't on the job, I saw it. The man who sat down in the barber chair next to me in Detroit, told me good morning, then pitched forward as if he had been snapped to the floor by an invisible bungee cord, and died, covered by the hair trimmings of the previous customers. It was all around me. And it seemed so wrong. Mystifying. Contradictory to the long and productive life I was led to believe was out there for all of us. My friend and mentor,

Dean Spencer, with whom I had written my first book and made my first real money, crashed his plane trying to land in fog. His last word was "Mayday," spoken calmly in a measured tone.

This could not be how it was meant to be.

And yet, this is how it has been since Cain killed Abel. It's all Mayday. "I don't mind dying," Woody Allen said. "I just don't want to be there when it happens."

Well, here we are again, Dean. It's your fault, of course. You keep forcing this correspondence. In the middle of your letters you always put these tough questions to me. This is what it was in the last letter. "What does it matter if we know that God hears? What difference does that make? Why is it enough to know that God hears?" I think you answered your own questions with one of your questions: "Because that's all there is, therefore it has to be enough?" We have to know that God hears, otherwise even the good stuff the church taught us when we were growing up is not true. We want it to be true. That's the Big Truth we keep holding on to. Not just that God is, but that he hears me. And I hear him. That's what we keep holding on to.

And I want to keep on hearing. Since my future is a little more uncertain than yours (more certain, maybe?), I'm scavenging for words to live by and to die by. Words are a way of hearing, a way of hearing from God. In moments of despair especially—and at times, at least for very brief periods, it is a despair—words lift me out.

God preparing a table for me in the presence of my enemies. My enemies these days? Finger's free translation: Fear. Uncertainty. Anxiety. Yes, at times, despair.

And all those other words in the other Psalms: Rock. Refuge. Fortress. Deliverance. Shepherd. O Lord God of my salvation. His steadfast love endures forever. Out of my distress I called on the Lord. Out of my distress I go on a scavenger hunt. Every night (the church taught me to say my prayers and read scripture before going to sleep at night), scavenging the Psalms, seeking, searching, listening for the voice. Yes, at times I'm a desperate man. It's like taking the Kingdom by violence. The violent bear it away.

And all the words of Jesus, the Gospel words, the Jesus words. Chapter by chapter, verse by verse, word by word. A desperate man.

I want to hear. The shepherds heard, however terrifying that hearing was. They were sore afraid, the beautiful King James has it. Yes, I want to hear even if the hearing makes me scared stiff.

And much of the time I'm scavenging for words in great silence interrupted from time to time with the hum of the refrigerator, a car passing, the furnace kicking on. I'm learning—finally—to stop my scavenging at times and listen. Listen to the silence.

There are two sides of silence with me, of course. I'm the great faith/doubter and the great doubt/believer. So at times silence is doubt, yes even despair. But silence, too, is becoming for me, I believe, more and more faith. Peace is perhaps a better word to describe this silence. God, having heard, manifests himself in the silence. Silence becomes peace. It sounds corny, preachy, pious, sanctimonious, but I'll say it anyway. I think—finally—I'm learning to rest, learning to relax in the arms of Jesus.

And now here a few days before Christmas—my little Christmas gift to you—let's you and I listen to some Christmas words from Buechner. He has one of the wise men, long after the journey to the manger, say these words:

"And now, brothers, I will ask you a terrible question, and God knows I ask it also of myself. Is the truth beyond all truths, beyond the stars, just this: that to live without him is the real death, that to die with him is the only life?"

We want a yes to that question, don't we? May it be a reality in your life and mine, living and dying. Living or dying—Immanuel!

The movement from this life to the next has to be more than just the shedding of this skin for another. It's more than molting. It has to be more than "getting rid of the old Ford" or "changing our address," or "slipping out of a pair of ill-fitting shoes." It has to be more than discarding our shells, as the Heaven's Gate cult said they were doing when thirty-nine of them committed suicide in order to meet a comet in the sky. Yet what is it? The veil between life and death is very thin. We have metaphors in the Bible, yet those point to something beyond our comprehension, something not contained in our alphabet. What are we left with? What, then, can we speak of? The sacrament of the present moment, while we are still with each other.

Recognizing the sacred nature of this stage of life emphasizes not the end result as much as the way there. It's still about the journey.

My friends D and Kacie Marsh, the couple who washed each other's feet at their wedding, found out about halfway through Kacie's pregnancy that their baby had a major birth defect. The doctors said that they still needed to go through the birth process, but the act of pushing the baby through the birth canal would be too much for its flawed system and the baby—if alive at all—would last seconds or a few minutes. I simply cannot imagine what life was like for D and Kacie as they proceeded toward this fatal five-month countdown. I talked with them, occasionally. They had named their unborn son Benjamin. They were trusting God. And they were in a great deal of emotional pain.

"Every day of our journey we woke up to the bitter realization that our son was not being formed correctly," D said. "There were mornings when it was a discipline to simply make the bed. And yet, for every single time the fear crept in to choke out our hope, the Lord was faithful to give us a scripture, a phone call from a friend to remind us we weren't alone, or a timely word of encouragement from someone who cared about us."

When Ben finally arrived, the doctor held him up, assessed his blue/gray color, checked for a pulse in the umbilical cord, and grimly put his lifeless body on Kacie's chest without even suctioning out his nose and mouth. The doctor shook his head slightly—no pulse, no breathing, no life. After several seconds of silence, Ben began to sputter. He tried to cough the mucus out of his airway and his gray color turned pink. As D said later, Ben was "FULLY ALIVE." Ben cooed, smacked his lips, smiled, looked his parents in the eyes, responded to their voices as they sang "Happy Birthday" to him, and squeezed their fingers. Not only did they experience that Ben was fully alive, they also sensed the same about God.

"He was more present than we've ever known him to be," D said. "He was there in Ben's first breath, in his little smiles, and in every bubble that he blew. And the Lord was supremely present when we looked at our little boy in his baby blue eyes and watched him peacefully breathe his last. God never left us and he never forgot us. Never."

Ben lived for more than seven hours. He drew pure love from his parents, the nurses, and the astonished doctor.

"I wish you could have been there for his last breath," Kacie said at the funeral for their son. "It was amazing. It was the moment that changed who I am and who I will be from this day on. Some people wonder what happens to a person after they die, but not me. That question was answered before my eyes. As Ben took his last breath, I have no doubt that I encountered the hands of God. It was as though I could physically see his hands wrap around my little boy's body as he took him back to heaven. In a moment that I anticipated would be so painful and devastating, I found myself humbled and in awe of the presence of God. I have never been so close to him. It was a sacred moment that I just don't have words for. I knew in that very moment that Ben was made whole."

It was not a Mayday moment for my friends. It was a I'm So Glad You Came.

Traveling Mercies

When my father-in-law was in his final days, before he was moved from the hospital back home under hospice care, the nurses asked the family if they wanted a priest to visit with him. My father-in-law was a Protestant evangelical pastor, and this was a Catholic hospital. My wife doubted that her dad would desire such a visit. The Reformation had occurred, after all. But she knew better than to decide without consulting him, even in his last days. Ever interested in creating an ecumenical moment, her dad said yes, he did want a visit. The young priest was quite respectful and polite in his conversation. When he asked my father-in-law about how he felt about his future, the reply was loud and clear enough for everyone in the room.

"Confident," he said.

That right there was a sacred moment. It was a voice from within him, as well as a Voice from the cosmos. It was also a message to his loved ones around him that he was not declaring "Mayday." It was a grace-filled moment that said, "I don't know where this is going, but I know who is going with me." Later, when he was moved home under hospice care, he drifted into a coma. A blood disease made his arms too painful and swollen to move without splitting the skin. Even in an unconscious state, movement would cause his face to go into a grimace of pain. And yet when it was time for him to go, with his daughters, son, and wife around his bed, he calmly, painlessly, lifted both arms toward the ceiling as if to receive a package. Or a Presence. It was as if he were getting assistance in stepping off of a curb, onto a street.

Walter Wangerin said, "Only the start is scary. The rest is endlessly marvelous, eternally beautiful."[3]

In our attempt to find the sacred and holy during something as profound and permanent as death, we sometimes try to change the outcome. That's wonderful and necessary if there are still medical procedures to be done, still prayers of faith to be prayed, still heroic acts to commit. But when those efforts are exhausted, and we stop pretending that things are going to get better, sometimes all that is left is an acceptance of what is, and life in the present moment. The Present Moment. And that is where grace appears, often in the form of another person, as a sacrament that merely involves being present for someone. Arriving when everyone else is hiding—whether it is during a crisis of death or any other kind of crisis—seems small. But your presence brings in another Presence, which makes the time holy.

What is the purpose of Mother Teresa's Home for the Dying Destitutes in Calcutta? To provide comfort in the final days of those who have no one else to be with them as they leave this life. People don't get well at this location. They are cared for as the transition occurs, and prayed for by sisters wishing them traveling mercies.

I had to be careful when I visited with my dying friend Dana, that I wasn't just being with him out of my own neediness. I didn't want to be like the people Morrie Schwartz complained about to Mitch Albom in the book *Tuesdays With Morrie*, who said that when it became well known that he was leaving this earth because of Lou Gehrig's disease people visited because they wanted him to tell them how to pack. So, with continual pulse-taking of my own motives, I would check with Dana's wife Lou Ann to see if I could come over. I'd read to him, tell him amusing things from the campus, news from mutual friends, recall stories from our past, or, if he was sleeping, just sit near him and rest and pray and weep.

One day when I was reading to him, he began to choke. His swallowing muscles weren't working, and he couldn't get out the gunk collecting in his throat. I yelled for his adult daughter Nicole, who was in the kitchen, and she ran in, well versed in this procedure. She pulled the suction machine from under the bed and stuck the plastic straw in her dad's mouth to remove the danger. After a couple of seconds, he lifted an emaciated hand and put it on the straw.

"Dad, there's still more in there, so I have to leave it in," Nicole told him. She had to speak loudly, because the brain tumor had taken most of his hearing.

He left his hand there, and tried to move it.

"You want to do it yourself? Is that what you're telling me?"

He weakly shook his head. Then he tried to move the straw again. Toward me.

"You want Dean to do this?"

He nodded.

She moved the straw to me, standing at the other side of the bed, so that I could participate in this living/dying moment.

"You're honoring me, Dana," I said, tears flowing onto his sheets below me.

He nodded again and smiled.

Thich Nhat Hanh said, "When you sit by the bedside of a dying person and you are calm and totally present in body, mind and soul, you will be successful in helping that person pass away in freedom."[4]

I went home that day, knowing Dana's eventual outcome. I didn't like it. It was too painful. I wondered if loving people was worth this kind of pain.

Then I wrote down all the uniquely Dana moments I remembered from our years of friendship. I wrote of frequently being flattened by him on the faculty basketball court. He would dribble methodically at the top of the key, then lower his head and charge toward the basket. "The Dana train had left the station, and I was usually on the tracks," I wrote.

I wrote about going to West Africa with him and, in the middle of the night, needing to use the bathroom. We both were having intestinal difficulty on that trip. I noticed a glow coming from the bathroom, and carefully walked in. There was Dana, buck naked, sitting on the toilet playing backgammon on his laptop computer. He had been there for hours.

And I wrote about something that didn't have near the meaning when it occurred as it does now. As I mentioned before, Dana and I met for breakfast once a week with one other man about our age. Daryl was an expert sailor, and occasionally the three of us and our wives would spend a day sailing on the ocean. On one particular day we were out into the late afternoon on a beautiful thirty-five-foot vessel, when we were unexpectedly surrounded by fog. We had seen it coming, but had misjudged how quickly. This marine layer, coupled with the sun going down, made it almost impossible to see our way back. The radio said the airport was abruptly closed. Highways were at a standstill. We knew we couldn't sail through it, so we brought the sails down and started the engine. Daryl sent Dana to the bow to tell us if he saw anything directly ahead, and he sent me to the stern, to the steering wheel. Dana and I weren't afraid, I don't think, because we completely trusted Daryl, who had done this countless times all over the world. Our wives did not share our confidence. I believe I heard my wife singing prayer choruses with a touch more desperation than praise.

The soup in the air was so thick that I could barely see Dana at the front of our ship. But this is what I did see. He was leaning as far forward as gravity would allow, with his arms outstretched in front of him, as if he were going to feel whatever it was we were about to hit. This was before the movie *Titanic*, too, so he wasn't trying to be Leonardo DiCaprio. He was just out ahead of us, feeling his way through the fog, letting us know what was ahead. We made it back to the marina without an incident.

E. L. Doctorow said that writing a novel is like driving a car through the fog with your headlights on. You can see only a few feet at a time, but it's enough to get you home. That's what Dana did for us on the boat. And on the bed where he was dying. He was just a little ahead of us in the fog. He had already taught us how to live—now he was teaching us how to die.

How good it is to hear from you, Dean. I wish I could report that I'm on top of the world. In recent weeks, the world's been on top of me.

I like what you say about filling the moments as you listen to your life, about allowing God to fill the moments. Deep in my valley I find encouragement in your letter. Your talk about your family is a simple reminder to me that I have a family, that exciting things are happening in my own family. One month from today Joli is to be married. So that's reason enough to get me out of the valley, you would think. Still, I find myself in the valley. It's as if I'm in a terrible state of numbness. Fact is, I'm not feeling well these days. I have a lot of nausea, on certain days of the chemo cycle, extreme nausea. I'm really wiped out. So I just go through those days trying not to throw up. But in recent weeks even during the days that are not as bad, I haven't been in charge of my moments. I think I've been overcome by a sense of my illness, an awareness that the cancer is in the process of taking my life. In recent weeks, I've done a poor job of living, really living, a day at a time, a moment at a time. In recent weeks, I've spent a lot of time resting and napping, and too much of that resting napping time allowing negative moments to control me.

Well, it looks like this letter has turned to be a confession—the confession of a Christian who is not acting very much like a Christian. But I'll come out of it. I believe that. I still have faith; it just happens to be under severe attacks at this moment in time.

And at this moment in time it helps me to be able to level with you about my current state.

So, good, dear friend, pray for me. I need your prayers. I need to improve my behavior, my Christian behavior. Your prayers will help me do that.

We live under a shadow. Deep down, we know we're going to die, and we know that the people we love are going to die. And we know that grief is excruciating. Grief is the companion of love, for when the person we love dies, our grief is the measure of that love. There may be some guilt mixed in there, too, but it is primarily the flip side of love. Grief is also how we experience eventual healing from what feels like an amputation. Grief has a job to do. It partially cauterizes the wound, without an anesthetic. It slows the bleeding. If we don't grieve, if we live in denial, the internal bleeding that still occurs will cause damage later and elsewhere. Grief's initial job is to show us how attached we were to a specific person. It slowly points to grace and gratitude, though, which shows us how much of that person is still all around us in our memories, our routines, and in the unexpected, if we are paying attention.

I began to grieve the losses of Dana and Larry well before they actually died. One of the ways I was able to grieve was to be with them in person, or letter, or spirit, as much as I, and they, could take. The grief is a little less when we've had a chance to say what needs to be said to those we love. It's far worse when death happens without warning. In that case grief has an even greater job to do—it has to deal with shock *and* loss. That's a more difficult task. Still, grief has to be allowed to do its work.

Letting grief enter us is how we let it do its work. How long does grief take to do its work? It depends on so many variables. Sometimes we are grieving not only the loss of a friend, companion, spouse, or family member, but also our expectations of what we hoped for in the future with that person. We suffer not just the death of a loved one, but also the death of what we thought was ahead. Grief needs to work on that, also. But it, too, will eventually give way to grace when we let it.

When people tell their grieving friends, "Don't you think you've grieved enough here? Isn't it time to move on?" those presumably well-meaning folks aren't part of the anointing process. They aren't part of the traveling mercies choir. They are static noise on the radio frequency.

A friend of mine whose husband died after they had been married for more than thirty years told me, "I feel like I walked through the door that said 'Emergency Exit Only' and now I can't get back in. I want my old life back. It's like I'm being punished because I had such a good relationship with my husband." Telling her that it's time to move on is not the kind of presence she needs. The sacrament that recognizes the passing is not just for the dying. It is also for us who are still here, grieving the loss. It is a way for God to tell us that he is present. Grief takes time. Mourning takes time.

When it comes to death, "What we must never do is get over it as soon as possible or make as little of it as we can," said Eugene Peterson. "'Get over it' and 'make little of it' are unbiblical and inhuman. Denial and distraction are the standard over-the-counter prescriptions of our culture for dealing with loss; in combination, they've virtually destroyed the spiritual health of our culture."[5]

My wife went back to Ohio to be with her dad when it became clear that he was not going to recover. She wanted to be with him throughout his last days, which ended up being five weeks. She slept in the living room near him in case he needed something in the night. She massaged his feet, rubbed what hurt, kept him clean—anointed the departure. When she came home, his absence in her life manifested itself in various ways. Tears, obviously. But other ways, too. Sometimes anger.

One night she was looking for the power cord that went from our video camera to the television so she could watch some tapes she had made. The camera was where it was supposed to be—in the case on the shelf in our bedroom—but the cord was not.

"Who was the last person to use the camera?" she asked.

"Blake," I said.

She went into his room where he was studying.

"Where is the cord for this camera?"

"How should I know?"

"You were the last one to use it."

"I never used the cord."

"It is always with the camera."

Everyone has heard conversations start out this way: Rational, informational at first, but then they gather some energy. What starts out as a breeze heats up and feeds on itself until it takes on the whirling fury of a tornado. The conversations become defensive, accusing, and then escalate into a major conflict, where the original point becomes collateral damage.

The cord was nowhere in the house. We searched every room. My wife accused my son of a lifetime of irresponsibility and wastefulness. Fortunately, he did not respond in generalizations or exaggerations. We did not find the cord that night, and my wife was a basket case. Over a cord! Her evening ended in tears of frustration, sadness, and anger.

When I went into my son's room later to tell him good night, he was in bed, crying. "This wasn't about the camera tonight, was it?" he said. At first I didn't understand. He continued. "This is about Grandpa, isn't it?"

Ah, the wisdom of youth. He got it well before I did. Here I thought this was an overreaction to a piece of equipment missing from an overpriced toy. But in reality, grief was doing its work, and Blake recognized it in his mom. That's why he wasn't defensive or disrespectful in his responses to her. He saw what was really going on, even though it was hurting his feelings, while I was still thinking it was about the cord. It *was* about a cord, but a different cord—one that attached a daughter to a father she adored who no longer existed in the form she had known for forty-seven years. Blake saw it as grief, and received it, providing grace to his mother.

Don't Forget

Part of grief's job is to remember. The fear component of grief is that we think others might forget our loved one who died, or that we will forget things about that person—significant dates, for instance. We want to remember, and we want the world to remember. So part of the job of those close to someone grieving is to help them remember. One day when Marcia and I were talking with Lou Ann, at least a year after Dana died, we said we didn't know if we should still bring up Dana in conversation, in case she wasn't thinking about him at the moment and the thought would make her sad. "I'm never *not* thinking about him," she said. "Talk about him as often as you can."

I am convinced that acknowledging the presence of death—of ours and of those around us—is one of the healthiest ways we can live. It is a way to let the present moment be full of life. In Walker Percy's novel, *The Moviegoer*, a character named Kate has survived a car accident in which her fiancé, Lyell, was killed. Years later she tells her cousin, the narrator, "Have you noticed that only in time of illness or disaster or death are people real? I remember at the time of the wreck—people were so kind and helpful and *solid*. Everyone pretended that our lives until that moment had been every bit as real as the moment itself and that the future must be real too, when the truth was that our reality had been purchased only by Lyell's death. In another hour or so we had all faded out again and gone our dim ways."[6]

The high school I attended had a practice that, when I attended there, I thought was grotesque and perverse. As I mentioned before, it was a private, all-male, college prep, Dead Poets Society-type school, and we had chapel services that no one took seriously in a beautiful old wooden cathedral. Toward the end of each school year, in one of the final chapel services, the headmaster would read a list of names of our graduates who had died since the previous May. Most of them were alums from classes more than 60 years before us—names of old dead men. There were dozens of names each year, each followed by the year he graduated. There were some hilarious names—hilarious to us in our immature, clueless state. After reading the list, the headmaster would intone, "You are not forgotten." I never gave the practice more than a moment's thought beyond those chapel services.

I went back to that school for a reunion, decades later. They conducted a chapel service just for us returning alums. At the end of the service the headmaster read the names of those departed from the previous year, which this time included some of my classmates, and concluded with, "You are not forgotten." Suddenly it was one of the most beautiful practices I had ever witnessed. It was part of the sacrament to declare that these people's lives counted, and will not be forgotten. It focused us, like Kate in *The Moviegoer*, at least for the moment.

A few years ago I trekked through Tibet with a couple of friends. One night we ended up in a small village seventeen thousand feet into the mountains, and asked some of the locals where we could sleep. They pointed to the large Buddhist Temple that had a monastery attached. We went to the monastery and the caretaker showed us a room upstairs. Early the next morning we heard a great deal of commotion outside the window. We looked out and saw some kind of ceremony taking place around a body that had been placed in the middle of the temple square. Lots of prayer flags and incense. Then a man picked up the body, put it over his shoulder and headed toward a path that led away from the village. My friends and I ran out of our room and followed the procession. Several people were on the path, and didn't seem concerned that we had joined them. After about a half-hour of walking, all uphill in very thin air, we noticed that the sky ahead was dotted with circling vultures. As we got closer to the top of this particular hill, we saw that the hills around us were covered—literally—by vultures. One even came in for a landing just over my head, and its wing swept across my face.

The procession of Tibetans ended at another small temple, where the body was laid out. After more ceremony, a man with a machete and—I kid you not—a black beanie with a Nike swoosh symbol on it, emerged from the temple and proceeded to filet the body and chop the parts into small pieces. Even the intestines came out. The vultures, now in the several hundreds, all sat in a circle around this display, shouting and clamoring as if they were ringside at a boxing match. When the body was sufficiently de-boned, the vultures attacked. They covered the area where the flesh had been tossed, covered the skeleton, fought and clawed and scratched each other until there was not an eyelash or fingernail left. Then the birds flew away.

The man with the machete now had a giant stone mallet, and he then mashed the bones of the skeleton. I'll spare you the description of the skull and brains. The vultures returned for another feast, and within hours of the ceremony that we witnessed out our window earlier that morning, there was not a trace of the body. This, we were told, is called a Sky Burial. No one seemed bothered by our presence. Except when I took out my camera. The man with the machete made it clear that I would be the next one fed to the vultures if I didn't put my camera away.

For the family of the one who had just been sent airborne, this was a ritual that spoke of their tradition and their view of one life ending, yet sustaining creation. It was gruesome to watch, but I thought it was beautiful in its meaning.

Remembering is one of the intentional things we can do to make moments holy. Sometimes helping others remember can be part of making the memory holy. Humanitarian Gary Morsch was serving with his Army Reserve unit in Kosovo a few months after Merita Shabiu, an eleven-year-old Albanian girl, was raped, murdered, and dumped in a snowbank by an American soldier. At the request of the U.S. general in charge of American forces in Kosovo, Gary visited

Merita's family to see how they were doing. When he asked about Merita, they broke down and cried, remembering their little girl. Gary asked if he could visit her grave to pay his respects. They took him to an area outside their village, where a few graves had been dug, none marked. The father pointed out Merita's, with the ground settling around it.

Gary asked why there was no marker at the grave indicating that Merita was buried there, and the answer was that there was no money for such an extravagance. Back at the Shabiu's small, ragged house, Gary pulled his laptop computer out of his pack and had the family members help design a proper gravestone. They brought out a picture of Merita—big smile, thin blonde hair. Gary scanned the photo into the computer and placed Merita's image in the middle of the stone he had drawn on the screen. The Shabius were flabbergasted. Did they want a message on the stone? Gary asked. They requested this: "She taught us to love one another."

Then they had a question for Gary. How are we going to pay for this beautiful tombstone? Gary had an idea.

He brought his computer back to the base and showed the image to other soldiers. Those who witnessed the visit with the Shabius talked about it among their peers. Without formal organization, a collection effort began. Within days the Army base had raised enough to pay for the gravestone's design and construction. Then a convoy of trucks, Humvees, and jeeps ascended the narrow mountain trail that led to the Shabius' village, and Merita was given a proper burial. There was money left over from the gravestone, so the soldiers brought the family some cows, too.

I visited the Shabius and Merita's gravesite about a year later. It is a beautiful setting, like a sunflower rising out of a field.

"Whenever I think of Gary, I know that Merita is still with me," her father told me.

You wrote me a letter about the details of your life. So I will respond with a few details about mine. One big detail right off. The wedding. I have good days and bad days and very bad days because of the chemo cycle. That cycle controls my days and gives me a hint as to what is coming: good day, bad day, very bad day, what the details of my life will be like. Truth is, I can't be assured of good days, can't plan my life assured that certain days coming up will be good days. So many days prior to the wedding I prayed, "Please let Saturday, Joli's Saturday, the Fingers' Saturday, be a good day." I asked God to pay attention to one of the details of my life. As it turned out I had a very good day for a beautiful wedding. I made it down the aisle feeling very, very good. Luck? God? To what extent did God pay attention to this detail in my life? Did God answer my prayer? I'd like to believe that he did. Maybe I should say that he did answer my prayer, he did pay attention to a detail in my life. God gave me a wonderful day when I really wanted it.

I mentioned earlier the chemo cycle. Well, it is the big detail in my life. It's a one-month cycle. Three days of taking the drug, then three to four days completely wiped out, followed by ten to twelve days of extreme fatigue, followed by a mixture of good days and bad days. The bad days are nausea days. Overall, the chemo is hard to deal with. I understand now what the oncologist meant before I started the treatment when he said, "Some choose not to take the chemo."

Well, the last time I wrote you I was overcome by numbness, or I was frozen in time. I was not paying very much attention to the details of my life. I was not in control. The tumor, the chemo, one or the other or both, had complete control. Well, things are much better now. I have a little more control, in fact, much more control. And how has this improvement taken place? I'm not at all sure I can explain it. An act of the will? Divine intervention? God answering my prayer, even the feeble effort at prayer at a time when I was not acting very Christian-like? More and more, I think I'm learning to relax, learning to accept my condition, learning to live with what I've got. Notice I say "learning to." I don't expect to master the task.

I'm no longer numb, no longer frozen. I'm reading again. It makes me less self-centered. It helps me understand myself. I've just finished Helmut Thielicke's little book, The Silence of God. *In numerous ways he says that God is most present in our lives when He is silent. As I read Thielicke, and others as well, I try to fix my mind on passages that will help me with the details of my life. I'm just now getting into Solzhenitsyn's* Cancer Ward. *Appropriate reading for me, don't you think?*

Experiencing the sacrament of the present moment in regard to passing from this life to the next can also be expanded to other transitions. I grieved a little when my kids went to kindergarten. My wife and I would no longer be the primary voices in their development. Could we trust the schools? Could we trust the future with our kids, without Marcia and me hovering over them? What we knew and celebrated in the present was about to change forever. Did that mean we had to declare Mayday? Or could we see the passing as a natural progression from one manifestation to the next? If they didn't go to school, that would be weird. Maybe against the law. What was happening was what *should* be happening. It was part of the cycle. But it didn't feel very good. Let me rephrase that. *Holding on to the past* didn't feel very good.

When they learned how to read, they no longer depended on their parents or teachers to tell them stories. I could take them into a library or bookstore, and they could look through books on their own, and decide what they thought looked interesting. I still had some say in this, but it essentially meant I had less and less control over them. *The Chronicles of Narnia* was replaced by *Goosebumps* and *Mary Kate and Ashley* books. The kids could read them for themselves. Mayday? I could have resisted this new stage and declared that my kids would only be able to take away my reading to them *The Lion the Witch and the Wardrobe* from my cold, dead fingers, or I could see that this was another passing—that God was in it and blessing it. It's how the rhythm gets tapped out. When they learned how to ride bicycles, I jogged for miles with them around the school parking lot, holding onto the bike seat, shouting encouragement, secretly letting go for more and more seconds at a time. So why did I cry when they *told* me to let go and they rode off on their own, and I was left squinting as they rode into the sun? It's the way it's supposed to happen. They needed me a little less. They passed from one level to the next. Little deaths. "Death is not a disaster, just a door, I suppose," said Tony Hendra.[7]

Don't even ask about how I reacted to their learning how to drive. Or started dating. Or when they went to college.

Eugene Peterson said, "It seems odd, even contradictory, that in order to live totally we must face death totally. But it's true."[8]

Eventually it dawned on me that these experiences of natural transformation from one state to the next could be sacred. We can't go back. It's not Mayday. It's traveling mercies. But we can only declare that if we're paying attention, and not trying to hold on to the bicycle seats. Little deaths occur throughout our lives. So do little births. Every moment of our lives is seen in Stanley Kubrick's *2001: A Space Odyssey*, where we are at the bedside of a dying old person, and we are also being born. Brian McLaren said, "The reality of death gives us an important gift every day: it reminds us that we can't keep putting off the work of becoming."[9] Little births, little deaths, every day. Every moment. It's how the disorder gets ordered.

Every hello is better because it involves a good-bye, said Robert Benson. "I am coming to believe that the thing God said just before 'Let there be light' was 'Good-bye dark' . . . 'Good-bye Egypt' turned out to be another way for the Israelites to say 'Hello Canaan.' 'Good-bye, Jesus of Nazareth,' whispers Mary through her tears at the foot of the cross on Friday afternoon. 'Hello Lord of the Universe,' she murmurs to the one she mistakes for the gardener, on Sunday morning."[10]

One of the more painful stages of living, or becoming, for kids is when they are confronted with an unfriendly, even hostile world, bursting the carefully crafted illusion we have created for them. We do our best to surround our kids with love and safety and encouragement, giving them perhaps a false sense of what the world is really like. When my daughter came home from elementary school and told us that their recess was cut short because a man assumed a combat position and aimed a gun at them in the schoolyard, I could only put my head in my hands and shudder. I lamented not just the prospect of what could have happened (alert teachers called the police, herded the kids inside, barricaded doors, and pulled blinds on windows; the man was in custody within eleven minutes), but I wept for the reality that my daughter now knew. She had passed from one stage to the next. Good-bye innocence. Hello violent world. She didn't seem traumatized by it, any more than I was traumatized by drills at school where we got under our desks to prepare for attacks by the Russians. Instead, she was excited to tell me because she thought I might want to cover the story for a newspaper. She was bringing home a story idea, looking out for me, and the thought of being a source pleased her. She didn't know it, but that afternoon she was at a different place from where she was when I walked her to school that morning. It was a passing worth noting, filled with fear and dread on my part, not unlike being with someone when he or she is dying. It's a New Reality that must be given to God.

Every elementary school kid sees this in the form of mean kids, insults, perhaps uncaring teachers. But those moments still need our presence and attention to keep the kids from declaring Mayday.

My son experienced the unfriendly world in a big way. He was about eight when our family watched the movie *Apollo 13*. Suddenly he wanted to be an astronaut. His career path was set. Or at least he wanted to be a movie actor, where he could get paid to pretend he was an astronaut. So later that week, when I saw that a real-life astronaut was going to be at a local bookstore to sign his new science fiction novel, I told Blake about it and we excitedly made plans to meet him. We got to the bookstore early, anticipating a line, and, sure enough, there were already about one hundred people ahead of us. It didn't matter, though. We were going to meet a member of the first crew that walked on the moon! This was more than celebrity worship, this was *hero* worship, and we were happy to genuflect.

I shelled out the twenty-five bucks for a book I knew I wouldn't read, and let Blake hold it for the astronaut to sign. Blake had also brought his autograph book that had signatures from some of his teachers and friends and a couple of minor league baseball players. It took about forty-five minutes for us to finally get to the star of the show. We handed him the book, made a little small talk, and asked him to write "To Blake," which our hero ignored. He signed his name in about a second and slid the book away. Blake extended his vinyl treasure that said "Autographs" in fancy cursive writing, holding it like one of the Magi offering myrrh, and said, "Would you please sign my autograph book?"

He shoved the book into Blake's chest and growled, "Can't you see the line behind you? Next!" Then he took the next person's book and signed it, as he had done mine. He had moved on.

I wanted to leap across the table and grab him by the collar and send that horse's astronaut back into orbit for a *real* moonwalk.

But I didn't. We had just crossed a threshold. Blake discovered that famous people could be jerks. He was crushed. I was furious. But I knew there was no crossing back. The toothpaste was out of the tube, and there was no putting it back. We could only try to redeem the moment. I could only look for an alternative to declaring Mayday. There was a video arcade nearby. We played air hockey, pinball, and some other noisy games. We got some ice cream. I tried to gauge how this was all playing out in Blake's head. He was snapping back. But he was different now, and I knew it. The secret was out: not everyone in this world is glad to see you. Nor do they all want you to be happy. It was a little death. I just had to recognize it, stand at the cross, and give it to God. Brian McLaren gets it right when he says, "We live every moment at the nexus of peril and possibility."[11]

When grace comes in these moments, it meets us where we are, as Anne Lamott says, but then leaves us in a better place. That's what makes them sacred, because we recognize that something bigger than us is at work. Being alert to the present moment, and to these stages in our lives and in the lives of those around us, helps us to see that we are continuously changing, being left in a better place. It is in that mindfulness that we see the work of God.

In a chapel service at the university where I teach, Brennan Manning spoke to us about the God who comes to us in all moments of our lives—even dying moments. In the chapel audience that day were the trustees of the university. I sat in the row behind them. Manning told of visiting a dying man who wanted to know some things about God. He had gotten books from a pastor, but they talked about concepts that were too lofty and confusing. He wondered if God even existed.

"Just begin by talking to God in your own language," Manning told him. "Imagine him sitting in this chair next to your bed, and you telling him all about your confusion and fear and doubt."

The man died a few days later, and his daughter said that he appeared to have died peacefully.

"But there was something strange about it," she told Manning. "When I walked into his room to check on him, he had already died, but he had laid his head on the chair next to the bed."

When Manning closed that chapel service one of our university's trustees looked around, and his wide, startled eyes finally locked on mine. "I will never be the same," he declared. I could only agree, and be happy that we were alert enough to be aware of the change.

Well, Dean, you probably think I have forgotten this cross-town correspondence. What happened is that this cross-town talk was interrupted by a cross-country trip to visit our extended family. I had lunch with about twenty-five aunts and cousins and uncles. They asked very little about my world, so I entered their world for a few minutes, hearing about their accomplishments, about their children, about their aches and pains. But it was good to be with them, good to be reminded of where I came from.

As I sat with them I got the chance to practice what I'm trying to practice every day: celebrate the moment, concentrate on the present moment. How easy it is to jump into the future. That seems especially true of me now. How much future do I have? What is the next test going to show? What is the next doctor's statement going to be? How foolish to ask questions about a time that I am not even assured of. How foolish to live in the future and pay little attention to the present moment. So I'm working hard at the task of trying to make the task not a task at all, but a moment to be enjoyed.

I practiced celebrating the moment today with Tam at lunch, and with a few of you this afternoon. I really did look at Tam. I really did see her. I really did listen to her. And this afternoon for an hour or so, I shared quite a few moments with a few of my cohorts—Mike, Kay, Charlene, Maxine, Kathy, Art, Phil, Sharon—not just names, not just faces, but people I like being with. So for a short period of time, not hindered by thoughts of the future, I celebrated the present. No earthshaking talk, just pleasant conversation.

The past. The present. The future. The flow of time. I have no control of time. But I can control my response to time. So, I'm working at it. Live in the present. Make the most of it. That is what I am trying to do.

And that is what's on my mind at this particular writing, this out-of-my-heart-and-mind, cross-town talk that we have going on. All that I have is the present moment. I will rejoice and be glad in it.

This was the last letter I got from Larry. He got much weaker in the next few weeks, and died at home. His Mayday in a previous letter had turned into traveling mercies.

What will it be like for us when it is our time to leave this world? Will it be like stepping off of a trolley as it slows down for us? Being helped off of the curb? Will it be just another stage, as we have been experiencing different stages all along? Will it be like labor pains, leaving the womb of this world into another kind of fullness? Will we be near enough to one another to help our Maydays become traveling mercies?

Let's listen to Buechner, as my friend Larry used to say, once again:

> The great craft lumbers its way to the take-off position, the jets shrill. Picking up speed, you count the seconds till you feel lift-off . . . Once airborne, you can hardly see the wings at all through the grey turbulence scudding by. The steep climb is rough as a Ford pick-up. Gradually it starts to even out. The clouds thin a little . . . The pilot levels off slightly. Nobody is talking. The calm and quiet of it are almost palpable. Suddenly, in a rush of light, you break out of the weather. Beneath you the clouds are a furrowed pasture. Above, no sky in creation was ever bluer.
>
> Possibly the last take-off of all is something like that. When the time finally comes, you're scared stiff to be sure, but maybe by then you're just as glad to leave the whole show behind and get going. In a matter of moments, everything that seemed to matter stops mattering. The slow climb is all there is. The stillness. The clouds. Then the miracle of flight as from fathom upon fathom down you surface suddenly into open sky. The dazzling sun.[12]

I look into the sky, and I know that there is turbulence ahead. I know it is true for you, and I know it is true for me. If we're attentive, we'll be able to run alongside of the craft for each other—maybe even stretch out beyond the bow of the ship—hold onto the seats for a while, shout encouragement, gradually let go, be each other's guides for a while, and tell each other that we're headed in the right direction.

8

Batting a Balloon

The New Sacrament of Service

If you would do good, you must do it in Minute Particulars.

William Blake[1]

The sacrament of service is not part of traditional church history—it isn't officially one of the big seven. But it should be. I hereby declare it so. Call it Vatican III. Even Catholic writers agree with me that this *could* be so—the additional sacrament, I mean, not the additional Vatican Council. "Once sacraments are understood for what they are—human creations which function as doors to the sacred—there is no intrinsic reason why new sacramental forms could not be invented to reach the same sacred realities that the old forms once revealed," wrote Joseph Martos.[2] The doors themselves aren't the point—they are merely the means to what lies beyond them.

My friend Bob Goff specializes in construction defect law in two different states. He's used to making deals with tough clients. But he made a deal with a different kind of group—his kids—and the deal ultimately shifted his focus from construction flaws to human ones.

He sat at his kitchen table with his wife and three kids a few days after the September 11, 2001, attacks in New York and Washington, D.C. They all knew that something had gone terribly wrong in the world, and in the middle of the conversation Bob tossed out an idea. He asked his kids, if they could have five minutes with a world leader, what would they ask?

Adam, age nine, said he would ask if the leader would like to come hang out at the Goff home for a while.

Richard, age eleven, said he would ask the leader what his or her source of hope was.

Lindsey, age thirteen, said she would ask that if the world leader could not come to the Goff home, could the Goff kids go to the leader's home and videotape the visit.

That got the Goff kids thinking. What if they wrote letters to world leaders and asked for a meeting with them to ask these questions? Bob Goff listened to the discussion, and put an offer on the table. "If you get a 'yes' from a leader," he told his kids, "I'll take you there."

The kids researched on the Web and wrote more than one thousand letters to presidents, vice presidents, prime ministers, and ambassadors. They received twenty-nine invitations for meetings—some in the different countries' government centers, and some in embassies the countries have in Washington, D.C.

One response, from the office of the prime minister of Malaysia, was curt, but accepting.

"I'll meet you in Kuala Lumpur in two weeks," the message said.

Before long, the U.S. State Department was calling, asking Goff if he knew that his kids were planning a trip to Bulgaria, and that they had been corresponding with government leaders around the world. "I told them, 'yeah, I'm taking them!'" Goff said, laughing.

In addition to meeting with leaders from Malaysia and Bulgaria, Team Goff, as Bob likes to call them, met with officials from Israel, Jordan, Egypt, Morocco, New Zealand, Bolivia, Norway, Switzerland, Liechtenstein, and others.

At the Hungarian embassy in Washington, D.C., the ambassador treated the kids to his own secret avocation. He told them he was in a rock band with other diplomats called the Coalition of the Willing.

Then he produced his favorite, fire engine red Fender Stratocaster guitar and showed his solo skills.

The meetings ended with the Goff kids presenting a gift to each leader. It was a small box, exquisitely wrapped. Each leader carefully opened the box. Inside was a key.

"This is a key to the front door of our home in San Diego," Lindsey would tell them. "All of our friends have a key to our house, and now you're our friend. Our house is open to you, just as you opened your house to us."

But while these meetings produced goodwill, they also revealed some deeper, more disturbing issues that meant the Goffs could not simply return to their San Diego lives as they had enjoyed them. After the Malaysia meeting with the prime minister, the Goffs traveled to India. On a drive through some cities and villages, the Goffs saw evidence of the rampant bonded labor market, where children are sold to slave traders so that families can pay off financial burdens such as medical bills and dowry debts. The children are put to work in the equivalent of a slavery camp, but the trader demands such high fees, with interest, and pays sometimes twenty-five cents per day. There is little hope for the children to pay off the debt and be released.

In Mumbai the Goffs saw the red-light district, where many of the prostitutes on the streets were young girls.

Statutes in India prohibit both bonded slavery and child prostitution, but they are mostly unenforced, Goff was told. Suddenly, his attention shifted from the most powerful people in the world to the least powerful.

"That trip ruined a perfectly good legal career," he said. "On that sixty-hour trip home I concluded that, while I loved the practice of law, I could not continue it in a business-as-usual fashion."

The experience gave him a sense of a higher calling, he said.

"I sensed that there was a better use of my skills than simply being a hired gun litigating civil matters," he said. "It was time for a change of trajectory, not because I didn't love practicing law, but because of the gravitational pull exerted by recognizing that I had something to contribute to ease the pain of others."

For two years he traveled back and forth to India in an effort to end illegal slavery, drawing inspiration from William Wilberforce, the

British Parliament member who fought for the abolition of slavery in the late-eighteenth century.

Goff and some local human rights workers met secretly with bonded slaves, documented their stories, then presented their findings and the statutes to local officials. Within days, police began raiding the slavery camps to arrest the operators and free the workers.

"We felt that the fight needed to be taken to the bad guys," he said.

But Goff knew that just setting workers free wasn't the answer. They still needed jobs. He and the others started a company called Snekethar, which means "friend" in Tamil, where the former slaves could make products out of bamboo.

Back in the U.S., the effort grew into a nonprofit group called Restore International, an organization created to get a country's own laws enforced and to take action on behalf of the poorest of the poor who have no voice in the system and are routinely taken advantage of.

At times the Restore staff has had to badger the local police into conducting raids on the slavery camps and prostitution rings. They have also been threatened by local brothel owners. Sometimes they receive more than threats. One investigator was recognized by a brothel owner who had been busted by the police. The brothel owner gathered a group and incited them to attack the Restore workers with rocks and fists. Soon the street was filled with angry men who bloodied Goff and the others, destroying their car.

"Here I was, a middle-aged American lawyer in one of the worst neighborhoods in South Asia, bleeding, surrounded by an angry mob, and yet I had a peace knowing that I was where I should be, doing what I should be doing—helping locate and rescue girls who were forced into prostitution and keeping them out of the sex racket for good," he said.

Doing Justice

More recently, Goff and Restore turned their attention to finding ways to help children in Uganda who had been caught up in the country's twenty-year civil war, where thousands were killed and more than 20,000 children abducted and made to be child soldiers. The war displaced 1.4 million people within its borders, which created "enormous justice issues," Goff said. So many Ugandan adults fled the country or were killed that the average age in Uganda is now just fifteen years old. The nation's future leadership is in their hands. So Restore started two schools in northern Uganda.

The organization also worked with local agencies and law enforcement to free girls from working in brothels. In one year more than thirty girls were rescued and placed into schools outside of the capital where they could recover and heal.

Restore also installed wells in internally displaced persons camps. The wells provide thirty-eight thousand people with fresh and clean water every day.

Justice issues remain at the core of Restore's objectives in Uganda. One of the differences from India, though, is that Uganda did not have laws against human trafficking. So Restore began working with the Judiciary and members of Uganda's Parliament to pass a law prohibiting the trafficking of persons. It also worked for Ugandan ratification of various United Nations conventions on human rights.

Because of the instability caused by the civil war in northern Uganda and schedule conflicts, judges had been unwilling to travel to the north. The situation left many justice issues unaddressed. Restore assisted Ugandan judges by having U.S. lawyers and law students from Pepperdine University and Seattle University write case briefs. Restore's attorneys and staff then organized what were called the Gulu High Court Sessions where Restore's people worked with the Ugandan judiciary to bring more than 150 human rights cases in northern Uganda to trial. The pilot project was so successful that it was implemented in five districts in the north.

Restore's next strategy was to gather the majority of the Ugandan Judiciary to discuss the rights of the country's children, the plight of those caught up in child prostitution and other forms of human trafficking. Taking a cue from his kids, Goff asked former U.S. Attorney General John Ashcroft and the former Chief Justice of the Missouri Supreme Court if they would accompany Restore's team and participate in a judicial conference. They also said yes, and even the president of Uganda attended to show support for the efforts to end human trafficking and protect the rights of the country's children.

"Wilberforce showed that individuals can make a difference if we care enough and are willing to act," Goff said. "The issues we work on are serious, grim, and revolting. But it doesn't really seem like work because it feels so good to be spending my days bringing justice to children around the world who are about the ages of my own kids. I'm naïve enough to believe that creativity, love, making friends, and even having fun can be a part of this work."

What Goff and Restore have achieved in Uganda and India come out of two understandings that Goff adheres to. The first is that God calls us to, and is experienced when we serve others. The second is that people have a right to justice. He became part of a much larger story when he decided to serve others. It was a burst of revelation.

One could argue that we experience God by serving others as understood through the sacrament of vocation, but I think it ought to be more specific. Jesus's example of washing his disciples' feet, of taking the position of performing a humble act for the benefit of another is a way to participate in the life of Christ. We experience Christ when we act like him.

Philip Yancey tells of a visitor to Vellore, India, where Dr. Paul Brand ran a leprosy hospital. The visitor was a French monk named Pierre, who showed up with all of his belongings in a single bag. Pierre had been raised in the upper class of France, was a member of the French Parliament, but became disillusioned at how long it took for any kind of change to take place. This was in the aftermath of World War II, when the streets of Paris were filled with homeless beggars, and all the politicians could do was debate about the problem. One winter, many of the beggars froze to death. At that point, Pierre could take it no longer, so he resigned his post and became a monk in the Catholic Church to try to do something about their predicament. He still couldn't get government to help, so he got the idea of organizing the beggars themselves. He divided them into teams to go through the city and collect discarded bottles and rags. He showed them how to build a warehouse out of discarded bricks to store the bottles and then recycle them.

He also gave each beggar the responsibility to find someone poorer than himself to serve. The effort became an organization called Emmaus, and it expanded into other countries. Within a few years the organization reached a crisis point. There were no more beggars to serve.

"I must find somebody for my beggars to help," Pierre told Brand. "If I don't find people worse off than my beggars, this movement could turn inward. They'll become a powerful, rich organization, and the spiritual impact will be lost. They'll have no one to serve."

Pierre mobilized his former beggars to build a ward for the leprosy patients in a Vellore hospital, to house the Untouchable caste—people in far worse conditions than the group from Emmaus. "It is you who have saved us," he told the leprosy patients. "We must serve or we die."[3]

Sounds a lot like what Babette said at her feast.

Or what Jesus said, when he said he did not come to be served, but to serve.

The Address of God

When my daughter was sixteen, I took her with me to the slums of Guatemala City, where we helped install a water filtration system in a church. The Sunday school class I teach raised the money for the system, so a few of us went there for the final work and inauguration. We knew that exposure to contaminated water is the chief cause of death among children around the world; this system was going to provide clean, inexpensive water to a community of about eighteen thousand people. My wife and I tried to raise our kids with the awareness that, as Americans, they lived in virtual Disneyland compared to how most of the rest of the world lives. Our country has created a culture that seems to believe we are entitled to what the rest of the world would consider an extravagance. Adequate health care, braces on our teeth, access to a car, a house with our own bedrooms, indoor plumbing, reasonable police, fire, and justice systems, and jobs, for instance. My kids called us Amish parents for not having cable television and high-speed Internet.

In addition, my daughter had some health issues where she did not digest her food properly, and that caused her a great deal of pain when she ate. She's paranoid about food being left out on a counter for five minutes anyway. She is convinced that salmonella and *E. coli* are her constant companions (like shame and remorse are to most of my friends), waiting to burst upon her at the most inopportune moment. Her Girl Scout troop spent a weekend at an Embassy Suites and had the gall to call it a *camping* trip. Still, she agreed to go with me to Guatemala.

We left the day after she passed the test for her driver's license.

While we were in Guatemala City, we visited the dump where anywhere from 4,000 to 10,000 people live. We watched them swarm over the garbage trucks that rumbled through, dumping their contents over the people scrambling for food or anything of value. Astonished, we witnessed the bulldozers pushing tons of refuse over the edge of a steep canyon, on top of the people below.

We ate in the homes of people who were going to be the recipients of the clean water we were helping provide. These were people who raised their own chickens and vegetables and made their own tortillas. Lunch was prepared in a kitchen about the size of the bathroom in my house. We ate outside on plastic chairs at a folding table set up in the dirt. The hanging laundry snapped overhead in the breeze like prayer flags. I looked at Vanessa as our hostess ladled soup into a bowl, and I raised my eyebrows as she ate ravenously. She saw me looking at her as she put a large piece of chicken in her mouth.

"I should be nervous," she said between bites. "But for some reason I'm not."

Actually, I knew the reason. The sacrament of serving others puts our own issues into proper perspective so that they don't dominate us. We see others as people to serve—we see them as Jesus sees them. We experience something of the nature of God as a result. What is service? Karl Barth says it is when we act not in self-interest, but "with a view to the purpose of another person and according to the need, disposition, and direction of others." God speaks in this action, Barth says.[4] It is recognizing God in others. When we don't, we tend to see each other as commodities, someone we can use, dominate, abuse, consume, oppress.

The word *latreia* means service that we do to help others. It is also where we get the word *liturgy*, which is the service we give God through worship. "The service we offer to God (in worship) is extended into specific acts that serve others," said Eugene Peterson. "We learn a relationship—an attitude toward life, a stance—of servitude before God, and then we are available to be of use to others in acts of service."[5]

Our purpose in life, Peterson said, is to serve one another. "We mediate to one another the mysteries of God," he said. "We represent to one another the address of God. We are priests who speak God's Word and share Christ's sacrifice."[6]

George Hill told National Public Radio that, after he left the Marine Corps, he was homeless for twelve years, addicted to drugs and alcohol. "I can't even begin to tell you the misery of rain," he said. "I don't even care how slight the rainfall is, it was misery beyond belief." One day, as Hill sat on a bag with his belongings on Skid Row, another homeless man approached him. This man was filthy. He had rags on his feet for shoes, and his hair was matted into two enormous dreadlocks. The man approached Hill, fished around in his pocket and pulled out a dollar. He gave it to Hill and said, "Here, man. I feel sorry for you." Then he shuffled away.

That act, that moment, changed Hill. He said, "Oh, no, no. I'm going to get some help." He took the dollar and paid for bus fare to a hospital psychiatric unit. He has been off the streets for ten years, has a job with the Veterans Affairs department, and has begun working on a college degree. "Now, every time it rains and I have keys in my pocket, I have a joy of life that you cannot believe," he said.[7] An act of service led to a transformation. Sounds like something sacred, doesn't it?

Martin Luther King Jr. said, "Human progress never rolls in on wheels of inevitability; it comes through the tireless efforts of men willing to be coworkers with God."[8] Coworkers. Sharing his nature. Entering into the Mystery of God's grace as we serve others.

There is a Hasidic parable that makes the point. A rabbi asked God about Heaven and Hell. God said, "I will show you Hell," and he took the rabbi to a round table filled with ravenously hungry people. It was a strange sight because in the middle of the table was an enormous pot of stew. The smell of the stew filled the room, even making the rabbi's mouth water. The people around the table had

spoons to get at the stew, but the spoons had very long handles—
so long that, even though the people could reach into the pot, the
spoons were longer than the people's arms. The people could not get
the food into their mouths. They were starving. The rabbi couldn't
believe how badly the people were suffering. Then God said, "Now
I will show you Heaven."

They went into another room that was identical to the first. Same
big, round table, same pot of stew, same spoons with handles longer
than the people's arms. But these people were happy and well fed.
God, seeing the rabbi's confusion, said, "It's simple, but it requires a
specific skill. They have learned how to feed each other."[9]

The difference between heaven and hell was the difference between
serving others and serving ourselves. Compassion instead of competition. The sacrament of serving others means there is enough for
everyone.

"So how can you be of service?" asks Henri Nouwen. "What is
your ministry to others? Where are you to spend your time? Go to the
place where people are in pain, but don't go alone. Go with others
who have learned how to be grateful for the good and bad of life.
Go with those who can sit with others in need, even if problems and
pain persist. Let your heart be broken, and rely on Jesus's example of
self-emptying so that you can be filled by God's strength. Then you
will find the Messiah in your midst."[10]

Anne Lamott asked the same question of how we can serve, and,
as you can imagine, puts her own personality into the answer:

> First, find a path, and a little light to see by. Then push up your
> sleeves and start helping. Every single spiritual tradition says that
> you must take care of the poor, or you are so doomed that not even
> Jesus or the Buddha can help you. You don't have to go overseas.
> There are people in this country who are poor in spirit, worried,
> depressed, dancing as fast as they can; their kids are sick, or their
> retirement savings are gone. There is great loneliness among us,
> life-threatening loneliness . . . You do what you can, what good
> people have always done: you bring thirsty people water, you share
> your food, you try to help the homeless find shelter, you stand up
> for the underdog.[11]

Power and Service

I co-wrote an entire book on this topic, along with the person who showed me the sacramental nature of serving others: Gary Morsch. Our book is *The Power of Serving Others*, and in it we describe incidents from relief efforts after hurricane Katrina in New Orleans, after earthquakes, after wars, after revolutions, and, as Lamott says above, in the little things that can transform a person's outlook on life. My personal favorite was the example of the little, bent-over neighbor lady who came my house just to provide relief to my son when he was still in half a body cast. In the sweltering heat of southern Ohio, he laid on his back in the living room floor, guffawing, as our elderly neighbor sat in a chair across the room and batted a balloon to him. Little things. Ordinary things. Transformative things. They brought us into the Mystery of Something Bigger than our frustration, pain, fear, and hopelessness. She served my son.

The premise *The Power of Serving Others* is that everyone has something to give, and that we can start right now, where we are. By doing so, we participate in the work of God in the world. Leo Tolstoy, in his short story *What Men Live By*, tells of an angel who disobeyed God, and was discovered as a naked, freezing man in a Russian winter by an impoverished shoemaker. The angel had been sent to earth to find the answer to the question *what do men live by?* The shoemaker, not knowing the man was an angel, provided him clothing and shelter. By the end of the story the man has discovered the answer to the question, and God returns his wings. "I learned that man does not live by care for himself, but by love for others," the angel said. "When I came to earth as a man, I lived not by care for myself, but by the love that was in the heart of a passerby . . . All men live, not by reason of any care they have for themselves, but by the love for them that is in other people . . . It is by love for others that they really live."[12]

When Jesus told the parable of the Good Samaritan, it was in answer to the question *who should we be serving?* Here is another NPR story. A man named Julio Diaz was on his way home to the Bronx one night when he got off the subway one stop early so he could eat dinner at his favorite diner. He stepped off the Number 6 train onto the empty platform and headed toward the stairs. A teenager appeared, showed a knife in a menacing manner, and demanded Diaz' wallet. Diaz gave it to him, but as the teenager started to run away, Diaz yelled to him. "Hey wait a minute. You forgot something. If you're going to be robbing people for the rest of the night, you might as well take my coat to keep you warm."

The robber stopped and looked at Diaz. Finally he said, "Why are you doing this?"

Diaz said, "If you're willing to risk your freedom for a few dollars, then I guess you must really need the money. I mean, all I wanted to do was get dinner and if you really want to join me, hey, you're more than welcome."

The teenager went with Diaz to the diner and sat in a booth. Throughout the meal the manager, the waiters, and even the dishwasher stopped by the table to say hello to Diaz.

"You know everybody here," the robber said. "Do you own this place?"

Diaz told him no, but that he ate there a lot.

"But you're even nice to the dishwasher."

"Haven't you been taught you should be nice to everybody?"

"Yeah, but I didn't think people actually behaved that way."

Diaz asked the boy what he wanted out of life. The boy's expression saddened and he couldn't, or wouldn't, answer.

When the bill arrived, Diaz told the thief, "I guess you're going to have to pay for this bill, 'cause you have my money and I can't pay for this. If you give me my wallet back, I'll gladly treat you." Without hesitation the teen returned the wallet. Diaz took out twenty dollars and gave it to him. Then he asked the boy for something—his knife—which the boy also turned over without hesitation.[13]

Something happened in that diner that night, almost as if it had been lifted off the page of *Les Miserables*. A boy, meaning harm, was served by his victim. Revelation broke through. The boy understands something about Mystery that he didn't understand before. I suspect that eventually it will dawn on him that he experienced a sacred moment in that diner. So did Diaz.

What keeps us from serving others? Lack of opportunity? I hardly think this can be true. I looked out my kitchen window on Christmas

Eve morning, and saw that someone had spray-painted racist graffiti on the solid wood fence of my black neighbor across the street. It took a few hours, but he and I eventually got the paint scrubbed off. All it took was a little time and some elbow grease. And noticing. Sometimes the opportunity isn't even across the street. A spouse, a child, a sibling, a parent—they're part of our service orbit, too. Remember, when we're serving others, by definition we give up power to dominate and control them. Which is part of the point.

Lack of money? It doesn't take money to serve others. A gift card to a grocery store for hungry people might take some money. But if money is limiting the service we offer, well, that's a failure of imagination.

Lack of talent? What talent did my elderly lady neighbor have for serving my family by playing with my son who was hostage to half of a body cast? She could bat a balloon across the room. From a chair! No special gifts needed there. She didn't need a sociology, child development, or ballooning degree.

Here's what I think is the biggest deterrent to people serving others: they think they have to have pure motives. But Dorothy Day of the Catholic Worker movement said, "If we were going to forbid hypocrites to work here with us, there'd be no one to do the work, and no one to do the forbidding."[14]

Serving others is easier than it appears, as are all of the other sacraments. It is a way of bringing order to the disorder, and revealing further that we are surrounded by the sacred and holy. Oscar Wilde once wrote, "The nicest feeling in the world is to do a good deed anonymously—and have somebody find out about it." The more we understand the sacrament of service, the less importance we'll place on people finding out about what we do.

Rabbi Lawrence Kushner said, "Everyone carries with them at least one and probably many pieces to someone else's puzzle. Sometimes they know it; sometimes they don't know it. And when you present your piece, which is worthless to you, to another, whether you know it or not, whether they know it or not, you are a messenger from the Most High."[15]

That's what serving others does—makes each of us more whole. And holy.

Conclusion

Weighing the Evidence

now the ears of my ears are awake and
now the eyes of my eyes are opened

e. e. cummings[1]

When I go to ice hockey games with friends or family members, we have entirely different experiences. I know the game intimately. Every year, with only one or two exceptions, from age fourteen to fifty I played in a competitive league. When the Minnesota North Stars became a team in the late 1960s, I went to their summer camp taught by my new local heroes. I played on my high school team. In college I played in the midnight factory leagues, which are sponsored by local companies, mostly factories, to let their employees (and some ringers like me) let off some figurative steam. I played in a pick-up league in Detroit, as well as through graduate school. On Marcia's and my first anniversary we went to Toronto. The Hockey Hall of Fame happens to be there. I told her I just wanted to see it while we were in town. She followed me around for a while, then waited for me on the front steps. "It was scary seeing how mesmerized you were by a jersey or a stick," she said. The company I mentioned in a

previous chapter, where I worked for three years, sponsored its own
league, and I was in it. In San Diego, surprisingly, there are several
leagues. I played on their most competitive teams where they had
tryouts and drafts. For a few years I had season tickets to the minor
league team that played in San Diego. I decide which national conventions I attend in part by seeing if there is an NHL team in that city,
and if there is a home game while I am there. The only time my house
gets cable television is during the Stanley Cup playoffs. Those are the
hockey fan's High Holy Days. More than once the cable installer has
arrived at our house on the exact same day as the year before. When
the champion is determined, the subscription is canceled.

I know this game.

When my kids were young and our family attended one of the
minor league games in San Diego, each of us had a different experience. Blake loved the fighting, the abusive fans who chanted horrible
things at the opposing goaltender (all things he was forbidden to say
at home), the obese, wacky guy who clanged the cowbell in our ears,
and the scoring, in that order. Vanessa, when she wasn't looking
for the cotton candy vendor, lived in fear that she was going to get
struck by a deflected puck hurtling into the stands, as she was when
she was five. Marcia indulges my love for the game, sees things most
people don't see, but at these games would get disturbed by the way
the cheerleaders looked like hookers. "This is what happens when
you don't go to college," she said to Vanessa during one particularly
provocative dance routine—on ice, amazingly.

People laugh when I say it, but I think hockey is an extremely subtle
game. It isn't about crashing one guy into the boards, or the fights, in
my view, although I have been involved in both. It is about the curve
of the stick, the precision pass, the anticipation of the goaltender,
the placement of the hands during a faceoff, the sharpness of the
skate's edge, and how wide apart the players keep their feet. And it all
makes sense during the Zen-like experience of watching the Zamboni
machine lay down a new sheet of ice.

Some fans, like Blake, see blood, teeth, and violence. I see those
things, too. But I see something else. Some, like Vanessa, see some
peripheral sweet thing, and then are brought back to their inherent
fear because of a bad experience. I see those things, too. And more.

Some, like Marcia, see the good stuff about the game, but the dumb stuff discourages her. Me too. But because I am used to seeing so much more than that, I see things they don't see, which makes me love the game even more, which draws me to it more intensely all the time.

Our sense of God is shaped somewhat the same way. There are people who know about God only through the fireworks and dazzling miracles, or they have a strange attraction to the shedding of blood (Mel Gibson, anyone?). Anyone can see this and be impressed. There are others who know about God only at the extremes of sugary sweet (we've all heard the choruses that make Jesus sound like your girlfriend), and fear of the unexpected tragedy. Some see glimpses that there is more of God to be experienced, but get too distracted by things that miss the point (hypocrisy, inquisition, DaVinci Code, etc.). But it is possible to see more. To see more deeply. To see more clouds as pillars. To see more bushes as burning. To see more hills as places of transfiguration. To see more grace at knee level. Or ankle level. On a pitcher's mound in the World Series.

What Do You See?

Charlotte Beck tells the following Zen story in her book, *Nothing Special*: A student said to Master Ichu, "Please write for me something of great wisdom." The master picked up his brush and wrote one word: "Attention." The student said, "Is that all?" The master wrote, "Attention. Attention." The student became irritable. "That doesn't seem profound or subtle to me." In response, Master Ichu wrote, "Attention. Attention. Attention." Frustrated, the student demanded, "What does this word *attention* mean?" Master Ichu replied, "Attention means attention."[2]

We could use the words *awareness* or *mindfulness* in this context, too. Are we paying attention to the everyday moments of our lives and seeing God in them, or are we living in such a chaotic frenzy that we hope we'll have time to look for the presence and mystery of God later, when we have more time—say, when the degree is finished, the kids have moved out, this project is completed, or we retire?

We have to look now. This is really all we have. *This* is the day the Lord has made. Let us look for, and see him in it.

In the play *Our Town* by Thornton Wilder, the character Emily dies in childbirth, and she asks the Stage Manager character if she can return to earth for one day. She is struck by the beauty of the ordinary, and she is despondent over the living's lack of awareness, or attention, to it. When she returns to the cemetery, she asks the Stage Manager, "Do any human beings ever realize life while they live it?" He thinks for a moment, then says, "No. The saints and poets, maybe. They do some."

Do we realize the sacred and the holy while it surrounds us? If we're paying attention, we do. There is reconciliation going on all around us—perhaps just momentary closures of distance between two human beings, or between human beings and other parts of creation. Meals are not always just means to satisfy physical hunger. Sometimes they are means to experiencing the Mystery around the table. We experience moments of illumination—that we are truly loved and known by God—throughout each day, creating a continual baptism. We have opportunities to abandon our shallow understanding of God and his purpose everyday by trusting and pursuing something deeper, riskier, less knowable, to experience the confirmation of this spiritual voyage. We see that our family is ever-expanding, and that the key to its success is not legislation, but inclusion, based on commitment, service, and self-sacrifice, and that marriage is about giving away power, not hoarding it. Every day we see how our true vocation is to be a needle on the compass pointing to God. Every day someone near us is passing from one significant stage of life to another—maybe even into the next life—and they need someone to acknowledge it, affirm it, and celebrate it.

"In the end, of course, our approach to the future comes down to how we feel about mystery," said philosopher Ram Dass.[3]

All of this grace is going on about us every day. When we see the sacraments as a way to experience something holy or sacred, we are recognizing them for what they truly are—the means by which God breaks through our ordinary days to remind us that he is with us. That he got here before us. That, through bursts of these sacramental revelations, there is order in the disorder.

"We must be ready to allow ourselves to be interrupted by God," Bonhoeffer wrote.[4] The interruptions come constantly. We see them as means of grace when we're paying attention. Maybe we can experience God as both an interruption and recognition.

A colleague and friend at my university, Dan Croy, showed a small group of us a video of his trip to Disneyland with his wife Kay, daughter, son-in-law, and their eight-month-old grandbaby. Dan and Kay stopped to pose for a photo with their beautiful granddaughter. Their daughter, Kacey, decided to videotape the impromptu photo session. The videotape showed Dan, Kay, and baby holding a pose while the photographer said, "Okay, hold still. Smile everyone. No wait. I need to wind it. Okay, now we're ready—smile everyone! Hold on—I can't get the flash to work. Okay. I think I got it. Smile real big now . . ."

This went on for several seconds. In the video we could see Dan and Kay's faces harden into forced smiles, barely hiding frustration that it wasn't happening fast enough. They muttered to each other about the incompetence of the photographer.

Here's what they missed, and what we saw on the videotape. While Dan and Kay focused on becoming statues in a wax museum, waiting for the expected thing to happen, and while the photographer was audibly on the verge of a meltdown because he couldn't get the camera to work, the baby turned to Dan's face and started touching it with her tiny hands. We could hear those beautiful baby vowels, ooos and aaaaas, while she touched Dan's face. The baby smiled and even leaned in to put her mouth on Dan's cheek. The baby then turned and stroked Kay's face. And Dan and Kay missed it because they were too busy posing, trying to fulfill someone else's expectations.

"Look at all the love we missed," he told us. "The love that came to us unannounced and unexpected and undeserved. It was there for us, but we missed it."

It was a love that they didn't initiate, and was there whether they recognized it or not. "What is essential is to know that the Christian life is mostly what is being done to you, not what you are doing," said Eugene Peterson. "*You* don't begin the spiritual life, the Holy Spirit does. And it began a long time ago. It was his idea before it was yours." It is not a matter of us taking on this sacred life. "God has already taken you on—you are his project."[5]

This is the conclusion the main character comes to in Wendell Berry's novel *Jayber Crow*. "So it is that the life force may take possession of a man—so that in the end he may be possessed by something greater, no longer at all belonging to himself."[6] As Crow realizes he is coming to the end of his life, he begins assessing how he has lived.

> I feel that I have lived on the edge even of my own life. I have made plans enough, but I see now that I have never lived by plan. Any more than if I had been a bystander watching me live my life, I don't feel that I ever have been quite sure what was going on. Nearly everything that has happened to me has happened by surprise. *All* the important things have happened by surprise . . . And so when I have thought I was *in* my story or in charge of it, I really have been only on the edge of it, carried along. Is this because we are in an eternal story that is happening partly in time?[7]

True Profanity

This entire book has focused on using the sacraments to give us clearer vision of God's activity in our everyday world. What happens if we don't see this activity? The word "profane" comes from the Latin "profanus," meaning "outside the temple." In other words, not sacred. If the universe is the temple of God, the place where his presence is seen and known, then there is no place that is outside the temple, or profane. It is when we treat this temple, or anywhere in it, as a place where God cannot be, we desecrate something that is already holy. My friend, philosopher Rick Power, says, "The only part of God's creation that can be off-limits to him is the will of a free person. When I treat others as means instead of ends in themselves, I desecrate something holy. When I adopt a materialist view that reduces all love, truth, and beauty to physics, I profane the God-bathed world. When I hate my own life and think nothing of value can happen here, I miss the unique ways the sacred can happen in and through me."

The profane, he says, is what happens when we are blind to the reality of the holy.

But sometimes, when we do see the holy, we don't know what to do next. If we find ourselves in the presence of the sacred, sometimes we are struck silent. Often, it seems, we do something dumb by making a big deal out of it. "Uneasy with the unknown . . . we run around crazily, yelling and screaming, trying to put our stamp of familiarity on it," said Eugene Peterson. "We attempt to get rid of the mystery by making our presence large and noisy."[8]

Our everyday activities provide us with ample opportunity to see it, when we're paying attention. "We are not here to show something to God," said Robert Benson.

> We are here because God—the One who wants to be completely known—has something to show us . . . We do not always see that we should be moving about our days and lives and places with awe and reverence and wonder, with the same soft steps with which we enter the room of a sleeping child or the mysterious silence of a cathedral. There is no ground that is not holy ground. All of the places of our lives are sanctuaries; some of them just happen to have steeples. And all of the people in our lives are saints; it is just that some of them have day jobs and most will never have feast days named for them.[9]

Jesus used mud to help a man see. Something found in the ordinary, everyday experience of life—right under our feet. Spirituality is about seeing. Recognizing the sacramental nature of our daily activities moves us into that improved state of vision. C. S. Lewis wrote that there are no ordinary *people*—"You have never talked to a mere mortal . . . It is immortals whom we joke with, work with, marry, snub, and exploit." He also says there are no ordinary *things*. Whether it is a row of cabbages, a farmyard cat, a wrinkled motherly face, a tiled roof, a single sentence in a book—each can be seen as a God breaking through our consciousness. Lewis called them "patches of Godlight" in the world.[10]

But usually we start missing the signs again. It all begins looking routine. Or at least it can. "Somewhere along the way this exponential expansion of awareness, this wide-eyed looking around, this sheer untaught delight in what is here, reverses itself: the world contracts; we are reduced to a life of routine through which we sleepwalk," said Eugene Peterson. "But not for long. Something always shows up to jar us awake: a child's question, a fox's sleek beauty, a sharp pain, a pastor's sermon, a fresh metaphor, an artist's vision, a slap in the face, scent from a crushed violet. We are again awake, alert, in wonder: how did this happen?"[11] Bursts of revelation.

Emily Dickinson said that "Consider the lilies of the field" is the one commandment she never broke. Annie Dillard, in describing an unremarkable muddy creek in Virginia wrote, "It's all a matter of keeping my eyes open. Beauty and grace are performed whether or not we will sense them. The least we can do is try to be there . . . so that creation need not play to an empty house."[12]

Toward the end of Richard Russo's novel, *Straight Man*, the main character, William Henry Devereaux Jr., lies in a hospital bed after fainting at the university where he teaches. His life had been falling apart, and he thought he was dying. But, realizing that he is still alive, and that his wife has returned to him, he drifts back into a medicated sleep with this thought: "I can't help thinking that it's a wonderful thing to be right about the world. To weigh the evidence, always incomplete, and correctly intuit the whole, to see the world in a grain of sand, to recognize its beauty, its simplicity, its truth. It's as close as we get to God in this life, and we reside in the glow of such brief flashes of understanding, fully awake, sometimes, for two or three seconds, at peace with our existence. And then back to sleep we go."[13]

Those brief flashes of understanding are often illuminated by the sacraments. But sacraments aren't static and fixed. Viewed rightly, they show us that virtually anything can carry something of God to us. "The kind smile of a Down's syndrome child, the bouncy jubilation of a puppy, the graceful arch of a dancer's back, the camera work in a fine film, good coffee, good wine, good friends, good conversation," said Brian McLaren. "Start with three sacraments—or seven—and pretty soon everything becomes potentially sacramental as, I believe, it should be."[14]

My own tendency is to look for God where he is "supposed" to be. On Good Friday I like to make my way to the original mission in the San Diego area, called Mission de Alcala. It's a preserved chapel, a few hundred years old, with stone, sweaty walls, some stained glass, a stone floor. It feels like a cave. I usually feel like I have found him there. I have also looked for him in the aftermath of Hurricane Katrina in New Orleans, and found him. And in some of the spectacular cathedrals of Europe. But Jesus said that the Kingdom of Heaven was more like a seed in the ground, a treasure in a field. There is always that possibility, you know—that God decided to hide the kingdom not in any of the extraordinary places that treasure hunters would be sure to check but in the last place that any of us would think to look, namely in the ordinary circumstances of our everyday lives," said Barbara Brown Taylor. "Like a silver spoon in the drawer with the stainless, like a diamond necklace on the bureau with the rhinestones; the extraordinary hidden in the ordinary, the kingdom of heaven all mixed in with the humdrum and ho-hum of our days, as easy to find as an amaryllis bulb in the dark basement that suddenly sends forth a shoot, or a child's smile when she awakes from sleep, or the first thunderstorm after a long drought—all of them signs of the kingdom of heaven, clues to all the holiness hidden in the dullest of our days."[15]

Final Blessing

I had a great uncle named Mel Anderson. He was a great uncle because he was my grandmother's brother. He was great for other reasons, too. He had been a pastor for more than sixty years. He lived in San Diego until he got too frail, and then he moved to be near his son and his family for the final year of his life. People didn't have discussions with my uncle. They had debates. He and I had very spirited debates, often about spiritual matters. "I can help you, if you'd just shut up and let me," he said repeatedly. I believe there is a psalm that says something similar. "Be still and know" is, in today's vernacular, "Shut up and let me love you," according to Bono.

But a statement like that from my bombastic uncle usually meant that he wanted to replace my not-knowing with his certainty. Still, it was a relationship that I cherished.

When it was time for him to move away, I paid him one last visit. Throughout his adult life he had lived in nice homes, usually provided by the churches he served. In his last few years, he and his wife lived in a modest trailer outside of San Diego. When his wife died, he moved into a senior citizen complex, which is where I went to visit him on his last day in town. In his mid-eighties, his energy, enthusiasm, and humor were seeping out of him at a rapid rate. All of his possessions were in a few boxes. His entire existence had been reduced to this one room with a bed, a television, a desk, and a chair.

He was sitting in the chair when I walked in. We chatted for a while, rehashed some memorable moments together. I even tried to start a mini-debate with him, but he didn't have the strength. Then I told him the real reason I wanted to see him one last time.

"I want you to give me a blessing," I said. "Just like they did in the Old Testament with the patriarchs. I don't have a particular request or dilemma. I just want your blessing."

His reply surprised me. He wasn't amused or surprised. He had no quick comeback. He simply said, "Okay." He reached out his hands to me, and he prayed for me. He prayed that God would continue to make himself known to me, and that I would continue to use my gifts for others to know God.

Then he did something else that surprised me. Keeping hold of my hands, he then said, "Now I want you to bless me."

I am forty years his junior—a child by comparison. He lived in the house where I was first raised. He is a respected force in his denomination. At first I hesitated. But I looked at him, and his eyes were already closed, his head bowed. "Bless me," he said, without looking up.

So I did. I thanked God for all of the lives my uncle had touched, for what a role model and mentor he had been to me, and for strength as he moved into this next stage of his life. A gap of years and experience evaporated in that moment. We engaged in the Mystery. We saw who we truly were before God—the unconditionally loved. It was a time of anointing for the voyage ahead, which within a year included another world for him. It was a sacred and holy time because we both saw the sacramental nature of this act. For that moment, anyway, our lenses were clear.

When Madeleine L'Engle was recovering from a time of fatigue from committing herself to too many projects, and also from an injury as a result of a fall, she was emotionally stressed and physically hurting.

One afternoon I had a couple of hours to myself, and so I limped to the sea wall and stretched out and closed my eyes and tried to let go all my aches and pains and tiredness, to let go and simply *be*. And while I was lying there, eased by the cool breezes, the warm sun, bursts of bird song, I heard feet coming to me across the water. It was a sound I recognized, a familiar sound; the feet of Jesus coming towards me. And then another noise broke in, and I was back in an aching body. But I had heard. For a moment in that hearing I was freed from the dirty devices of this world. I was more than I am. I was healed.[16]

Jesus said, "Here I stand knocking at the door; if anyone hears my voice and opens the door, I will come in and sit down to supper with him and he with me." Jesus proposes a meal together to those who are listening. The proposal is ongoing, usually in the everyday stuff of our active lives.

Buechner said,

All the absurd little meetings, decisions, inner skirmishes that go to make up our days. It all adds up to very little, and yet it all adds up to very much. Our days are full of nonsense, and yet not, because it is precisely into the nonsense of our days that God speaks to us works of great significance—not words that are written in the stars but words that are written into the raw stuff and nonsense of our days, which are not nonsense just because God speaks into the midst of them. And the words that he says, to each of us differently, are '*be brave . . . be merciful . . . feed my lambs . . . press on toward the goal.*'. . . . These words that God speaks to us in our own lives are the real miracles. They are not miracles that create faith as we might think that a message written in the stars would create faith, but they are miracles that it takes faith to see—faith in the sense of openness, faith in the sense of willingness to wait, to watch, to listen, for the incredible presence of God here in the world among us.[17]

Waiting, watching, listening. Attention.

The sacraments point us to God's presence all around us, coming toward us, arriving before us, if the ears of our ears and the eyes of our eyes are awake.

It really comes down to our imagination. If we are completely bound by what can be articulated and explained, then we will lead lives of not noticing. But if we allow our imaginations to work, then we see things differently. Czeslaw Milosz, the Nobel Prize-winning poet, said that imagination, particularly when it is used in religious practice, provides us with the capacity to view everything that confronts us as a means to the greater Mystery. "Imagination can fashion the world into a homeland as well as into a prison or a place of battle," he said. "It is the invisibles that determine how you will view the world, whether it is a homeland or as a prison or place of battle. Nobody lives in the 'objective' world, only in a world filtered through the imagination."[18]

Whether we see the sacred and holy in everyday life is not a matter of whether it exists. Rather, it is a matter of whether we see it. The sacraments are tools for improving our vision.

> This life's dim windows of the soul
> Distorts the heavens from pole to pole
> And leads you to believe a lie
> When you see with, not thro,' the Eye.[19]

Notes

Introduction

1. Walker Percy, *The Moviegoer* (New York: Vintage Books, 1960), 13.

2. Quoted in Marcus Borg, *The God We Never Knew* (San Francisco: HarperSanFrancisco, 1997), 47.

3. Ibid.

4. Eugene Peterson, *Under the Unpredictable Plant* (Grand Rapids: Eerdmans, 1992), 128.

5. Frederick Buechner, *Now and Then* (New York: HarperCollins, 1983), 108.

6. Ibid., 87.

7. Peterson, *Under the Unpredictable Plant*, 133.

8. Anne Lamott, *Plan B* (New York: Riverhead Books, 2005), 162.

9. Quoted in Karl Rahner, *Belief Today* (New York: Sheed and Ward, 1967), 14.

10. Philip Yancey, *Rumors of Another World* (Grand Rapids: Zondervan, 2003), 17.

11. Eugene Peterson, *Subversive Spirituality* (Grand Rapids: Eerdmans, 1994), ix.

12. Thomas Merton, *The Living Bread* (New York: Farrar, Straus, Giroux, 1956), 92.

13. Joseph Martos, *Doors to the Sacred* (Liguori, Mo: Liguori/Triumph, 1981), 469.

14. Ibid., 5.

15. Thomas Keating, *Open Mind, Open Heart* (New York: Continuum, 1995), 37.

16. Martos, *Doors to the Sacred*, 467.

17. C. S. Lewis, *Letters to Malcolm* (San Diego: Harcourt Brace, 1964), 75.

18. Theodore Runyon, *The New Creation* (Nashville: Abingdon Press, 1998), 159.

19. Ibid., 206.

20. Jean-Pierre De Caussade, *The Sacrament of the Present Moment* (San Francisco: HarperSanFrancisco, 1982), xi.

21. Thomas Kelly, *A Testament of Devotion* (New York: Harper & Row, 1941), 96.

22. De Caussade, *The Sacrament of the Present Moment*, xix.

23. Ibid., 77.

24. Quoted in Borg, *The God We Never Knew*, 47.

25. Michael Lerner, *The Left Hand of God* (San Francisco; Harper San-Francisco, 2006), 65.

Chapter 1

1. Joseph Campbell, *The Power of Myth* (New York: Anchor, 1991), 85.

2. Parker Palmer, *A Hidden Wholeness* (San Francisco: Jossey-Bass, 2004), 60.

3. Parker Palmer, *Let Your Life Speak* (San Francisco: Jossey-Bass, 2000), 25.

4. Donald Hall, *Life Work* (Boston: Beacon Press, 1993), 54.

5. Ibid., 4.

6. Palmer, *Let Your Life Speak*, 4.

7. Ibid.

8. Studs Terkel, *Working* (New York: Pantheon Books, 1974), 1.

9. Campbell, *The Power of Myth*, 146–50.

10. Mark Salzman, *Lying Awake* (New York: Knopf, 2001), 181.

11. Frederick Buechner, *The Alphabet of Grace* (San Francisco: HarperSanFrancisco, 1989), 109–10.

12. Matthew Fox, *The Reinvention of Work* (San Francisco: HarperSanFrancisco, 1994), 133.

13. Tony Campolo, *Letters to a Young Evangelical* (New York: Perseus, 2006), 243–44.

14. Quoted in Campolo, *Letters to a Young Evangelical*, 250.

15. Eugene Peterson, *Leap Over a Wall* (San Francisco: HarperSanFrancisco, 1997), 27–33.

16. Quoted in Os Guinness, *The Call* (Nashville: W Publishing, 1998), 2.

17. Peter van Breemen, *The God Who Won't Let Go* (Notre Dame, IN: Ave Maria, 2001), 102.

18. Barbara Brown Taylor, *Bread of Angels* (Cambridge, MA: Cowley, 1997), 155.

19. Peterson, *Under the Unpredictable Plant*, 46–47.

20. Ibid., 35.

21. Quoted in Guinness, *The Call*, 34.

22. Ibid.

23. Frederick Buechner, *Secrets in the Dark* (San Francisco: HarperSanFrancisco, 2006), 38–40.

Chapter 2

1. Robert Benson, *Between the Dreaming and the Coming True* (New York: Tarcher/Putnum, 1996), 68.

2. Merton, *The Living Bread*, 126.

3. Quoted in Marcus Borg, *Meeting Jesus Again for the First Time* (San Francisco: HarperSanFrancisco, 1995), 136.

4. Kathleen Norris, *The Cloister Walk* (New York: Riverhead, 1996), 162.

5. Merton, *Living Bread*, 126.

6. Rahner, *Belief Today*, 33.

7. James Fowler, *Stages of Faith* (San Francisco: HarperSanFrancisco, 1995), 180–81.

8. Campolo, *Letters*, 70–71.

9. Tony Hendra, *Father Joe* (New York: Random House, 2004), 73–74.

10. Sara Miles, *Take This Bread* (New York: Ballantine, 2008), xi–xiv.

11. Ibid., 175.

12. Thich Nhat Hanh, *No Death, No Fear* (New York: Riverhead, 2002), 117.

13. Ron Hansen, *A Stay Against Confusion* (New York: Perennial, 2002), 233–34.

14. Jim Klobuchar, *Pursued by Grace* (Minneapolis: Augsburg, 1998), 66–67.

15. Ibid., 53.

16. Taylor, *Bread of Angels*, 10.

17. Henri Nouwen, *Life of the Beloved* (New York: Crossroad, 1999), 88–89.

18. Eugene Peterson, *Christ Plays in Ten Thousand Places* (Grand Rapids: Eerdmans, 2005), 174.

Chapter 3

1. Philip Yancey, *Prayer* (Grand Rapids: Zondervan, 2006), 55.

2. Buechner, *The Alphabet of Grace*, 44.

3. Klobuchar, *Pursued by Grace*, 21, 85.

4. Walter Wangerin Jr., *Ragman* (San Francisco: HarperSanFrancisco, 2004), 21–22.

5. Frederica Mathewes-Green, *At the Corner of East and Now* (New York: Tarcher/Putnam, 1999), 21.

6. Ibid., 65.

7. Frederica Mathewes-Green, *Facing East* (San Francisco: HarperSanFrancisco, 1997), 20.

8. Ibid., 21.

9. Yancey, *Prayer*, 32–33.

10. Lauren Winner, *Real Sex* (Grand Rapids: Brazos, 2005), 13–14.

11. Ibid., 160.

12. Anne Lamott, *Grace (Eventually)* (New York: Riverhead, 2007), 57–58.

13. Ibid., 252.

14. Michka Assayas, *Bono* (New York: Penguin, 2006), 336.

15. Henri Nouwen, *Here and Now* (New York: Crossroad, 1994), 41.

16. Henri Nouwen, *In the Name of Jesus* (New York: Crossroad, 1989), 46.

17. Dietrich Bonhoeffer, *Life Together* (New York: Harper & Row, 1954), 112, 115.

18. Donald Nicholl, *Holiness* (New York: Paulist Press, 1981), 54–55.

19. Frederick Buechner, *The Hungering Dark* (New York: Seabury Press, 1968), 47.

20. Hendra, *Father Joe*, 57–59.

Chapter 4

1. Walker Percy, *Lancelot* (New York: Picador, 1977), 4.

2. Richard Foster, *Celebration of Discipline* (San Francisco: Harper & Row, 1978), 1.

3. Philip Yancey, *Soul Survivor* (New York: Doubleday, 2001), 215.

4. Thomas Keating, *Invitation to Love* (Rockport, MA: Element, 1992), 67.

5. Nicholl, *Holiness,* xiv.

6. Keating, *Invitation to Love*, 90.

7. Richard Rohr, *Everything Belongs* (New York: Crossroad, 1999), 67.

8. Keating, *Invitation to Love*, 3.

9. Ibid., 36.

10. Nicholl, *Holiness*, 85.

11. Keating, *Open Mind, Open Heart*, 137.

12. Rohr, *Everything Belongs*, 27–28.

13. Palmer, *Let Your Life Speak*, 83–85.

14. Keating, *Invitation to Love*, 35–36.

Chapter 5

1. Richard Rohr, *Simplicity* (New York: Crossroad, 1991), 114.

2. Lerner, *Left Hand of God*, 241.

3. Richard Russo, *Straight Man* (New York: Vintage, 1998), xvii.

4. Quoted in Palmer, *A Hidden Wholeness*, 62–63.

5. Nouwen, *Here and Now*, 118.

6. Thomas Keating, *Intimacy With God* (New York: Crossroad, 1994), 30.

7. Walter Wangerin Jr. *Little Lamb, Who Made Thee?* (Grand Rapids: Zondervan, 1993), 136.

8. Richard Louv, *The Web of Life* (Berkeley, CA: Conari Press, 1996), 17.

9. Henri Nouwen, *Reaching Out* (New York: Doubleday, 1975), 56.

10. Campbell, *The Power of Myth*, 6.

11. John Michael Talbot, *The Lessons of St. Francis* (New York: Plume, 1997), 225–26.

12. Reuben Welch and Dean Nelson, *Come As You Are* (Kansas City: Beacon Hill Press of Kansas City, 1999), 32.

13. Mitch Albom, *Tuesdays With Morrie* (New York: Doubleday, 1997), 149.

14. Campbell, *The Power of Myth*, 7.

15. Nouwen, *Here and Now*, 129.

16. Frederick Buechner, *Whistling in the Dark* (San Francisco: Harper & Row, 1988), 79.

17. Ibid., 47.

18. Keating, *Invitation to Love*, 88.

19. Margaret Guenther, *The Practice of Prayer* (Cambridge, MA: Cowley, 1998), 117–18.

20. Lamott, *Grace (Eventually)*, 128.

21. M. Craig Barnes, *Sacred Thirst* (Grand Rapids: Zondervan, 2001), 129–30.

22. Buechner, *Whistling in the Dark*, 47.

Chapter 6

1. Quoted in Palmer, *A Hidden Wholeness*, 34.

2. Anne Lamott, interview by Dean Nelson, "Writer's Symposium by the Sea," UCSD-TV, February 19, 1998.

3. Anne Lamott, *Traveling Mercies* (New York: Pantheon, 1999), 231–32.

4. Peterson, *Christ Plays in Ten Thousand Places*, 23.

5. Frederick Buechner, *The Faces of Jesus* (Brewster, MA: Paraclete Press, 2005), 44.

6. Merton, *The Living Bread*, 102.

7. Frederick Buechner, *Telling Secrets* (San Francisco: Harper SanFrancisco, 1991), 44–45.

8. Benson, *Between the Dreaming*, 80.

9. Lamott, *Plan B*, 303–7.

10. Vincent Donovan, *Christianity Rediscovered* (Maryknoll, NY: Orbis, 2005), 68.

11. Lamott, *Traveling Mercies*, 261–62.

12. Philip Yancey, *What's So Amazing About Grace?* (Grand Rapids: Zondervan, 1997), 282.

Chapter 7

1. Peter Matthiessen, *The Peter Matthiessen Reader* (New York: Vintage, 1999), 196.

2. Quoted in Eugene Peterson, *Traveling Light* (Downers Grove: InterVarsity, 1982), 186.

3. Wangerin, *Little Lamb, Who Made Thee?*, 216.

4. Hanh, *No Death, No Fear*, 192–93.

5. Peterson, *Leap Over a Wall*, 120.

6. Percy, *The Moviegoer*, 81.

7. Hendra, *Father Joe*, 265.

8. Peterson, *Leap Over a Wall*, 115.

9. Brian McLaren, *A New Kind of Christian* (San Francisco: Jossey-Bass, 2001), 91.

10. Benson, *Between the Dreaming*, 38.

11. McLaren, *New Kind of Christian*, 91.

12. Buechner, *Whistling in the Dark*, 39.

Chapter 8

1. Quoted in Peterson, *Under the Unpredictable Plant*, 129.

2. Martos, *Doors to the Sacred*, 469.

3. Philip Yancey, *Reaching for the Invisible God* (Grand Rapids: Zondervan, 2000), 239–40.

4. Quoted in Eugene Peterson, *A Long Obedience in the Same Direction* (Downers Grove, IL: InterVarsity, 2000), 60.

5. Peterson, *Long Obedience*, 66.

6. Ibid., 181.

7. Story Corps, "A Transformative Moment Sparks Change of Life" (NPR). www.npr.org/templates/story/story.php?storyId=19252578 (accessed March 31, 2008).

8. Quoted in Philip Gulley and James Mulholland, *If God Is Love* (San Francisco: HarperSanFrancisco, 2004), 281.

9. Timothy Miller, *How to Want What You Have* (New York: Henry Holt, 1995), 94.

10. Henri Nouwen, *Spiritual Direction* (San Francisco: HarperSanFrancisco, 2006), 142.

11. Lamott, *Plan B*, 307–8.

12. Gary Morsch and Dean Nelson, *Serving Others* (San Francisco: Berrett-Koehler, 2006), 2.

13. Story Corps, "A Victim Treats His Mugger Right" (NPR). www.npr.org/templates/story/story.php?storyId-164759 (accessed March 31, 2008).

14. Morsch and Nelson, *Serving Others*, 2.

15. Ibid., 108.

Conclusion

1. e. e. cummings, *100 Selected Poems* (New York: Grove Press, 1959), 114.

2. Charlotte Joko Beck, *Nothing Special* (San Francisco: HarperSanFrancisco, 1993), 168.

3. Ram Dass, *Still Here* (New York: Riverhead, 2000), 134.

4. Bonhoeffer, *Life Together*, 99.

5. Eugene Peterson, *The Wisdom of Each Other* (Grand Rapids: Zondervan, 1998), 32.

6. Wendell Berry, *Jayber Crow* (New York: Counterpoint, 2000), 198.

7. Ibid., 322.

8. Peterson, *Christ Plays*, 41.

9. Benson, *Between the Dreaming*, 68, 141.

10. Quoted in Os Guinness, *The Call* (Nashville: W Publishing, 1998), 200.

11. Peterson, *Christ Plays*, 51.

12. Quoted in Yancey, *Soul Survivor*, 232

13. Russo, *Straight Man*, 366.

14. Brian McLaren, *A Generous Orthodoxy* (Grand Rapids: Zondervan, 2004) 225–26.

15. Barbara Brown Taylor, *The Seeds of Heaven* (Louisville: Westminster John Knox, 2004), 44.

16. Madeleine L'Engle, *Walking on Water* (Wheaton: Shaw, 1980), 197.

17. Buechner, *Secrets in the Dark*, 20–21.

18. Quoted in Peterson, *Under the Unpredictable Plant*, 170–71.

19. Quoted in Huston Smith, *Why Religion Matters* (San Francisco: HarperSanFrancisco, 2001), 147.